BABYLON RESURRECTED

Benjamin Nehemiah

Thinking Critically Presents...

ISBN-13: 978-1519108197

ISBN-10: 1519108192

Follow the author on Twitter:
https://twitter.com/BenNehemiah

For further publications, please visit Academia.edu:
https://essex.academia.edu/BenjaminNehemiah

About the Author

Benjamin Nehemiah graduated from the University of Essex with a bachelor's degree in computer science before pursuing a post-graduate certificate in information systems. In 2010, his path of study took a new direction when he set out to uncover the mysteries surrounding the origins of life and civilisation. His diverse research interests include: biocybernetics, the philosophy of information, biology, the origins of life, UFOs, theology, history and ancient civilizations.

For further publications, please visit Ben's Academia profile:
https://essex.academia.edu/BenjaminNehemiah

For updates, please follow Ben on Twitter:
https://twitter.com/BenNehemiah

This work is concerned with gaining a strategic awareness of mankind's origin and destiny, embarking upon the ultimate quest for knowledge.

Contents

1. Opening Statements

"All truth passes through three stages. First, it is ridiculed. Second, it is violently opposed. Third, it is accepted as being self-evident."

Arthur Schopenhauer

A Challenging Literary Adventure

When was the last time you had to exercise your mind beyond the limited scope of normality? Have you ever tried to comprehend a conspiracy against mankind, or process a belief that goes against the curriculum taught to you as a child? I'm not talking of rumours you hear from friends, watching the occasional documentary or reading a newspaper that may lead you to conclude yourself as being well-informed. I'm talking about disregarding mainstream media stories, researching a variety of sources and taking the time to form your own opinion rather than allowing the corporate media to form the opinion for you. There is an extremely fine line between "pressing news" and media drivel. This work is concerned with gaining a strategic awareness of mankind's origin and destiny, embarking upon the ultimate quest for knowledge. For any newcomers to these subjects I intend to divert you away from the pseudoscience, the deception, the delusions and the false prophets. Indeed, the vines of life are ripe with relative truths and morals, but what does it mean to be human?

Upon investigating some of the myths, legends and enigmas of the past, we will be confronted by monumental mysteries and controversial theories. As we explore some of the most complex building projects from antiquity, we will gain an insight into the advanced abilities of ancient man and will be left speculating over why some of their achievements are unparalleled, even today, with the use of modern technology. Whilst this work is a partial investigation into the mysterious world of secret societies, we will explore the nature of reality and the claim that mankind exists within a virtual domain, transcended by a non-physical reality. Today, the laws of nature are well-understood and various scientific breakthroughs have revealed a coherent picture of the universe; thus, the absolute truth of its origin (and, subsequently, the origin of life) can now be discovered. Life is extremely delicate; our planet can only support advanced life due to the remarkable fine-tuning of the universe. Although there may be no advanced physical life in neighbouring galaxies, it does not rule out the possible existence of UFOs. Towards the end of this work, we will investigate the *true* nature of UFOs, the issues surrounding transhumanism and the Hybrid Age. We will also assess the concept of a universal creator (God) and put His possible existence to the test before we voyage through Babylon to trace the origins of civilisation and reveal how an agenda born in this remote period of human history is coming to fruition today.

Objectives

- To attempt, through the use of logic and the laws of nature, to discover the absolute truth of the origins of the universe, information and life.
- To demystify the history and agenda of the ruling oligarchs and their New World Order.
- To study the origins, philosophies and mysteries of various secret societies.
- To investigate sophisticated ancient monuments (which are testimony of technology comparable with machine manufacturing and GPS satellite navigation).
- To gain insight into the nature of reality and the holographic universe.
- To evaluate animal and human-hybrids and the "alien" agenda.
- To identify the *true* nature of UFOs.
- To explore prophecies and the resurrection of Babylon.

A Cynical Perspective

Whilst many within society would assume the success of a chart-topping music single to be the result of an individual's songwriting ability, it is more apparent than ever that becoming famous is a reward for those who are willing to break ethical boundaries. Celebrity culture pervades aspects of modern life, and there are many sly techniques of inserting idle gossip into the minds of those unsuspecting. From a young age children are absorbed into the idolatrous and shallow culture of the 21st century. Increasingly today, fame isn't the result of talent or success, it is the objective. The art form dictates the culture and the spirit of the age has raised us to romanticise self-destructive behaviour and idolise the celebrities who promote it. Since the days of Elvis Presley's hip-shake, which caused outrage just over fifty years ago, society has been gradually desensitised, as I will demonstrate throughout this work. This steady yet disturbing moral decline is being led by a New Age agenda – even those who do not hold a belief in God can agree upon the moral decline and the breakdown of the traditional family during the 20th century. But with that being said, upon whose authority should we base our "moral code"? Using society or the government as a metric for right and wrong didn't work for the citizens of Nazi Germany. Adherents of atheism or nihilism *may* even argue that morality doesn't actually exist – at least, not in the objective sense. On this subject, Louise Anthony, an atheist philosopher, stated: "Any argument for moral scepticism is based upon premises which are less obvious than the reality of objective moral values themselves." In other words, a debate on the possible existence of morality can never be truly justified.[i]

Is a Belief in God Viable?

The answer to this question *should* be scientifically and logically ascertainable and not just speculative faith. If an attempt to demonstrate the existence of God were to be successful, scientific naturalism and materialism would need to be falsified. Naturalism simply states that the origin and development of living systems are the result of natural processes, i.e. there is no creator God. Materialism says that all that exists is matter, i.e. there are no non-material entities such as a spirit or a soul. The various books that I have read which attempt to answer questions about God have always left me unsatisfied, feeling that presented arguments were enforced by the author's opinion in an attempt to prove their preconceived ideas. Answering the age-old question of "does God exist?" does not solely depend upon science or theology, but requires aspects of philosophy, logic, sociology and history. After committing myself to research for this project, I began to notice the logical fallacies on both sides of the argument, from those who believe in God and those who do not. Growing up as an atheist and a "free-thinker", and after studying computer science and areas of physics and biology, I came to accept that discoveries in modern science *may* complement the theory of a "Universal Designer", but I also agreed with Professor Antony Flew when he stated: "The burden of proof is on those who believe God exists."[ii]

Scientific Discovery

In his book, *Temple at the Centre of Time*, author David Flynn stated: "Isaac Newton solved the riddles of space, time, gravity, light and invented mathematics to predict the motion of objects."[iii] The mind of Newton was nurtured in an era when the acquisition of knowledge through observation and testing had become the scientific method. His achievements in natural philosophy were merely a part-time study in comparison with his work on the Bible. Newton was intrigued by a universe that he perceived to be designed by God, and he wrote more about the Bible than any other subject. It was the study of mysticism (such as Kabballah and alchemy, which modern scientists consider pseudoscience) that assisted Newton in becoming a scientific icon and the capstone of the scientific revolution. Living in the Post-Information Age, the modern mind is rightfully suspicious of anything "supernatural". In between the modern separation of science and theology (God) comes philosophy, and whilst many people consider science and theology to be mutually exclusive, what do they have in common? One commonality would be higher dimensional geometry, or hyperspace, which, as Chuck Missler states, is the: "... ultimate source of unity in our conceptions of the universe."[iv] A major aspect of science is to discover the natural laws that govern the universe and, through observation and testing, scientists study "cause and effect" – surely man has reached an age where the scientific method can be used to discover the absolute truth of our origin. Charles Darwin stated that his theory of evolution had gaps, but he held faith that someday his theory would be proven true. Furthermore, with the advances in modern science, we are yet to discover a physical or chemical process which can account for the origin of life.

Bioinformatics

Since the discovery of DNA, it has been realised that "information" is present in all biological systems. It is this information (a term which shall later be concisely defined) which differentiates life from inanimate matter. Nobel Prize-winning biologist David Baltimore stated: "Modern biology is a science of information." Before one can begin to talk of the observable pragmatic functions within the cell, it must be recognised that coding systems are fundamental to all life – coding systems and the processing of a prescription for the manufacture of molecular machinery is what distinguishes biology, or living systems, from

4

complex organic chemistry. It is the coding systems and computation of algorithms, not just blind chemical reactions, which govern life to achieve metabolism and replication for the continuation of life on Earth. Dual-PhD-wielding scientist Dr. Donald Johnson stated: "Life is an intersection of physical science and information science. Both domains are critical for any life to exist, and each must be investigated using that domain's principles." Thus, life *must* adhere to the principles of semiotics, coding and information theory. Furthermore, if it could be demonstrated that the prescriptive algorithmic information present within life is not reducible to nature, it would rule out a "naturalistic" origin of life scenario. From a naturalistic perspective, just how did the first three-dimensional cellular architecture assign formal meaning to physical symbols, before constructing a coding system and processing a dynamic prescription to produce an output that gave rise to life on Earth? If such an event could occur naturally, life takes on a new meaning when we realise that these initial processes, against all odds, were able to steer clear of a non-functional dead-end. The challenges surrounding Darwin's theory and the naturalist worldview are non-trivial in nature, yet the school curriculum taught to me as a child conveyed evolution as a proven explanation of how biological systems self-originated and self-organised, thus eliminating the need for God. Has man's rational thinking been exploited? Is the argument for atheism more "philosophical" than scientific? Is modern society driving a philosophical apartheid, separating the logic of atheists from the supposedly incoherent and primitive beliefs of the theists?

In the Beginning...

One of the most glorious discoveries of modern cosmology is that the universe had a beginning. This realisation is partially based upon the discovery that the universe is expanding (a discovery which is commonly credited to Edwin Hubble's measurement of galaxies). Prior to this, even up until the mid-20th century, scientists and philosophers could never agree as to whether the universe had a beginning in finite time, or if it was infinite, i.e. static, and had no beginning. Many experts were inclined to believe that it was infinite and evidence to counter this belief was met with resistance. Following the discovery of a cosmic beginning, man is naturally inclined to investigate the characteristics and properties of the *cause* of the universe. In 1970, Stephen Hawking and Roger Penrose published a paper titled *Singularities of Gravitational Collapse and Cosmology* after turning their attention to the theory of general relativity. The singularity theorems of Hawking and Penrose, which fuelled their increasing academic recognition, demonstrated that the universe began from a singularity: an infinitely dense point in which all the matter of the universe was compressed – the "expansion" of this singularity marked the beginning of space and time. There are various ramifications of this Big Bang singularity theory, such as the breakdown of the laws of physics and the inability to define events before the Big Bang. Thus, if the singularity could be proven true, it could pose an obstruction to understanding *why* we originated. Stephen Hawking even admitted: "It would be very difficult to explain why the universe should have begun in just this way, except as the act of a God who intended to create beings like us."[v] Today, the Big Bang theories are widely recognised and it can now be argued that the cause of the universe transcends space and time, is non-physical and is not restricted by the laws of physics. Hawking is either an atheist or a deist (similar to Einstein, he seems to be a deist who believes in a "non-personal" Creator) and he has battled with the question of *why* the universe began throughout his entire career.

Cause and Effect

Furthermore, many discoveries have been made which demonstrate just how delicate life is and how the universe *appears* to have been designed to precise specifications. In fact, throughout the universe, the degree of fine-tuning on which life depends is so extensive that it is almost incomprehensible and, as Albert Einstein once stated: "The most incomprehensible thing about the world is that it is comprehensible." The strongest evidence for a beginning of space and time, together with a century of testing of Einstein's theory of general relativity (which is now regarded as an accurate description of space, time and gravity), introduces a new paradigm for both atheists and theists alike: the law of causality says that, along the dimensionality of time, a material effect must have an antecedent or simultaneous cause – this is "cause and effect". Following this, the Cosmological Argument states that the universe is a physical "effect" and the current understanding of this physical "effect" demonstrates a non-physical "cause" (based on the singularity theory, there can be no material cause). According to the atheistic worldview, the attributed cause is non-intelligent, or "randomness". According to the theistic worldview, the cause of the universe is an intelligence, an "uncaused-cause" (God) that transcends our universe and independently upholds space and time. Astrophysicist

Dr. Hugh Ross states: "Astrophysics and theoretical physics has now established non-physical reality as a part of the scientific tool base." As stated by Dr. Ravi Zacharias: "The physical universe reduced in any form cannot explain its own origin... the universe as we see it has to have something that is non-physical as a first cause."[vi] Throughout this work we shall delve into the evocative topic of non-physical reality before I present what I have found to be the most logically coherent worldview.

2. Ancient Engineering

"Condemnation without investigation is the height of ignorance."

Albert Einstein

As Above, So Below

Throughout the ages, all the greatest artists, pharaohs, popes and kings have shared the fascination of encrypting messages within art and architecture. Encoded within artistic masterpieces, road alignments, monuments and urban architecture are extremely modest harmonics which link man to the solar system – it is a subtle connection of the microcosm to the macrocosm and, to the untrained eye, these marvels go unnoticed. For those who have been initiated within esoteric brotherhoods, such designs reveal illuminating messages. Various diligent researchers have decoded these messages and various ex-occultists have revealed such secrets, some of which will be presented in this work. Even at the most novice level of initiation, we shall be discovering some of the secrets handed down throughout the ages within the Mystery Schools. As you progress through this work, you will come to realise how pervasive the concept of "As above, so below" is, and in the final chapters it shall be revealed how truly profound it is. The Mystery Schools trace their roots back to ancient Sumer and Babylon (situated in modern day Iraq along the Tigris and Euphrates Rivers) and to Egypt – societies in which religions were used to keep a closed population (the masses) under control of the ruling elites who had a desire to be worshipped as gods, or at least to act as the interface between the masses and the gods. Rituals and ceremonies, bewildering philosophies, altered states of consciousness, drug-induced trances, alchemy, numerology, astrology, occult technology and black magic are all rooted in the Mystery Religions of antiquity. Originally, the craft of Masonry (known as Operative Freemasonry) was concerned with architecture and construction – the showcasing of complex geometry through the design of buildings and monuments is a highly skilled art merged with science.

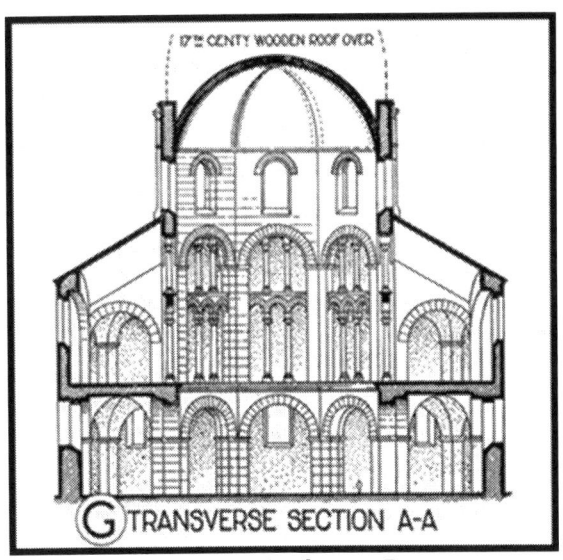

Image 2.1 Aachener Dom
(A History of Architecture on the Comparative Method, 1921).

The techniques of the most highly skilled Knights and Freemasons throughout medieval Europe were closely guarded secrets and many of their cathedrals and castles still stand today. In order to maintain their status as the most highly skilled workers and be commissioned for the most important projects, guild members would keep their trade skills a secret. By the end of the 17th century, various Freemason guilds were focused on more esoteric knowledge and identified with King Solomon of Israel and Nimrod of Babylon. Today, Nimrod is considered the founder of the fraternity – he is known as the "first and most excellent master". Author Daniel Beresniak states: "He gave Masons their signs and symbols in order for them to distinguish themselves from other people."[vii] Nimrod ruled over various great cities in Babylonia and headed one of the earliest building projects in recorded history, the Tower of Babel.

Speculative Freemasonry

By the Age of Enlightenment, in the 18th century, the Freemasons were initiating members who had no experience in the building trade and the fraternity became known as Speculative Freemasonry. Freemasonry is one of the oldest existing fraternal brotherhoods and producer Chris Everard states: "It has commonly acted as a middle-management system throughout the democratic world."[viii] Today, the Freemasons are

9

a misunderstood organisation and some of their symbols shall be decoded in this work. With truly radical implications, we will gain an insight into extraordinary philosophies, ancient technology, craftsmanship and cabals that have been overlooked and understated within conventional academia and the mainstream media. In regards to the ancient monuments discussed in this coming chapter, the full scope of anomalies has proven extremely challenging to explain, even by the most competent experts, so the purpose of this chapter is merely to highlight those anomalies and allow you to come to your own conclusion.

Ancient Engineers

Image 2.2 The Great Pyramid of Giza
(image courtesy of Mstyslav Chernov).

The Great Pyramid of Giza casts a shadow of doubt over everything we think we know about our past. The archaeological records reveal that the only tools available to the ancient Egyptians were mallets, copper chisels, hemp rope and wood (the wheel had not yet been invented). As we begin to investigate some of the pyramid's technical aspects and consider the logistical implications of the building project, we will see why it is recognised as the most remarkable building project ever completed. Technical and scientific specialists (such as architects, structural engineers, stone cutters and geologists) are left bewildered by some of the marvels of the ancient world. When talking about the

Great Pyramid, Chris Wise, the structural engineer of the London Millennium Bridge, claimed that many modern builders could not match the accuracy of this ancient design.[ix] Whether it is intentional or merely coincidental, embedded within this ancient monument is advanced mathematical and geometrical knowledge such as pi, the golden number and even the speed of light. The Great Pyramid also has interesting astronomical relationships and a near perfect alignment with true north. The most complex monument ever constructed is over 4,000 years old, demonstrates breathtaking precision and alacrity, yet was achieved using the most primitive of tools – how is that possible? The answer to that question merely depends upon which theory you believe, and there are plenty of them. In an attempt to sidestep the pseudoscience and address the non-trivial issues, consider the extraordinary precision of the granite sarcophagi in the Serapeum of Saqqara located near Memphis, Egypt. The quality of craftsmanship is truly amazing and the precision of the interior angles would be envied by the most skilled of modern stone cutters (see Image 2.3). The impeccable design of these ancient granite monuments is testimony to the engineer's true sophistication.

Image 2.3 Engineer Christopher Dunn measures the interior precision of these monolithic structures at the Serapeum of Saqqara (image courtesy of Christopher Dunn).

The Sophistication of the Ancient Egyptian Sarcophagi

Christopher Dunn, an experienced engineer who has worked at almost every level of high-tech manufacturing, has spent an extensive amount of time analysing the ancient wonders in Egypt, including the remarkable 70-ton boxes at the Serapeum of Saqqara (these boxes are known as sarcophagi, weigh approximately 70 tons and have 20 ton lids). In antiquity, a sarcophagus was a box in which dead bodies (mummies) were placed. These boxes are monolithic – single blocks of granite were hollowed out to create the box structures – which is a method of design that modern engineers would not usually attempt. The feasible alternative for replicating these monolithic box structures would be to join five separate slabs into position and create a box structure (...if IKEA did sarcophagi). Today, diamond-tipped circular saw blades are used for cutting slabs of granite and do so with ease, but these tools are prone to wear and tear.

Image 2.4 The scale of the granite sarcophagi
(image courtesy of isida-project.ucoz.com).

In reference to replicating this monumental task, Dunn states: "Even though after contacting four precision granite manufacturers I could not find one who could replicate their perfection, I would not say that it would be impossible to make one today – if we had a good reason to do so. But what would that reason be? For what purpose would we quarry an 80-ton block of granite, hollow its inside and proceed to craft it to such a high level of accuracy?" Like many engineers, Dunn wonders why the ancient designers chose to complete their building projects using much tougher methods than those that would be used today, especially if they only had primitive hand tools. What was the real purpose of these structures? If their sole purpose was to entomb a dead body, why were they built with such breathtaking precision? More important, how were they built and what tools were used? There is no practicality in a theory which states that hand saws or copper chisels can be used to cut granite in the fashion demonstrated in the sarcophagi (see Image 2.4). Ask a professional stone cutter – it simply is not feasible. The multi-ton blocks used in the construction of these ancient monuments were quarried at Aswan, 500 miles away, which demonstrates that a highly efficient transportation method must have been used to move the blocks to their location – the archaeological records reveal that the wheel had not even been invented in Egypt at this time (see Image 2.5).

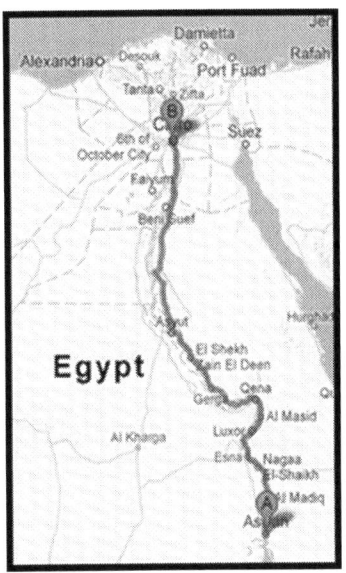

Image 2.5 The quarry at Aswan (A)
is over 500 miles south of Cairo (B).

After a thorough investigation of these structures, Dunn summarised his opinion: "As an engineer and craftsman, who has worked in manufacturing for over 40 years and who has created precision artefacts in our modern world, in my opinion this accomplishment in prehistory deserves more recognition. Nobody does this kind of work unless there is a particularly high purpose for the artefact. The only other reason that such precision would be created in an object would be that the tools used to create it are so precise that they are incapable of producing anything less than precision." It is the sophistication of these granite monuments that Dunn believes to be the "smoking gun" evidence of an advanced technology used in antiquity. The conventional theory of Egyptologists which suggests that primitive hand tools were used in their construction has been falsified by modern engineers. It is only after we assess the combination of all the workings involved that we can begin to value their level of sophistication. The origins of this civilisation remain a great mystery. At the very least, there are some serious discrepancies within the history books:

- Using primitive methods, how were monuments made from igneous rock that weigh up to 80 tons, quarried and transported, before being cut to a precision that modern engineers would find challenging to match?

There is plenty of speculation and fanciful conjecture surrounding these monuments because the conventional theories fail to account for the major anomalies. Consequently, in an attempt to address these issues, many revisionist historians and alternative researchers (including scientists, engineers and architects) have revisited and reinvestigated a wide scope of physical evidence to draw alternative theories that do not conform to the traditional, tightly bound views of history. Practical investigations (including the analysis of building materials) have led various engineers to conclude that advanced tools, comparable with disc saws and drills cutting at a high velocity, were used by the engineers of antiquity and that their level of skill surpasses our own. Our capabilities are nothing new and, in many ways, we are not the most technically advanced we have ever been. As stated by author David Flynn: "The highest achievements of modern science lay not in the realm of discovery but rediscovery."[x] So what happened to these cultures? If high technology was used, what are the implications for the conventional theories on the origins of civilisation? There are reasonable answers to these questions, but before we review them, let us look a little deeper.

A Common Influence...?

Advanced culture was not unique to ancient Egypt – various civilisations across the globe (isolated by location and time) show signs of a common influence. Various researchers of the antiquities have concluded that an unknown mediator guided the development and beliefs of various cultures around the world in the regions of Mexico, South America, Europe, Africa and Asia. With regard to this common influence, researcher Richard Cassaro has documented *many* archaeological riddles that illustrate striking and mysterious similarities in architecture, iconography, mythology, rituals and religions of various ancient cultures all over the globe. Are the similarities merely coincidence, or is it possible that these cultures were the offspring of an unknown "mother culture"? Image 2.6 is a comparison of civilisations from Egypt, Mexico and Cambodia.

Image 2.6 Mexico, Egypt and Cambodia
(image courtesy of Richard Cassaro for www.richardcassaro.com).

These three ancient civilisations were on separate continents and not thought to have had any connection to one another. There is an interesting similarity in the design of pyramids and corbel arches and that each of the cultures practised the mummification of dead bodies.

Image 2.7 The monuments of Bali (Asia) are similar
to those of the Mayans located in South America
(image courtesy of Richard Cassaro for www.richardcassaro.com).

Image 2.7 is a comparison of some more monuments, this time showing interesting similarities between the ancient cultures of the Balinese people of Asia and the Mayans of Mexico. Again, both cultures were on separate continents and built immense stepped pyramids with temples on top. The pyramids have fierce dragons/serpents protruding from the sides of the construction.[xi]

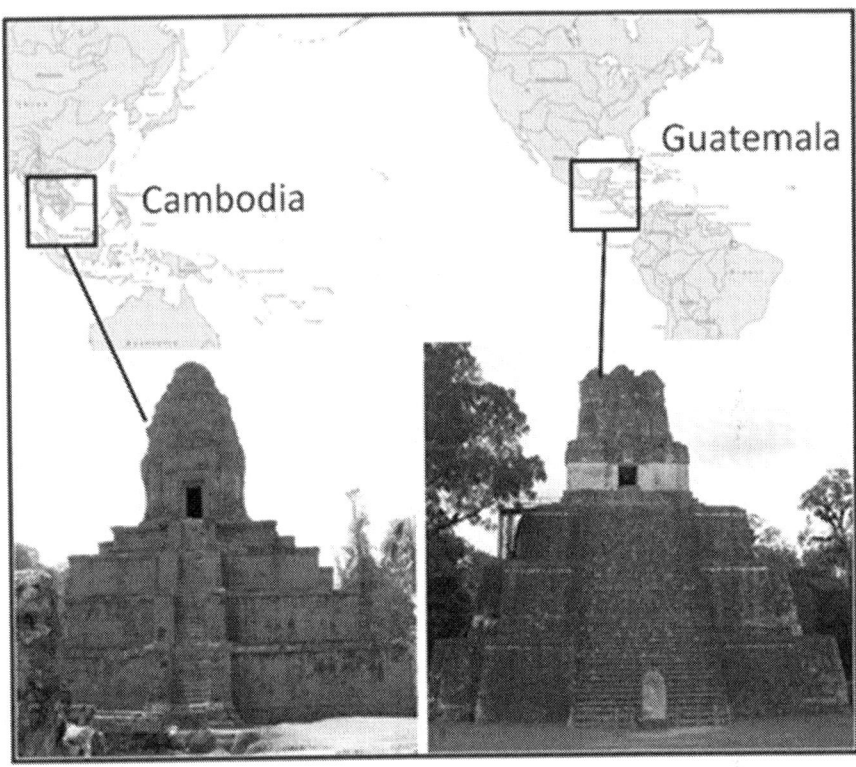

Image 2.8 An ancient temple located in Cambodia in Asia (left) and Guatemala in South America (right).

Image 2.8 is a comparison of a stepped pyramid located in Cambodia (Asia) and a stepped pyramid in Guatemala (South America). Although they are separated by the Pacific Ocean, the pyramids are very similar and both cultures appear to have had similar practices.

Similarities between South American and Northern African Cultures

As Richard Cassaro further points out, there are striking similarities between the ancient cultures of the pre-Incan or Incan peoples of South America and the Egyptians of Africa. Once again, both cultures developed on separate continents and are not thought to have had any connection to one another. In terms of architecture, mythology, rituals and religions, some of the following images show how these geographically distant people had much in common.

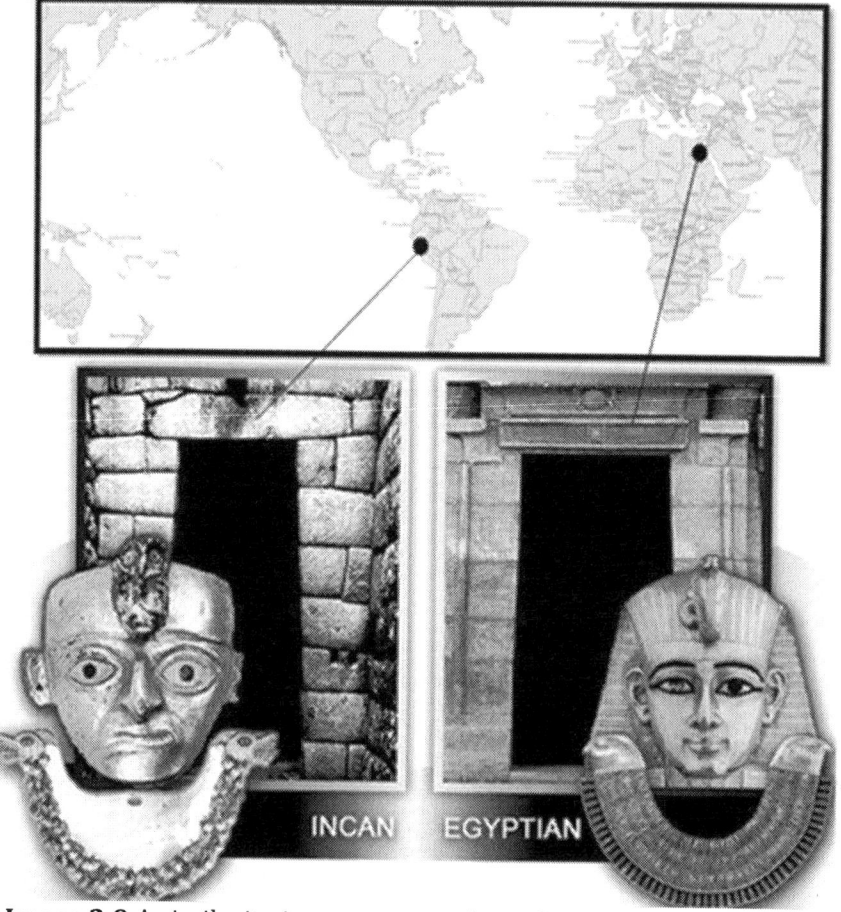

Image 2.9 A similarity in monuments from the pre-Incans or Incans of South America (left) and the Egyptians of Africa (right).

Image 2.10 Both the pre-Incan or Incan peoples and
the Egyptians mummified dead bodies
(image courtesy of Richard Cassaro for www.richardcassaro.com).

Image 2.11 The similarity in stonemasonry of both cultures and the
precision of the monuments is remarkable – both cultures were
capable of producing high-quality monuments which were designed
to be earthquake-proof
(image courtesy of Richard Cassaro for www.richardcassaro.com).

Image 2.12 Both cultures erected obelisks
(image courtesy of Richard Cassaro for www.richardcassaro.com).

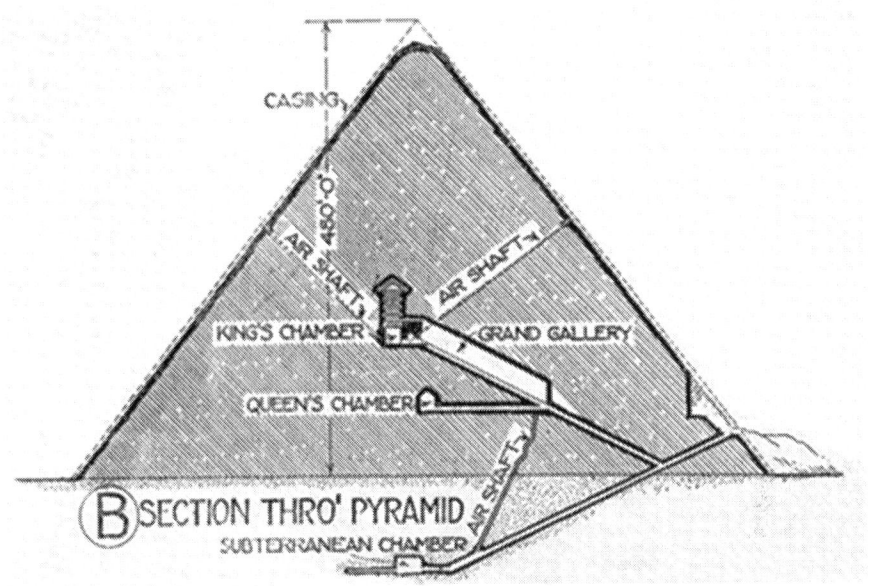

Image 2.13 A Sectional View of the Great Pyramid of Giza
(*A History of Architecture on the Comparative Method*, 1921).

The Great Pyramid of Giza is considered to be one of the ancient Egyptians' first – and mankind's greatest – building achievements, so why has this accomplishment never been paralleled? Egyptologists believe that the Great Pyramid was built around 2560 BC for Pharaoh Khufu and was completed within a 10-20 year period. It was designed to be earthquake-proof and remained the tallest man-made structure for almost 4,000 years. It was the most accurately aligned building on Earth (within three minutes of a degree from true north) until the construction of the Paris Observatory.[xii] The pyramid actually has eight sides, not four, which makes the planning and construction process *much* more of a challenge – so challenging, in fact, that this kind of monument has never been bettered. The pyramid contains three burial chambers, one of which is subterranean, carved into the bedrock (see Image 2.13). Various air shafts and pathways, hundreds of feet in length, were cut through solid rock and would have proved extremely challenging to construct – compound angles require precision tools and exceptional skill to design, especially with the level of accuracy demonstrated in the pyramid. In his book *The Giza Power Plant*, Christopher Dunn talks of his intrigue as to how such consistent tolerances were managed by supposedly primitive methods. The standard of precision is evident throughout the entire construction – thousands of the outer-casing blocks, reporting to weigh between 16 and 20 tons each, were manufactured with a tolerance of 1/100 inch (0.010) and installed with a gap of 0 to 1/50 inch (0.020).[xiii] This level of accuracy is not even required by modern building standards. In addition, 1/4 inch (0.25) tolerance is adequate for limestone blocks used in construction projects today, thus the ancient engineers once again demonstrate superiority over modern standards.[xiv] Dunn's experience with precise dimensional tolerances is extensive, and he says that he finds it amusing when Egyptologists claim that ancient monuments and artefacts were constructed freehand using only hammers and chisels (naturally, one is inclined to trust the analyses of a professional engineer over the speculation of an Egyptologist).

The pyramid contains an estimated 2.3 million blocks, made up of many different sizes and shapes – over 30 Empire State Buildings could be built using the stones from the Great Pyramid. The average weight of a single block is 2.5 tons, but some blocks weigh over 50 tons. Many of the limestone blocks were quarried from nearby sites, but remarkably, the King's Chamber (see Image 2.13) contains granite blocks that weigh in excess of 50 tons – they were quarried and transported from Aswan, 500 miles away, and raised to heights of over 150 feet before being installed with remarkable precision. Even with modern tools and the most skilled workers, it is unlikely that this project could be replicated today. In a documentary titled *The Revelation of the Pyramids*, the construction project is well summarised as follows: "4,700 years ago when the rest of the planet was still wandering around in animal skins, the ancient Egyptians flattened a limestone hillock, paved an area the size of six football pitches, piled up two million blocks of stone to the height of a 42-storey building, drove a narrow 300-foot long passage utterly straight through the rock, fitted the stone in the inner chamber with complete precision, built the outside of the pyramid with eight sides instead of four, made it earthquake-proof, lined it up precisely with true north and got the whole job done in 20 years using only chisels, mallets and rope."[xv]

Implausible Discoveries and Inevitable Speculation

Due to the implications of these monumental mysteries, many theories arise and plenty of speculation occurs. On that note, consider the following: the latitude of the Grand Gallery is 29.9792458° north. This number resonates with the speed of light (c), which is 299,792,458 metres per second. Although the units of measurement differ, 29.9792458° and 299,792,458 m/sec are the same numbers. So, whether it is accidental or deliberate, the speed of light is encrypted within the design of the Great Pyramid. The metre, as a unit of measurement, is said to be a modern invention that wasn't known to the ancient Egyptians. In 1983, the General Conference on Weights and Measures defined a metre as the length of the path travelled by light in the time interval of 1/299,792,458 of a second (prior to this, the definition was based upon a wavelength of krypton-86 radiation). It begs the question: is the definition of a metre an esoteric expression of our relationship with the Sun? If so, it is a subtle connection of the microcosm to the macrocosm ("As above, so below") and a demonstration of how esoteric philosophy has filtered down throughout the ages. As shall be reviewed later, the early Egyptian culture was influenced by that of the Sumerians, and it is the Sumerians who are credited with inventing the advanced base-60, or sexagesimal, number system, which is still in use today for the measuring of angles (360° in a circle), geographic coordinates and time. The Sumerians divided a single day into two lots of 12 hours before dividing an hour into 60 minutes. Thousands of years later, the minute was divided into 60 seconds – "time" literally began in Sumer. Considering that the division of a minute into 60 seconds is a rather modern invention, it would seem preposterous to claim that the speed of light (measured in metres per second) was deliberately encoded into the design of the Great Pyramid. Either way, it appears as though advanced metrology was involved with the design of the Great Pyramid.

In the construction industry, land surveying is a science that utilises various observational techniques to accurately calculate terrestrial or dimensional points, positions, angles and distances. One modern tool used for surveying is GPS (Global Positioning System) for which testing began in the 1970s before Full Operational Capability was declared in 1995. The Great Pyramid lies three minutes of a degree from true north and the mathematical constant of pi (π) is also concealed within the design of the pyramid. Either these "implausible discoveries" are merely coincidental or they are testimony of advanced surveying techniques that rival modern-day GPS.

Image 2.14 The Great Pyramid of Giza.

The Logistics of the Great Pyramid

Using the supposedly primitive methods of the ancient Egyptians, completing the project within 20 years would be a logistical nightmare or impossibility. When it comes to the logistics of a large group of people such as those involved in the pyramid construction project, the level of planning and preparation would have been enormous even by modern standards. An overall timeline would have been created with a breakdown of how much food, water, tools and other supplies would be required throughout the entire project. That is not to mention the painstaking process of creating a design on papyrus (or a 3D model) and calculating the size and shape of every block (there were a variety of different shapes and sizes). Organising the workforce would have involved recruiting quarrymen, hauliers, installers, farmers and many highly skilled workers. In comparison, Merle Booker, technical director of the Indiana Limestone Institute of America, conducted a Great Pyramid feasibility study in 1978. Consisting of 33 quarries, the Institute is considered by many architects to be one of the world's leading authorities on limestone. Booker concluded that it would take 27 years just to quarry, fabricate and transport the required materials if the entire Indiana Limestone Institute's facilities (33 quarries) could be used with a sufficient number of railroad cars. The study did not account for the installation of the blocks and assumed that there were no delays or equipment downtime during the entire project.[xvi] The requirements of the Great Pyramid were spectacular, even by modern standards. There are various ways to estimate the logistics for the Great Pyramid and many researchers have drawn vastly different conclusions, but in order to paint a basic picture, consider the following analysis:

The conventional theory states that the Great Pyramid was built in 20 years and is composed of an estimated 2.3 million blocks. Assuming that the work was non-stop for the entire 20 years (this would require round-the-clock effort), then approximately:

- 115,000 blocks would have to be moved every year, equivalent to 9,583 blocks every month, or 319 blocks every day.

Thus, approximately 13 blocks were positioned every hour. So, with the labourers working around the clock, they would have to install one stone every four-and-a-half minutes for the entire 20 years. How much manpower would that have taken? If just one stone was mislaid, installation in the immediate area would have to be halted and the erroneous process would have to be reversed before installing the block in its correct position. How many master builders/planners would have been involved to ensure that every single block was laid in its correct position? There was no time for mistakes and the precision of each block is amazing. The stones were made up of various sizes and shapes, and many master planners would have been needed to ensure that the appropriate blocks were cut and arranged ready for installation at the right time. It would have required communication between hundreds of people over distances that are not even linked by line of sight – there are so many logistical issues to consider. This estimation does not account for the amount of workers required to repair and replace the tools (rope, chisels, mallets and other materials such as clothes) each day, nor for the amount of workers required to lift and position the blocks. How many animals would have to be born and slaughtered just to feed the construction workers in a single day? How many animals would that be during a week or an entire month? It would require hundreds of farmers and workers just to manage the food preparation each month. And what about the granite stones that were quarried from Aswan, 500 miles away? There is no plausible explanation of how 50-ton blocks could be cut, lifted and installed using only wood, rope and other primitive tools. There is a *serious* discrepancy in the conventional theory of how and when the Great Pyramid was constructed. Thus, based on the conventional theories, this project would have been a logistical nightmare or *impossibility*.

Image 2.15 The Great Pyramid of Giza
(courtesy of a 19th-century stereopticon card photo).

Monumental Mysteries – Summary

The geometric precision, overall accuracy and sophistication of the Great Pyramid's design, combined with its geographical and astronomical relationships, testify to an impeccable observational science and advanced technology used for its construction, implying that ancient man had capabilities that we cannot account for. The structures in Egypt (and many other ancient building sites around the world) are testimony to technology comparable with stone-fabrication machinery that was used to cut, grind, sand and polish the materials used during the construction process. These ancient monuments were not produced by primitives, but were the products of advanced surveyors, engineers and scientists. Where did these exceptional skills come from and, more importantly, why were they lost? Whilst many conventional academics will not reassess their theories on the origins of civilisation, some sites of exceptional archaeological interest have been greatly restricted, systematically preventing much-needed research. My personal opinion is that the conventional date of the construction of the Great Pyramid (2560 BC) is totally wrong. Rather, it is a prehistoric monument built by an advanced civilisation – apart from the remaining structure, there is no real evidence to prove conclusively how it was built. Before investigating the demise of this advanced prehistoric civilisation, let's look further at some intriguing testimonies and see how esoteric knowledge can be encoded into architecture.

Image 2.16 The Great Pyramid
(image courtesy of Mstyslav Chernov).

3. Monumental Mysteries

Another perfect example of understated ancient ability is the site at Baalbek in Lebanon (this land, north of Israel, was once known as Phoenicia or Canaan). It is said to be one of the oldest building sites on Earth and again, much conjecture and mythology surround this site. It is home to one of the most ambitious construction projects ever completed – laid here are some of the largest cut stones on Earth, including one named the *Stone of the Pregnant Lady*. This single block is some 65 feet in length, 14 feet in height and estimated to weigh over 1,000 tons (see Image 3.1).

Image 3.1 The Pregnant Lady at Baalbek, Lebanon
(image courtesy of Oregon State University Collections and Archives).

The sheer size of this colossal block is bewildering. The men sitting on top look tiny in comparison and one has to wonder what methods would have been used to cut and transport it. As stated by researcher Andrew Collins: "It lays at a raised angle – the lowest part of its base still attached to the living rock – cut and ready to be broken free and transported to its presumed destination."[xvii] In his book *History of Baalbek*, the ex-curator of the Baalbek monuments, Michel Alouf, reveals how the ancient site has undergone minor transformations throughout various epochs, and says that the true origins of this site are unknown. The Romans undertook one of their largest building projects at Baalbek (which was never completed) and 2,000 years ago, during the peak of the Roman Empire, the original Baalbek fortress was *already* ancient. The antiquities of Baalbek in Lebanon are believed by some to be the only pre-diluvian (before the deluge or "great floods") monuments left on Earth.[xviii] Modern engineers and construction workers have great difficulty in explaining how the site at Baalbek was constructed – some of the original stones are much larger than anything we can feasibly manage today – let alone explain how it could have been managed thousands of years ago. The local legends state that the impeccable Baalbek fortress was built by Cain, son of Adam, in the year 134 of creation. As recorded in the Bible, Cain was banished from the Garden of Eden after he committed the first murder by killing his brother, Abel. The legends say he constructed the original fortress at Baalbek after a fit of rage and populated it with a race of giants.

Geographical Alignments

An architect, and producer of the documentary *Secrets in Plain Sight*, Scott Onstott, discovered a theoretical connection between the Baalbek monuments in Lebanon, Silbury Hill in England and the World Trade Centre in Baltimore, USA. What is the relevance of this alignment? Perhaps nothing, but it is worth discussing as it will provide a basic understanding of how sacred knowledge can be encoded into the design of cities, monuments and megaliths.

Image 3.2 The World Trade Centre in Baltimore (far left), Silbury Hill in England (centre) and Baalbek in Lebanon (far right) (image courtesy of Google Earth).

As shown in the aerial view of Earth (Image 3.2), a horizontal line has been placed over all three sites to connect Baalbek in the Middle East to Silbury Hill in England and the World Trade Centre in Baltimore, USA. After briefly discussing the wonders of Baalbek, let's investigate some points of interest in England.

Prehistoric Monuments, England

Image 3.3 Stonehenge is estimated to be 5,000 years old.

What was the purpose of Stonehenge and why was it built? Was this location chosen specifically? How was it built? These are all questions that archaeologists can't answer with absolute certainty. Perhaps we can gain an understanding of the ancient builder's mindset by taking a look at the aerial view of the Stonehenge Station Stones on Google Earth.

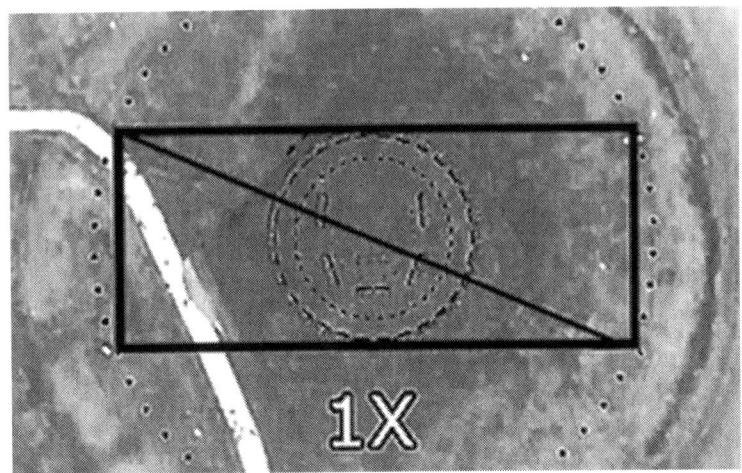

Image 3.4 An aerial view of Stonehenge's Station Stones (image courtesy of Google Earth).

Image 3.4 is an aerial view of the Station Stones rectangle (which encompasses a 5:12:13 triangle). Increasing this rectangle 2,500 times reveals a *possible* indication of why this location was chosen. See Image 3.5:

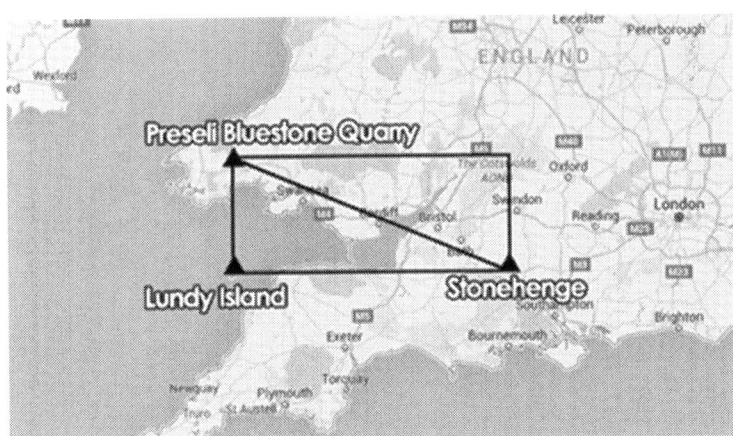

Image 3.5 Stonehenge (bottom right), Lundy Island (bottom left) and the Preseli Bluestone Quarry (top left). These three sites form a 5:12:13 triangle.

Increasing the dimensions of the Station Stone rectangle 2,500 times connects Stonehenge to the Preseli Bluestone Quarry from which the bluestones were quarried for the construction of Stonehenge. At approximately 130 miles away, one has to wonder how these stones were transported such a great distance and why it was necessary to use these particular bluestones. Directly below Preseli, in the Bristol Channel, is Lundy Island, and while Lundy is not usually associated with Stonehenge, there is a potential esoteric connection. A horizontal path of 123.4 miles runs from Stonehenge to Lundy Island (this distance can be measured on Google Earth). As reported by Richard Heath in his book *Sacred Number and the Origins of Civilisation*, the measurement 123.4 miles is equal to 108 Egyptian royal miles where 1 royal mile = 8/7 statute mile – the importance of the numbers 1234 and 108 will be discussed shortly.

Now consider Silbury Hill, a prehistoric artificial chalk mound near Avebury, located in the English county of Wiltshire (it is a part of the Stonehenge World Heritage Site). It is 130 feet in height and is one of the largest prehistoric man-made structures left in Europe; the purpose of its creation is also unknown.

Image 3.6 Silbury Hill is one the largest
prehistoric man-made structures in Europe
(image courtesy of Tony Grist).

The base of Silbury Hill (shown in Image 3.6) is located in close proximity to the prehistoric Stonehenge site and the distance between them is 86,400 feet. As was speculated in the previous chapter, it is possible that the definition of a metre is merely an expression of our relationship with the Sun. The Sun had a spiritual importance for the pagans and druids of antiquity, who worshipped its life-creating ability. With this in mind, consider the following: one complete rotation of the Earth takes 24 hours, or more specifically, one complete rotation of the Earth is divided into 86,400 units because there are 86,400 seconds in one day. Consider the Sun's mean diameter of 864,000 miles[xix] (99.8% accuracy) – in reality, solar astronomers have had great difficulty in accurately measuring the Sun's diameter and some even suggest that the Sun is shrinking.[xx]

Notice how one Earth rotation is divided into 86,400 units, a number which resonates with the Sun's mean diameter of 864,000 miles. Is the number of seconds in a day merely an expression of Earth's unity with the Sun – a subtle connection of the microcosm to the macrocosm ("As above, so below")? The number of feet between the prehistoric sites at Silbury Hill and Stonehenge (86,400) resonates with the mean diameter of the sun in miles (864,000) *and* the amount of seconds in a day (86,400). Once again we are left wondering if the prehistoric sites at Silbury and Stonehenge were purposely designed to express this esoteric harmony.

Summary

- The number of feet between Silbury Hill and Stonehenge: 86,400.
- The number of seconds in a day: 86,400.
- The mean diameter of the sun in miles: 864,000.[xxi]

Finally, before a conclusion is made, let's briefly look at the modern-day World Trade Centre located in Baltimore.

Baltimore, USA

The Baltimore World Trade Centre, USA, runs in alignment with Stonehenge, Lundy Island and Baalbek. The Baltimore World Trade Centre is the tallest regular pentagonal building on Earth. Its height measures precisely 123.4 metres. The numbers 1, 2, 3 and 4 feature in

Pythagoras's sacred Tetractys and interestingly:

- The Moon-to-Earth mass ratio is 1.23%.
- The Moon has a radius of 1,080 miles.

To summarise:

- The height of the World Trade Centre measures 123.4 metres.
- The distance between Stonehenge and Lundy Island is 123.4 statute miles, equal to 108 royal miles.
- The Moon-to-Earth ratio is 1.23% and the Moon has a radius of 1,080 miles.

The distance between Stonehenge and Lundy Island in statute and royal miles resonates with the Moon-to-Earth ratio and the Moon's radius in miles. Were the modern designers of the World Trade Centre aware of its geographical alignment with Silbury Hill and the possible significance of the numbers 1234 and 108? We can only speculate over whether these connections are merely a coincidence or an indication of something profound.

The Esoteric Connection

With an atomic weight of 108 grams per mole, silver is commonly associated with the Moon (as previously mentioned, the mean radius of the Moon is 1,080 miles). Perhaps it is merely coincidental, but the number 108 is found to be sacred to various religions. According to the Shiva Purana, the Hindu god Shiva has 1,008 names. There are 108 prayer beads on the holy rosary used by Sikhs, Hindus and Buddhists – the Muslims have adapted the holy rosary beads, as have the Roman Catholics, who use it to recite the Hail Mary prayer. As will be discussed in a coming chapter, the influence of Eastern mysticism led members of the Roman Catholic Church to elevate the Virgin Mary to the status of a deity. To the esotericists within the church, Mary represents the queen of heaven or the mother goddess who is commonly represented by the Moon, Venus or the star Sirius. Mother goddess worship is an ongoing theme of various mythical religions and esoteric brotherhoods, even in the modern world. The mother goddess pagan deity has various identities and characteristics depending upon the era and location in which she is being worshipped. She was known as Diana to the ancient Greeks, Isis to the ancient Egyptians, Parvati to the Hindus, Virgo to astrologers and Columbia to the early settlers of America. She is sometimes personified as a virgin or the queen of heaven, and naturally, critics of the Bible claim that the story of Jesus is simply a retelling of this ancient pagan myth – these claims will be addressed later as there is actually a more profound reason for these parallels. Perhaps you are familiar with the Statue of Liberty (designed by a French Freemason) located in New York or the icon of the American film production company, Columbia Pictures – these pagan idols represent the mother goddess (it is often claimed that America is a Christian nation, yet the pagan idols are plentiful). Interestingly, Washington DC, or the *District of Columbia* (in reference to Columbia, the mother goddess), was designed by Freemasons and corresponds to the celestial Virgo. In fact, the entire design of Washington DC embodies a remarkable quantity of esoteric symbolism and the capital is stylised as an ancient Egyptian necropolis (a temple for the dead). Interestingly, it was in the 18th century that the state of Virginia and the state of Maryland donated land for the establishment of the newly formed District of Columbia. It is remarkable, and also no coincidence, that two states containing the words "Virgin" and "Mary" gave birth to Washington DC – this offspring, constructed by esotericists, grew up to house the world's most formidable military force and is now the "murder management" capital of planet Earth.

Image 3.7 Parvati: Hindu Mother Goddess

Conclusion

From the ancient Egyptian sarcophagi to the Great Pyramid of Giza and the ancient megaliths of Baalbek and Stonehenge, the methods used for the construction of these monuments remain an exceptional mystery. Without speaking to the original designers, we can only speculate over the correlations which are mere coincidence and those which are esoteric and deliberate. For reasons unknown, the ancients appear to have encoded messages within the designs of their monuments. So what happened to the ancient technology used to construct such marvels?

4. The Lost Civilisation Hypothesis

The lost civilisation hypothesis requires a multi-disciplinary analysis; indeed, it has become increasingly recognised amongst researchers and academics. This following chapter presents scientific analyses, physical evidence and documented history that support the theory of a recent global transformation. Regardless of personal worldviews, many scientists and historians agree that the Earth underwent some dramatic changes just a few thousand years ago.

The Deluge: Ice Age

As defined on Wikipedia: "An ice age, or more precisely, a glacial age, is a period of long-term reduction in the Earth's surface and atmospheric temperature resulting in the presence of continental ice sheets."[xxii] According to a common theory of geologists, the last glacial period ended several thousand years ago (meaning the Earth is currently in an interglacial period), and the last series of glaciations covered North America and Eurasia in huge sheets of ice.[xxiii] The Earth's climate was profoundly impacted by the ice sheets, leading to droughts, desertification and a dramatic drop in sea level.[xxiv] It is suggested that the most recent glacial period could have ended just over 10,000 years ago when the ice began to melt, causing a huge rise in sea-level – various super-floods would have submerged coastal regions beneath the water. Sea levels rose by 120 meters around the world, resulting in more than 27 million km^2 of land being submerged beneath the sea.

The Deluge: Catastrophic Plate Tectonics

Geophysicist Dr. John Baumgardner has spent 25 years investigating evidence of a vast geological transformation. After extensive research, he concludes that a planetary-scale tectonic catastrophe caused a vast transformation on the Earth. Although Dr. Baumgardner doesn't agree on the timescale for the aforementioned glacial periods, his research has led him to conclude that extensive flooding covered the entire Earth and that it was caused by a phenomenon he calls *catastrophic plate tectonics*. The conventional theory of plate tectonics assumes a level of uniformitarianism (i.e. the Earth's plates drift at a constant rate which has remained unchanged for millions of years), but Dr. Baumgardner's research led him to conclude that a worldwide catastrophe caused a rapid global flood. Research geologist Dr. Steven Austin favours this theory and states: "If uniformitarian assumptions are discarded... then a catastrophic plate tectonics model explains everything that slow-and-gradual plate tectonics does plus most everything it can't explain."[xxv]

The Deluge: Physical Evidence

Doggerland is a region of a former landmass that once connected Great Britain to mainland Europe. Recent research suggests that tens of thousands of inhabitants once occupied this region, making it the heartland of Europe before it gradually became submerged beneath the rising sea level.

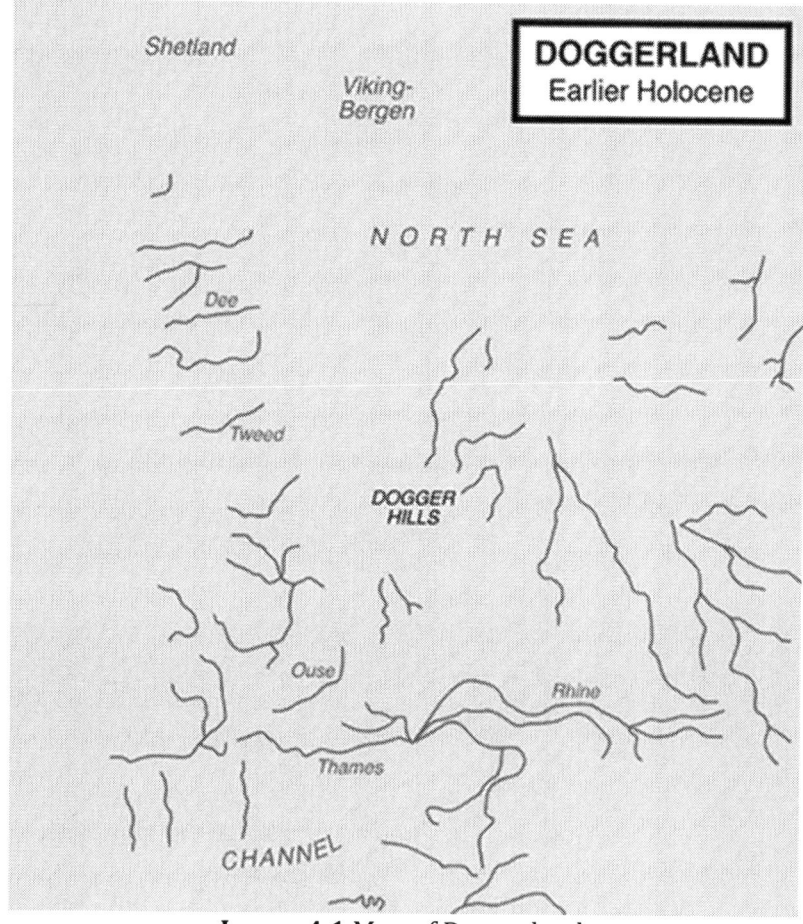

Image 4.1 Map of Doggerland
(image courtesy of Max Naylor for Creative Commons).

Image 4.1 illustrates the hypothetical extent of Doggerland that connected Great Britain (located to the left) to mainland Europe (located to the right). Interestingly, a recent hypothesis claims that much of the land was flooded by a devastating tsunami around 8,000 years ago – thousands of people could have been killed in the disaster which submerged the region underwater (was this due to catastrophic plate tectonics or the end of a glacial period?).

Yonaguni Island: Underwater Monuments

Another site of interest, which lays amongst a small chain of islands south of Japan, is Yonaguni (Image 4.2). In this region, approximately 80 feet underwater, are what appear to be the remains of an ancient civilisation; however, as with the great pyramid structures in Bosnia, Europe, it is debated as to whether these marvels are man-made or natural.

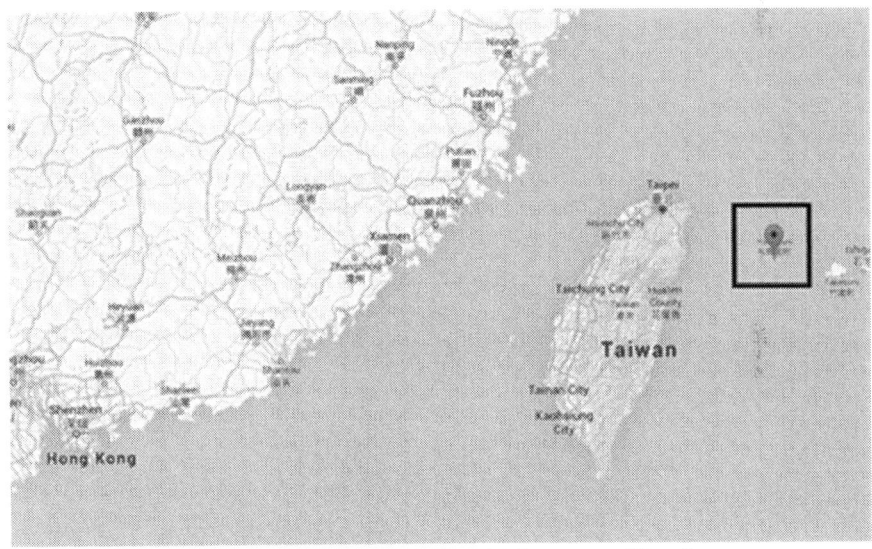

Image 4.2 Yonaguni Island, Yaeyama District.

After first-hand investigation that began in 1997, researcher of antiquities Graham Hancock became convinced that these structures were man-made. His systematic programme of underwater photography and research continued until 2001.

Image 4.3 A monument lying at depths of 30 metres below the sea (image courtesy of Santha Faiia, 1999).

If these monuments are manmade, they would have been constructed over 5,000 years ago, when sea levels were much lower. Sundaresh, an experienced marine archaeologist from the National Institute of Oceanography in Goa, India, is one expert who, after an expedition back in September 2000, concluded that these structures were man-made: "The terraced structures with a canal are undoubtedly man-made, built by cutting an existing huge monolithic outcrop."[xxvi]

Indeed, scattered all around the world are traces of various coastal civilisations submerged beneath the water, helping to fuel the legends of Atlantis which were popularised by Plato just over 2,000 years ago (although Plato originally stated that Atlantis was one specific island located in the Atlantic). As the scientific analysis reveals, our Earth has recently been subjected to huge cataclysms and it appears as though a deluge (a severe flood) could have been responsible for wiping out various civilisations across the world. It is difficult to be certain of when this event (or events) happened and how severe the flooding was – some experts say that only coastal regions would have been affected, whilst others believe that entire countries were submerged beneath the water.

The Deluge: The Legends

There are hundreds of different tales from all over the world that speak of a devastating flood that wiped out civilisation. From South America, Europe, Africa and Asia to Australia, various civilisations, isolated by location and time, each speak of a great flood with many common characteristics. From ancient Sumer, it is the Epic of Gilgamesh that talks of a great flood – this is one of the earliest surviving works of literature known to man. In ancient China it is the Gun-Yu myth, and in India it is the story of Manu (a man who survived the great floods in a boat). Of course, in the Bible, this is the tale of Noah's Ark – an enchanting story that many children are told from a young age. With so many of these ancient tales on every continent, one has to wonder whether they originate from an actual event – a global cataclysm that almost wiped out mankind. The Epic of Gilgamesh could, in some respects, be considered as the start of recorded history, before which mankind is essentially mute. Found in Babylonian and Sumerian culture, the original Gilgamesh writings can be dated as far back as 2000 BC, but the story was certainly an oral tradition before the invention of writing. There are various aspects of this story which align with Noah's Ark (such as the story originating in the Middle East and there being a few survivors in a boat) and if these were the only two stories, Noah *could* be considered a retelling of the Epic of Gilgamesh. However, with overwhelming evidence of a mass flood and an apparent retelling of this event throughout countless generations all over the globe, it is reasonable to conclude that these stories originate from an actual event – in fact, in light of the evidence, it seems ignorant to dismiss such stories as pure mythology.

The Sumerian King List

One particular region to which modern archaeologists trace the birth (or *rebirth*) of civilisation is ancient Sumer (the region of present-day Iraq). As shall be reviewed later in this work, the Sumerians were a mysterious yet highly sophisticated people who are credited with inventing writing and are said to have over 100 "firsts" as testimony to their achievements. In fact, the history of Iraq is, in many ways, a history of Western civilisation. But is it any wonder that they were so advanced, if they were descendants of a sophisticated pre-diluvian culture? Recently discovered in Iraq, the Sumerian King List (Image 4.5) is an immensely valuable 4,000-year-old cuneiform manuscript that provides a unique insight into the deepest antiquity. This intriguing artefact contains a chronological list of the kings of ancient Sumer and the lengths of their reigns. Although some of the kings are known to have existed, there is still scholarly debate on how much of the Sumerian King List is mythological and how much is factual (for example, the manuscript claims that some of the kings reigned for elaborate lengths of time). With specific reference to the great flood, it claims that kingship descended from heaven and records the kings who ruled the pre-flood world. It is evident that the Sumerian people believed civilisation (and the skills required to maintain a civilisation) was a gift from the gods, and that the monarchy was a divine institution – the kings of ancient Sumer were gods on Earth.[xxvii] Although this tradition of the "divine right" of kings appears to have originated in ancient Sumer, it was present in many ancient cultures all over the world – it has even trickled down to the modern day.

Image 4.5 The Sumerian King List.

The Lost Civilisation Hypothesis: Conclusion

The scientific analyses, the physical evidence and the similarity in worldwide accounts all support the theory of a deluge, and this explains why the technology and techniques used in the construction of ancient monuments have disappeared. The accounts of Gilgamesh and Noah are clearly based on genuine events – they are a record of the most cataclysmic event in known history, yet today, the story is given little consideration. Conventional theories on the origins of civilisation do not account for the pre-diluvian life (neither the inhabitants nor their technology). Some of the most astonishing building projects ever completed are attributed to primitives who had just emerged from the Stone Age. Various engineers have falsified these conventional theories – it's apparent that some of these monuments were built in a forgotten epoch in which the building techniques and level of technology were comparable with the present day. It's quite unlikely that these forgotten civilisations harnessed fossil fuels, machinery and the internal combustion engine, but instead used alternative energies and technologies. Today, memory and understanding of our past is fragmented. Hundreds, maybe thousands of civilisations could have been obliterated in a global cataclysm that occurred just a few thousand years ago. One has to wonder why an advanced race wasn't better prepared for such an event. After all, they had the ability to build complex monuments that survived earthquakes and all the extremities of Mother Nature. With an apparent high mortality rate, a few surviving members of the human race had to start from scratch, re-learning the basic skills to build and maintain a civilisation.

The Rebirth of Civilisation

Philosophers can look back at the Epic of Gilgamesh, found in Babylonian and Sumerian culture, to see some of the earliest recorded thoughts of mankind. Gilgamesh is presented as a tyrant who is seeking to find the meaning of life. It is a work of intriguing and despairing philosophy and morality, and tells of man seeking a relationship with the divine. The origins of this quest for immortality will be discussed later, as it has some genuine implications on the religions and esoteric orders of today. Modern philosophers and theologians battle with the same questions as those presented in the Epic of Gilgamesh: origin, meaning, morality and destiny[xxviii]. In terms of aspirations, mankind has changed very little over the course of several thousand years. Since the 2003 Western-led invasion and occupation of Sumer (now known as Iraq), the country's infrastructure has been destroyed and the land has been mired in violence. Saddam Hussein spent over 20 years re-developing Babylon and identified with the legendary King Nebuchadnezzar II (605-526 BC). Babylon was a bustling commercial hub and played an influential role in world history for hundreds of years. It was on Tisha B'Av (the ninth day of the month of Av in the Hebrew calendar) in 587 BC that King Nebuchadnezzar II destroyed the Jewish-built Temple of Solomon in Israel before the Israelite tribes were sent into exile.

בית־המקדש הראשון—שיחזור
בכניסה אל בית־המקדש ניצבים שני עמודים—יכין ובועז.

Image 4.6 A depiction of the First Jewish Temple:
The Temple of Solomon.

The Regeneration of Babylon

In 2009, construction of the largest and most expensive embassy *ever* built was completed – in close proximity to the ruins of ancient Babylon, near the present-day city of Baghdad. Costing the Americans over $700 million to construct, it has left many people wondering why such an extravagant foreign project of this kind was implemented. As stated on the embassy's website: "Our second largest grant is the Future of Babylon Project, which is funded by the United States Government."[xxix] With an increased Western presence throughout the politically unstable Middle East, efforts have begun to rebuild Iraq's offensive military capabilities and its economy – are we witnessing the attempted resurrection of an empire that once ruled the world? In his 2005 Inaugural Address, George W Bush compellingly stated: "When our Founders declared a new order of the ages... they were acting on an ancient hope that is meant to be fulfilled." To understand this "ancient hope", which is central to the theme of this book, an analysis of the geopolitical climate is first required. An agenda is currently unfolding which can be traced right back to this remote period of mankind's history... welcome to Babylon Resurrected.

5. The Oligarchs and Politics

A New World Order

Fast forward to the near present day, when in 1994, speaking at the UN Ambassador's dinner, David Rockefeller stated: "This present window of opportunity, during which a truly peaceful and interdependent world order might be built, will not be open for too long." In recent years, various politicians and prominent businessmen (including Henry Kissinger, Tony Blair, Gordon Brown and Barack Obama) have all spoken of a "New World Order". The Vatican called for a universal jurisdiction and, on World Day of Peace in 2004, the pope declared: "More than ever, we need a new international order."[xxx] Speaking on the New World Order, Winston Churchill stated: "The creation of an authoritative world order is the ultimate aim toward which we must strive."[xxxi] All the world's greatest business, religious and political figures are talking of a New World Order – but what is a New World Order and why is it so imperative? The potential implications of this movement can ultimately be realised based upon the ideologies, policies and proposals of the globalists, thus eliminating any conspiracy theories. For example, elitist David Rockefeller stated: "Some even believe we are part of a secret cabal working against the best interests of the United States, characterizing my family and me as 'internationalists' and of conspiring with others around the world to build a more integrated global political and economic structure – one world, if you will. If that's the charge, I stand guilty, and I am proud of it."

The Political Spectrum

To gain an understanding of the current geopolitical climate and the potential implications of a New World Order, a basic understanding of the political spectrum is required. This political spectrum is defined by the amount of control a government has over an individual. At one end of the spectrum is individualism, where individuals are independent and self-reliant. At the other end of the spectrum is statism, where the state has substantial control over an individual. The introduction of taxes, laws or regulations increases the amount of control a government has and decreases the freedom of an individual. The following basic representation of the political spectrum scales from "total" individual freedom on the right to "zero" individual freedom on the left:

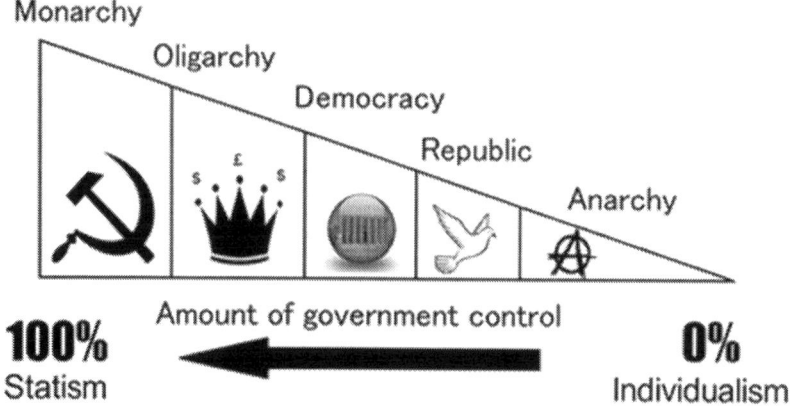

Image 5.1 The Political Spectrum (from right to left): individualism (total freedom) to statism (where an individual has no freedom).

Anarchy: No rule. Anarchy is a society that has no government, laws or taxes (the concept of individualism). This is usually a transitional period between the downfall of one government and the establishment of another.

Constitutional Republic: The rule of law, not of men. This system is designed to restrain a government and give individuals the freedom to live and prosper. Every law or tax enforced gives the government a higher level of control and the individual less freedom.

Democracy: The rule of people. This can be a disadvantage as the majority can rule over the minority (mob rule leads to tyranny and corporatism and can act as a stage show, giving individuals the impression that they are in control).

Oligarchy: The rule of an elite network or an expansive government. This system has similar characteristics as a monarch; it leads to high taxes, wars, conquest of other nations and the loss of individual freedom (the concept of statism).

Monarchy: The rule of a single person (king, queen or dictator). This system has similar characteristics to oligarchy.

To make this political spectrum more simplistic, anarchy can be removed from the scale as this usually occurs within a transitional period. A monarchy (the rule by one) can also be removed as, typically, kings, queens or dictators operate within an elite network of peers and advisors. Remaining on the political scale is:

- Republic.
- Democracy.
- Oligarchy.

Monarchs and Oligarchs

Since the rebirth of civilisation, the most common form of rule has always been that of a monarch (a single head of state who inherits the right to rule over a kingdom) or an oligarch (a super-wealthy elite network), both of which have similar traits. Monarchs and oligarchs practise intermarriage and inbreeding in order to solidify their power and wealth. In his book *Oligarchy*, political scientist Jeffery Winters presents his research into a wide range of oligarchs, ranging from antiquity to contemporary Indonesia, and he defines the oligarch as a "system of wealth defence". Revealing that the existential motive of the oligarch is to accumulate wealth, Winters demonstrates how oligarchs continue to operate throughout Europe, America and various other parts of the world[xxxii] (as shall be demonstrated throughout this work). Based on a historical analysis, the general ideologies and characteristics of oligarchs and monarchs are as follows:

- Moral, legal and constitutional constraints are totally absent.
- Monarchs typically inherit the throne by birth.
- They believe themselves to be elite or divinely appointed. In the days of antiquity, they believed themselves to be gods (this is common on most continents in every era, from South America, Europe and Africa to Asia).
- The intention to perpetuate oligarchy: to conquer foreign territories and resources, to accumulate wealth and to defend it by any means necessary (imperialism).
- They practise inbreeding and intermarriage. Their children inherit their wealth and power (the continuation of their legacy).
- They believe individuals are incapable of managing their own lives and they don't like independent individuals (the concept of individualism) within a society – dependence on the state is preferred.

- They don't like industry, creativeness or innovation (especially if it is foreign), as it leads to individualism and potential threats, but they will exploit, use and suppress technology for their own benefit.
- They see people as a burden on society and the planet – the removal of the middle-class from society is preferable.

These are the undying prejudices of an oligarch and they are accompanied by an irrational thirst for domination; their main objective has always been to *perpetuate oligarchy*. Under the rule of such a system, every aspect of civilisation comes under attack. Elitists play the game of geopolitics and use practices such as usury (the practice of lending money at high rates of interest), monetarism, genocide, slavery, looting, physical warfare, psychological warfare (also known as the "war on consciousness") and drug cultivation. So have these barbaric practices and ideologies died out?

Venice and the Great British Oligarchs

Historian Webstar Tarpley states: "The oligarchical system of Great Britain is not an autochthonous product of English or British history. It represents rather the tradition of the Babylonians, Romans, Byzantines, and Venetians which has been transplanted into the British Isles through a series of upheavals."xxxiii This statement is perhaps debatable, but Britain's pre-industrial rise to imperial greatness was certainly during an age of oligarchy, of which Tarpley states: "The world centre of gravity for the forces of oligarchism was the oligarchy of Venice." Founded upon the marshy lagoons of the Adriatic Sea, the Serene Republic of Venice was extremely prosperous and lasted for over a thousand years (whilst there are no historical records of when Venice was officially founded, refugees escaping from Roman cities which underwent invasions by Germanic and Hun tribes, began settling in Venice in around the 6th century AD. The first Doge or Duke of Venice was elected in the early 8th century). Venice incorporated one of the most influential and longstanding oligarchs in history and served as a great fascination for the British Whig political party during the 18th century. In fact, the 19th-century British Prime Minister, Benjamin Disraeli, revealed a well-known secret amongst oligarchs in his novel *Coningsby* when he stated: "The great object of Whig leaders... was to establish in England a high aristocratic republic on the model of the Venetian."xxxiv

The House of Saxe-Coburg and Gotha and the House of Schleswig-Holstein-Sonderburg-Glücksburg (alias the "House of Windsor")

In all its supremacy, the British Empire has a great history of savagery and occult strangeness. Europe's royal households are predominately inbred. Consider the current British monarch, Queen Elizabeth II, who, as a descendant of William the Conqueror, is related to the heads of many European reigning and non-reigning royal houses. Queen Elizabeth II (of Saxe-Coburg and Gotha) is married to her second cousin once removed, Prince Philip (of Schleswig-Holstein-Sonderburg-Glücksburg), the Duke of Edinburgh. Perhaps more remarkably, various American presidents, including the Bush family, are related to the British royal family, thus the true extent of this trans-oceanic bloodline is vast. Various genealogical researchers, such as Harold Brooks-Baker, who worked for Burke's Peerage Partnership, are advocates of the "most royal candidate theory", which claims that *every* US president since George Washington can have their bloodline traced back to various European royals.[xxxv] Queen Elizabeth II is considered by some experts as a "divinely ordained" royal succession that descends from ancient Israel's Royal House of David. The Royal College of Heralds in Britain holds in its archives some manuscripts which repeat this "traditional" genealogy of the medieval English Kings. British-Israelism is rife amongst the upper echelon, some of whom believe themselves to be descendants of the Twelve Tribes of Israel. Although this hypothesis of British-Israelism has been refuted by various researchers, it continues to have various significant adherents, including some of the elitists themselves. The fuel for these rumours is the fact that the British monarchy is rooted in Hebrew traditions (for example, as a baby, Prince Charles was circumcised by a rabbi). Some researchers suggest that the very name "British" is Hebrew for "covenant man" or "man of the covenant" (the Hebrew word "b'rit" means covenant and "ish" or "eesh" means man). According to the Old Testament, God made an unconditional covenant with David and promised that his descendants would inherit the throne, thus Queen Elizabeth II has the "God-given" right to rule. Following the Great Fire of London in 1666, Christopher Wren, who was working with the Royal Society, had the vision of rebuilding London as the New Jerusalem or "Zion" (Zion is a synonym for Jerusalem). In approximately 1804, William Blake, who had connections to Freemasonry, wrote the famous poem *Jerusalem*, which speaks of rebuilding God's chosen nation in England:

I will not cease from Mental Fight,
Nor shall my Sword sleep in my hand:
Till we have built Jerusalem,
In England's green and pleasant Land

After London was chosen to host the 2012 Olympic Games, it was interesting to note how both the opening and closing Olympic ceremonies were riddled with creepy and occult symbolic gestures. In an obvious reference to the two most frequently mentioned cities in the Bible, Babylon and Jerusalem, the ceremony opened with an orchestra playing *Nimrod*, from Edward Elgar's Enigma Variations, followed by a choir singing William Blake's *Jerusalem* before the event descended into an outright bizarre pagan ritual. It was the London-based company, Wolff Olins, that was responsible for designing the highly criticised 2012 logo which could be re-ordered to spell "Zion". Iran's Olympic committee threatened to pull out of the Olympics due to "subliminal pro-Israeli propaganda".

Oligarchs and the "isms"

Typically, monarchs and oligarchs favour systems such as communism, fascism or totalitarianism – the "isms" (where taxes are high and individual freedoms are limited or where individuals are *entirely* subject to the state). Although a democracy can be congenial, briefly consider the following:

- Socialism (an economic system) advocates either severe limitation or total ownership and regulation of property, production, distribution and trade by the community or state. Many societies throughout the world practise varying levels of socialism.
- Communism is a system in which the state (a single party) owns all property with little or no restraint. Communist Russia, North Korea and China are familiar examples of communism in which the state governs most aspects of society.

Communist nations generally require the removal or complete regulation of religion – the state replaces God. National Socialism, blended with fascism, was the political ideology of Hitler and the Nazis. Nazi biological racism and race superiority were rooted in the occult philosophy of the "Aryan master race", as shall be reviewed later in this work. Karl Marx is regarded as the father of modern communism and the Marxist theory states: "Socialism is merely a transitional state between the end of capitalism and the start of communism." Huberman and Sweezy stated: "Socialism is the first step in the process of developing the productive forces to achieve abundance and changing the mental and spiritual outlook of the people. It is the necessary transition stage from capitalism to communism."[xxxvi]

What is a New World Order?

The New World Order is a system in which every society on Earth will be subject to a central global authority. Since the days of antiquity, all the greatest monarchs and oligarchs have dreamt of conquering the known world. After highlighting the common ideologies of oligarchs and defining the political spectrum, a coherent understanding of the modern New World Order agenda can now be achieved. This transnational order has progressed significantly over the past century, yet many individuals within society are *totally* unaware of what is taking place. With state-enforced "political correctness" and multiculturalism, the poorly managed mass immigration into America and Europe (and specifically Britain) is deliberate and is fostering the death of patriotism, individualism and cultural identity. It has been engineered to destabilise nations, demoralise the natives and to undermine their values. The media is a tool which is partially used for the erosion of social and family cohesion. People often accuse their governments of being incompetent, but they are far from it – they are conniving, corrupt and merely following an agenda which aims to dismantle sovereign nations from the inside. In Europe, we are witnessing the undermining of national sovereignty as democratic power is being transferred from the local and national governments to unelected centralised bodies. The aim is to implement a transnational government who will come to rule over all relevant political, economic, ecclesiastic and military issues on a local, national and international scale. Today, a New World Order is possible due to the network of globalists and elite families, consisting of royal, religious, political and corporate bodies, who have established power bases on a global scale – it's a kind of polycentric oligarchical system. This ancient and ambitious dream is becoming a reality for the modern-day globalists, so is there a subversive agenda behind it? The extent to which the members of this system will go to achieve their goal is unbelievable, but as will be demonstrated throughout this work, many of the major events that have shaped history are merely components of this New World Order objective.

6. The Nature of a Conspiracy

In his memoirs, Winston Churchill labelled the "reconstitution of society" as a conspiracy: "This worldwide conspiracy for the overthrow of civilisation and for the reconstitution of society on the basis of arrested development and envious malevolence, an impossible equality, has been steadily growing. It has been the mainspring of every subversive movement during the nineteenth century."xxxvii By definition, a conspiracy is some form of subversive agenda or treacherous plot. Conspiracy theories thrive in times of widespread panic, disorder or any major event involving a nation's government (such as an election, assassination or economic crisis). Living in the Information Age, conspiracy theories spread like wildfire via the media, mobile phones and social networking sites, and leave an indelible mark on society. Naturally, conspiracy theories are prone to ridicule, especially if the political or economic climate is in turmoil – misinformation can act as a barrier to people who wish to discover the truth or take effective action in changing the situation. With that in mind, the aim of this work is to form an objective view of reality by exercising caution and critical thinking and to make a distinction between conspiracy *theory* and *fact*. Although the next few chapters dwell on some rather negative aspects, the aim is to demonstrate why society is heading into such uncertain times, to encourage individual prudence and activism and ultimately to share the greatest of all revelations.

When trying to comprehend the magnitude or implications of a conspiracy, consider the Manhattan Project, which saw the production of the first atomic bomb used in World War II. The project was led by the United States who collaborated with Canada and the United Kingdom. Multiple research and production sites were created throughout each of the Allied countries and the cost of this project reached an estimated $25 billion (in modern value).xxxviii The project employed over 130,000 people, but no more than a few dozen men knew the full meaning of the project.xxxix The Manhattan Project is certainly an extensive conspiracy and the dropping of atomic bombs over Japan led to the death of more than 100,000 people (some estimates suggest around 200,000). The explosive power of an atomic bomb is devastating, and the lethal after-effects of nuclear fallout and radiation poisoning are catastrophic to life and the environment. Today, the United States and the United Kingdom are the dominant stockpilers of nuclear, chemical and biological weapons (weapons of mass destruction), whilst at the same time they impose sanctions, threaten war and condemn other nations who may possess such capabilities. The United States has continuously demonstrated bellicosity like no other nation in history, bombing over 25 countries since World War II.[xl] In fact, since the country was established just over 230 years ago, this nation seems to have been at war for most of its existence. And, of course, the United States is not faceless, so who are the people behind the wars and policies?

Anti-Patriotic Activity

Consider the late US senator, Prescott Bush (1895-1972), who founded the Bush political dynasty and was one of several directors of the Union Banking Corporation. In 1942, the Union Banking Corporation assets were seized under the Trading with the Enemy Act after an investigation discovered they were holding gold on behalf of the Nazis. Union Banking Corporation (including Prescott Bush who was the grandfather of George W Bush) was involved in severely anti-patriotic activities, working with the very businesses that financed Hitler.[xli] Rewind even further, almost a decade, to the year 1933 when allegations of a political conspiracy emerged, now referred to as The Business Plot. A Major General in the US Marine Corps named Smedley Butler testified to the Special Committee on Un-American Activities (a congressional committee), stating that various wealthy businessmen were plotting to overthrow the American president and implement a Nazi-styled fascist regime (complete with Nazi-styled labour camps) – the committee regarded these allegations as credible. Funded by the Du Pont and Morgan dynasties (with involvement from Prescott Bush and various others), a military-style coup was planned, which Major General Smedley was recruited to head. Thankfully, as a true patriot, Smedley exposed the conspiracy and the plan was foiled.[xlii]

The Brotherhood of Death

Before working in investment banking, collaborating with Nazis and conspiring against the US government and its citizens, Prescott Bush graduated from Yale University after being initiated into a mysterious order known as the Skull and Bones Society. Family tradition saw both George H Bush and George W Bush become members of this exclusive fraternity, known as the Brotherhood of Death, before they entered the White House as presidents. Young initiates of the Skull and Bones are destined for some of the most powerful job roles in America. The 2004 US election saw John F Kerry and George W Bush go head to head campaigning for the presidency. However, Kerry and Bush are both members of the same Skull and Bones order, so regardless of who won the 2004 election, a Bonesman was once again destined to rule the country. Economist and historian Anthony Sutton (1925-2002) revealed the purpose and power of the Skull and Bones fraternity: "The Order has either set up or penetrated just about every significant research, policy and opinion-making organization in the United States, in addition to the church, business, law, government and politics."[xliii] Bonesmen undertake dark oaths, hold bewildering philosophies and perform bizarre death, rebirth and sex rituals, but what implication does this have on their political and business careers? The skull and crossbones symbol is commonly identified with the Jolly Roger (and 17th-century pirates) and the god of death. The origin of this society and its logo will soon become clear.

Figure 6.1 The Skull and Bones logo represents
the god of death – Osiris or Satan
(image courtesy of Yale University Archives).

A New World Order: Background Study

When George H Bush famously announced plans for a New World Order before a Joint Session of the Congress, the date was September 11th 1990. He stated in a later speech: "We can find meaning and reward by serving some higher purpose than ourselves. A shining purpose, the illumination of 1000 points of light."[xliv] What higher, shining purpose is he talking of? After his son, George W Bush, was elected, he asked twice during his inauguration speech: "Do you not think an angel rides in the whirlwind and directs this storm?" Whether or not you choose to acknowledge the esoteric overtone in the Bushs' historical speeches, we are moving towards a New World Order. The author of *Apollyon Rising*, Tom Horn, states that during the American Revolution and establishment of the United States of America, the number of secret societies was at an all-time high.[xlv] From behind the scenes, members of the Jesuits, the Vatican, the Freemasons, the Rosicrucians, the Illuminati and other mysterious orders were guiding the geopolitical climate and economic matters, as they still do to this day. When talking on the objectives of the Jesuits (Pope Francis, the most recently selected pope, is a Jesuit, and the Jesuits will be reviewed later in this work), historian and author Bill Hughes stated: "The Jesuits failed in their attempts to have a world governing body following World War I. They accomplished their sinister goal after World War II. Following the war, the weary, aching world was conditioned to accept an international government, and the United Nations was born. Since the creation of the United Nations in 1945, this so-called 'peace-keeping' body has failed miserably in keeping peace around the world. Why? Because keeping peace is not their purpose, even though they continue to claim that it is."[xlvi]

7. Prophets of the Money God

As stated by an organisation named The Rules: "The richest 300 people on Earth have as much wealth as the poorest 3 billion... the equivalent of one-third of the world's annual income – $21 trillion – is being hidden through tax havens where the rules that apply to the rest of us... don't apply to corporations and the super-rich... One of the biggest and most important tax havens for the entire global system is the City of London."[xlvii] Many of the world's governments are covertly headed by a cartel of international bankers and corporate elites who are not restricted by national laws or constrained by national boundaries. Together with the royal and religious elites, over the past three centuries, they have enslaved and bankrupted entire nations and financed major wars. They further profit from their investments in weapons manufacturers and contracting firms (e.g. £40 billion of taxpayers' money has been spent to rebuild Iraq since 2003[xlviii]). Consider the British multinational weapons manufacturer, BAE Systems, which had sales of £17.8 billion in 2012.[xlix] Despite the recent economic downturns, the highly concentrated industry of arms manufacturing saw a growth in profits for over 10 years and sales of weapons and military services exceeded £250 billion in 2010. As an example of a conflict of interests, in 2009 it was revealed that the leader of the Conservative Party, David Cameron (who went on to become the British Prime Minister), had accepted £100,000 funding from a Lebanese former arms dealer. The globe-trotting, warmongering Prime Minister now travels the world to promote arms sales and helps to clinch multi-million pound arms deals whilst also pursuing a policy of "liberal interventionism". As the largest debt generator, war is big business – so what gives this sinister system such a rude legitimacy?

The Federal Reserve

Hundreds of millions of lives were lost in warfare in the last century (the 20th century was known as the American century and was the bloodiest in human history). Whilst 190 million Americans are overweight or obese,[l] one in seven people throughout the world go hungry. India and China are the largest producers and exporters of food,[li] but these same two countries are home to some of the largest populations of people who are starving. Why is there no balance? Why is the global economy so unstable? Why do the media focus our attention on mind-numbingly trivial issues? The United States of America, also known as Land of the

Free, was established as a constitutional republic – apparently *some* of the founding fathers were aware of the inherent risks of a democracy. The constitution (the rule of law) was designed specifically for the citizens by giving the government limited power. Although prudent citizens would never willingly surrender their liberties, today there is little restraint on the regulatory powers that the government has over its people. Average American citizens may believe themselves to be somewhat under the protection of their constitution, but the country has slipped into a "democracy" and the people have had their constitutional rights removed incrementally. Various political commentators claim that socialism is creeping into the American way of life and, as previously stated, the father of communism, Karl Marx, stated that socialism was a transitional state between the end of capitalism and the start of communism. The American Federal Reserve is the central banking system of the United States. Despite the deceptive name, this institution is not federal; it was privatised in 1913. According to Article 1, Section 8 of the US Constitution, the privately owned Federal Reserve is an illegal enterprise. The Federal Reserve Act was implemented under deceptive and cunning tactics and, as a result, the citizens of the United States have lost control over their government, economy and constitution. Today, the US dollar is the most widely traded currency on Earth, but this currency is essentially worthless and is not backed by gold or silver – not only is the Federal Reserve not federal, but it has no reserves either. America has been pushed into bankruptcy and the privatisation of the Federal Reserve has consolidated political, economic and military power in the hands of unnamed shareholders – if a government is not in control of its currency, it is not in control of much else. Obama amassed a further $5 trillion debt during his time in the White House and the US national debt now exceeds $16 trillion.[lii] The inherent danger of privatising a central bank is clear – the ability to create economic booms and busts is so obvious that it's bewildering that such events are still perceived as random or accidental.

Debt Saturation

Martin Wolf, a former member of the Independent Commission on Banking, stated bluntly: "The essence of the contemporary monetary system is a creation of money out of nothing by private banks' often foolish lending." Within the economy today, only 3% of money is in paper form. A total of 97% of all the money in the economy is in the form of electronic deposits that banks have created through issuing loans.[liii] Money is created out of thin air by privately owned, for-profit corporations before it is loaned out. With every loan comes a new debt. This current system creates a "debt trap" – over time, personal and national debt increases and it is difficult (or impossible) for a nation to reduce its debts without causing a recession. Over the past 40 years, the banks have increased the amount of money they have pumped into the economy, which has caused the price of property to rise.[liv] The more money that comes into circulation, the less one's money is worth. With the cost of living rising, there will never be enough money in circulation to pay off the debt – not until the banking system is completely reformed. Currently, the banking system does not serve the interests of the people. According to journalist Seumas Milne: "The financial system has already failed at huge economic and social cost. It has been shown to be corrupt, incompetent, rapacious and economically destructive. The City's claims to be an indispensable jobs and tax engine for the British economy are nonsense: the bailout costs of 2008-9 dwarfed the financial tax revenues of the boom years, which were below those of manufacturing even at their peak."[lv] Hidden behind complex-sounding economic jargon, this unsustainable system has been strategically designed as a perpetual debt machine to enslave the population. Various transoceanic oligarchs all have a vested interest in these intricate criminal enterprises – it is these oligarchs who dominate the financial markets. As stated by author Henry Makow: "They have bought the wealth of the world using our credit."[lvi] Henry Ford reportedly once said: "It is well enough that people of the nation do not understand our banking and monetary system, for if they did, I believe there would be a revolution before tomorrow morning." When talking about the 2008 crash, the former US federal government analyst, Richard Cook, stated: "The Housing Bubble and its crash were engineered from the highest levels of the US government, the Federal Reserve, and the financial industry."[lvii]

Everything is Under Control

The engineered economic crises throughout American history have allowed the corporate elites to further consolidate their power through the redistribution of wealth – they are robbing the poor to give to the rich. The Hegelian dialectic is the technique of thesis and antithesis, which results in syntheses. It is the deliberate act of causing friction between two entities in order to achieve a desired outcome or "order out of chaos". In terms of politics, it does not matter if one is "left wing" or "right wing" as they both belong to the same bird which, in turn, is owned by unaccountable financiers. This current capitalist system is a means to bring about the end. We are being manipulated by a cabal of oligarchs into accepting globalisation as the default solution to the problems they have caused. It is being forced upon us and it is quite obvious that this push towards globalisation is the cause of the large increase in inequality – *this is the product of oligarchy*. What could be more degrading for humanity than soldiers killing women and children for an elitist agenda that they don't understand? It is the shedding of blood for gold, oil and drugs, and a lifetime of debt for every individual on Planet Earth – we are the ones paying the bill. The ability of man could elevate us and set us free, but instead we are being misled, degraded and enslaved by monumental debts.

The Bane of Oligarchy: Industry and Innovation

An orchestrated assault upon the middle-class of America (demonstrated in the post-industrial zero growth agenda) has seen local industry throughout the US (and other countries) outsourced to lesser developed countries (such as China) where slave labour is abundant – multinational corporations place no value on human life. After centuries of being subjected to the British Empire's drug trafficking, military intimidation, organised crime and widespread famine, China is now an emerging superpower and the largest foreign owner of American debt.[lviii] This communist nation has been a testing ground for the inhumane policies of the New World Order, such as eugenics, state-controlled media, state-controlled family planning (which has seen over 300 million forced abortions and over 190 million sterilisations[lix]) and restrictions on the right to protest and to practise religion. As previously mentioned, oligarchs have no requirement for a middle-class. They desire to rule over a docile lower-class society which is dependent on, or subject to, the state – this was one reason for the weakening of America's industrial backbone. This de-industrialisation has led to a sharp decline in the American standard of living and, as of 2013, there were over 11 million people unemployed[lx] and an astonishing 35-50 million living in poverty. Stamped on the iconic dollar bill is the Latin phrase *Novus Ordo Seclorum*, which translates to *New Order of the Ages* and is often interpreted as *New World Order*. As shall be reviewed later, the US currency displays the arcane language of symbolism, such as the pyramid and All-Seeing Eye:

Image 7.1 The All-Seeing Eye on the US dollar bill.

The Abstract Wars

Why do we invest such vast amounts of money into the wars on terror and drugs – wars that have no real enemy or definitive outcome? Why do we not invest equal efforts into wars against poverty and starvation for the elevation of mankind? Since the Western-led invasion of Afghanistan in 2001, opium output has exploded – 90% of the world's heroin now originates from Afghanistan.[lxi]

Prior to the Western invasion, in 2001, Afghanistan produced only a mere 180 tons of the crop which can be turned into heroin. By 2007, under the watchful and approving eye of British and allied NATO troops, production skyrocketed to 8,000 tons.[lxii]

Image 7.2 An Opium Field in Helmand Province, Islamic Republic of Afghanistan (a marine with 3rd Battalion, 4th Marine Regiment, greets local children working in the farmlands near the base).

A vast quantity of opium grows in southern Afghanistan, including the British-controlled Helmand province – these southern provinces are essentially run by drug lords and militias who are left to guard their fields of opium. The "crop-eradication missions" are merely a smokescreen that has allowed for the ongoing British control of the international opium trade. A prime motivation for the invasion of Afghanistan was to halt poppy production, yet Afghanistan's heroin is now valued at over $60 billion[lxiii] and a fraction of this money finances the recruitment, armament and training of thousands of al-Qaeda and Taliban mercenaries. If the mission of the War on Drugs was to maintain control of the international opium market and provide a method for the terrorists to finance themselves, it has been a *huge* success.

8. The Licensed Pirates

By no means is the international opium trade a new venture for those working behind the scenes. Various European oligarchs consolidated their wealth in the first half of the last millennium before the advances in navigational techniques allowed for trading across international waters rather than land. As author David Flynn states: "From the greatest antiquity, the art of navigation has demonstrated a link between the heavens and the Earth."[lxiv] The early mariners, who developed adequate techniques for navigating large bodies of water, kept their knowledge a secret (as did the highly skilled Freemasons) in order to avoid competition in trade or war. The British East India Company was established in the year 1600 and went on to conduct 50% of world trade, forming the solid foundations of the British Empire. As one of the first multinational corporations, the British East India Company (together with the Dutch East India Company) dominated commerce (including the lucrative slave trade) after establishing trade routes throughout Europe, Africa, Asia and the Middle East – these trade monopolies produced immeasurable profits for the governors and investors of the shipping companies. As one of the most influential flowers of all time, the opium poppy (also known as the cash-crop) was one particular global commodity that generated vast fortunes for the aristocracy and evidently still does today. In his book *The Committee of 300*, Dr. John Coleman states: "The truth is that the supply of Indian opium to China was a British monopoly."[lxv] Historian Carl A Trocki states: "The accumulations of wealth created by a succession of historic drug trades have been among the primary foundations of global capitalism and the modern nation-state itself."[lxvi]

60 Million Dead

Supported by the British Crown, the British East India Company acted as a network of cut-throat pirates who governed territories larger than the United Kingdom. They started out as a mere trading presence along the coast of India but, by the middle of the 18th century, they had begun to intervene in Indian politics and engage in wars. In the year 1764 they waged war in Bengal to secure ascendancy in the region before ruthlessly stealing the revenue-collecting powers and becoming the de facto ruler of Bengal. Historian Romesh Dutt states: "Land tax income was doubled and most of the revenue flowed out of the country."[lxvii] After the British remorselessly destroyed food crops to cultivate opium, food production was greatly reduced and 10 million people starved to death (around a third of the Bengali population). During the savageries of the British rule of India from the 18th-20th centuries, there were approximately 60 million recorded deaths due to famine alone – the economic and administrative policies of the British were a main contributor to such high mortality.

Image 8.1 The East India Company iron steam ship *Nemesis*, Commanded by Lieutenant W H Hall (Edward Duncan, 1803–1882).

The Opium War

After opening an office in the Chinese port city of Canton in the early 18th century, the British East India Company fostered a mass Chinese drug dependency. It acted as a relentless pusher, forcing the highly addictive and euphoric opium painkiller upon those who fell under its spell. Opium became a part of Chinese culture and, in the year 1836, 30,000 chests of opium were delivered to the country.[lxviii] Millions of Chinese became hopelessly addicted and the nation was subjected to degradation and a state of backwardness (this was merely an additional bonus for the British Crown, which detested foreign industrial development). The Chinese government reacted by waging its own war – a war against drugs. It began seizing opium and associated paraphernalia and making arrests. This greatly angered the investors and governors of the British East India Company and as a result, they sent in the Navy to engage in the First Opium War in 1839 (the Second Opium War soon followed). The mighty gunships of the licensed pirates were victorious in their assault – the opium trade continued and the Crown managed to acquire some of China's land, including Hong Kong Island (for which the UK recently transferred sovereignty in "the Return" of 1997). In 1865, in the aftermath of the First Opium War, the Hongkong and Shanghai Banking Corporation was established, primarily to launder the profits made from opium.

Skull and Bones

Many of the lucrative trading companies were run by esoteric brotherhoods – pirates were running drugs, slaves, spices and tea across international waters. From the shareholders to the ships' captains, these companies were dominated by an allegiance of occultists. During the early days of Speculative Freemasonry, lodges were established shore to shore, from Africa to India, along the trade routes. Initiates of the Freemasons visit a darkened room known as the "Chamber of Reflection" in which a skull and bones is present – many of the early mariners used the skull and crossbones logo on their ships' sails, such as the infamous Jolly Roger. One governor of the British East India Company who made a vast fortune was named Elihu Yale and, in 1718, the American-based Collegiate School was renamed Yale to commemorate this drug dealer who gave them a healthy donation (Yale University graduates include five US presidents). A family-run business named the Russell & Co trading company was one of the largest American opium smugglers and, in 1832, Alphonso Taft and General William Russell (of the Russell & Co opium smugglers) established the Skull and Bones headquarters on Yale University campus – not only was this esoteric society founded by pirates, it was funded by opium. Alphonso's son, William Taft, later became President of the United States and played a key role in the nation's narcotics control.[lxix]

Demonstrating their imperial aggression throughout the last millennium, barbaric oligarchs used the force of arms to protect their business interests and removed anybody who constituted an obstacle. The ruling elite have sacrificed the lives of untold millions throughout the past few centuries; they have blood-stained hands and great experience in exploiting and bankrupting nations. In the 17th century, Freemasonry and Britain's international opium trade combined to produce an offspring in the form of organised crime such as the Triads (Chinese Mafia) and the spin-off of the Order of Zion named B'nai B'rith. Today these infamous crime syndicates oversee a portion of the drugs trade and are involved with contract killings, gun-running, political corruption and countless other illicit activities.

HSBC

In recent years, various law firms and banks based in the City of London have come under investigation for laundering profits from gun-running, contract killings and drug trafficking for clients who consist of South American cartels and cocaine barons, the Italian and Sicilian Mafia (which is dominated by families of Roman Catholics, some of whom are tied directly to the Vatican) and Eastern European crime syndicates.[lxx] As a conduit for criminal enterprises, HSBC, one of the world's largest banks, has played a *key role* in the laundering of billions of pounds through many of its branches. After it was found guilty for its criminal activities in 2012 and fined £1.2 billion, one report stated that: "... [HSBC] failed to monitor a staggering £38 trillion of money moving across borders from places that could have posed a risk."[lxxi] All HSBC employees were spared criminal prosecution and 78 of its London staff were paid more than £1 million each that year – not only are these banks "too big to fail", but they are clearly too big to jail. All of this should come as no surprise considering that HSBC was founded in 1991 by the Hongkong and Shanghai Banking Corporation, which itself played a key role in laundering profits from opium. Headquartered in London, the international opium trade is one of the most efficient production and distribution systems of any commodity. The City of London is, and has always been, one of the world's largest money-laundering centres. Together, the Vatican and British Crown are the world's greatest drug dealers and, in order to manage the billions of pounds from which they profit yearly, various underground economies have been created, such as the infamous offshore banks in the Cayman Islands (which is British territory). In 2012, one study estimated that the Caymans hoarded over £13 trillion, a sum of money that is greater than the Japanese and US GDPs combined.[lxxii] Indeed, a large proportion of international banking and financial activities has been established primarily to handle the oligarchs' dirty cash. The oligarchs are waging a war against humanity and some of their weapons include cocaine and opium – many societies throughout the world are brimming with drug addicts. Whilst the police fight against the low-level drug-related crimes in local communities, the international drugs market is controlled; it is being fought with one hand while being fed with the other. During its peak, the British Empire had dominion over almost a quarter of the Earth's landmass – but the British Crown is *not* the monarch, it is a *corporate entity* and, because of the many nations it has plundered, the British Crown stands accused of crimes against humanity. Today, as one of the leading sponsors of global organised crime, the Club of the Isles, referred to as the "invisible empire", is the unincorporated successor to the British East India Company. According to the editors of Executive Intelligence Review, the Club of the Isles is composed of various elites who have vested interest in "… such corporate giants as Royal Dutch Shell, Imperial Chemical Industries, Lloyds of London, Unilever, Lonrho, Rio Tinto Zinc, and Anglo American DeBeers. It dominates the world supply of petroleum, gold, diamonds, platinum and many other vital raw materials; and deploys these assets not merely in the pursuit of wealth, but as resources at the disposal of its geopolitical agenda."[lxxiii]

9. Revolution Business and the Terrorist Franchise

In 2011, seemingly isolated and random civilian uprisings throughout Africa and the Middle East led to major political upheavals, the overthrowing of governments and civil wars. The Arab uprising (or Arab Spring) swept through Morocco, Algeria, Tunisia, Libya, Egypt, Syria, Bahrain and Yemen. The Egyptian revolution saw the shameful downfall of President Hosni Mubarak, yet unbeknown to a global audience following the intense media coverage, this revolution was organised in Belgrade, Serbia, by revolution consultants working for an organisation known as Optor. Optor (meaning resistance) began as an underground movement in Serbia in the 1990s and, through funding from the American taxpayer, it became instrumental in the overthrow of Slobodan Milosevic. The Washington-based National Endowment for Democracy spent almost $3 million in Serbia in the late 1990s, of which a significant amount went to Optor.[lxxiv] Following Optor's success, one of its founders went on to create a revolution training school called CANVAS (Centre for Applied Nonviolent Action and Strategies).

Image 9.1 The raised fist - the signature of resistance –
has been used world-wide since the overthrow of Slobodan Milosevic.

Egyptian revolutionaries were trained in workshops on the outskirts of Cairo by CANVAS, and the strategy used for overthrowing Slobodan Milosevic in Europe proved successful once again in the 2011 Egyptian revolution. Now active in over 30 countries (many of which the oligarchs have a great interest in), Optor has played a key role in training revolutionaries in non-violent resistance and their logo of the raised fist (Image 9.1) has become recognised as the international signature of resistance. Political commentators such as William Engdahl are convinced that Optor is still funded by the US and is being used to orchestrate regime changes throughout the world for the West's benefit.[lxxv] As a further demonstration of hypocrisy and ulterior motives on behalf of the West, armed forces spent ten years fighting against radical Islamists in Iraq and Afghanistan (apparently to combat terrorism and bring about democracy for "the freedom agenda"), while at the same time, they funded and armed the same kinds of terrorists in Syria and Libya in an attempt to overthrow governments.[lxxvi] With a longstanding interest in Libya as far back as 2001, the Pentagon had drawn up plans to invade the oil-rich North African country and the Arab Spring was the perfect excuse for "intervention". When speaking on countries in which the US had an interest, General Wesley Clark of the US Army stated on *Democracy Now* in 2007: "There were a total of seven countries, beginning with Iraq, then Syria, Lebanon, Libya, Iran, Somalia and Sudan."[lxxvii]

The Libyan Revolution

As a result of the Libyan revolution and the removal of Muammar Gaddafi, there has been a huge expansion of the al-Qaeda terrorist franchise as heavily-armed rebels have filled the power vacuum. Libya, a war-torn nation, has been left in the hands of violent militias who raised the flag of al-Qaeda, freed hundreds of prisoners (many of whom were convicted terrorists) and enforced Sharia law. Torture, unlawful killings and a brutal ethnic cleansing of black Africans has become widespread since NATO (the North Atlantic Treaty Organisation) unlawfully dropped several thousand bombs to destroy the country's infrastructure in 2011. And, of course, the mainstream media failed to report on the devastating consequences of NATO's intervention. So what was the real reason behind the Western intervention in Libya and was it legal? It's very difficult to keep an open mind without factoring in all the biased propaganda that the media has fed us. Although Gaddafi was a tyrant, he was responsible for making his country one of the most prosperous in the region. The Libyan uprising was led by violent militants who were portrayed by the media as "freedom fighters" – this is utter nonsense. NATO forces (on behalf of the oligarchs) proactively supported the al-Qaeda franchise for their own personal benefit, and it has proven devastating for an entire nation. If you are still unconvinced by the hypocrisy or ulterior motives on behalf of the elite, let's dig a little deeper.

Intervention in Libya

In 2010, Chevron Corp (one of six supermajor oil companies) and Occidental failed to extend their oil and gas licence in Libya (which is home to Africa's largest proven oil reserves). This was due to mounting pressure from Gaddafi, who rightfully demanded compensation for the UN-imposed sanctions which had previously ruined Libya's economy and abused the human rights of the Libyan people. In more ways than one, Gaddafi was becoming a burden for the oligarchs and his plan was to introduce a new gold dinar (a single African currency made from gold) to rival the euro and the dollar. He called upon neighbouring Arabic and African nations to implement this gold dinar and only conduct trade in their new currency. Of course, this would have totally shifted the global economic balance by undermining the oligarchs' fractional reserve banking system and their worthless fiat currency. A similar situation had arisen in 2000 when Saddam Hussein proposed plans to trade oil in euros rather than dollars – this was followed by sanctions and an invasion (various political commentators speculate that the invasion was due to Saddam's inconvenient plans).[lxxviii] Astonishingly, in March 2011, only a few weeks after the Libyan revolution had commenced and left the country in tatters, a "rebel council" had established the Central Bank of Benghazi as the central monetary authority alongside a national oil company. A couple of weeks into an uprising, in the midst of a life-or-death civil war, a central bank was established by rebels who were keen to sign international trade deals! Clearly, foreign agents assisted them in the creation of new trade policies and the establishment of a new central bank. The Libyan revolution saw the targeted and illegal assassination of Muammar Gaddafi (and his family) by NATO, who carried out 9,700 strike sorties and dropped over 7,700 precision bombs which murdered thousands of civilians and destroyed the country's infrastructure.[lxxix] NATO failed to acknowledge and examine these causalities but, by mid-July 2011, the Libyan Health Office stated that there had been 1,108 civilians killed and 4,500 wounded with a later death count of at least 30,000. This was not humanitarian intervention; this was the progression of Middle-Eastern conquest by an international confederacy which illegally conspired against Libya's oil, gas and monetary system.

Objectives of the Central Intelligence Agency

Ralph McGehee, an ex-CIA (the Central Intelligence Agency of the US government) agent turned critic of the agency, published an exposé titled *Deadly Deceits: My 25 Years in the CIA*, in which he states: "The CIA is not now, nor has it ever been, a central intelligence agency. It is the covert action arm of the President's foreign policy advisers. Disinformation is a large part of its covert action responsibility, and the American people are the primary target audience of its lies."[lxxx] After the transition from coal to oil, 20th-century Britain (its factories, vehicles and the armed forces who had just finished fighting a world war) was powered by Persian resources, and it was the antecedents of British Petroleum that had exclusive rights over Iran's resources – through exploitation, a British-based company was making healthy profits from Iran's oil whilst the Iranian nation received little in return. In 1951, with an economy in tatters, Iran's parliament nationalised the oil industry in an attempt to save the Iranian economy. This was met with hostility from the investors in British Petroleum, so with assistance from British intelligence, as one of the CIA's earliest assignments, the democratically elected Iranian government was toppled in 1953 and the British monopoly over Persian oil was maintained. The 20th century, also known as the American century, saw US corporations became increasingly involved in overseas trade. The days of licensed piracy and gunships were long gone and obviously Wall Street couldn't directly participate in warfare to protect its own business activities (like the British East India Company who used gunships just a couple of centuries earlier), thus an organisation was established to protect the overseas interests of corporate America – this organisation was none other than the CIA.

The CIA and the Muslim Zealots

Unbeknown to many, it was the 1980s' multi-billion-dollar "Operation Cyclone", led by the CIA, that armed, financed and trained over 30,000 Muslim zealots known as the Mujahideen (some of whom went on to become the Taliban). In order to fight the Soviets, this Middle-Eastern terrorist franchise was a creation of the CIA, but has since been used to justify intervention in the Middle-East for the conquest of oil, opium and land. In more recent years, public awareness of the CIA's malevolent agendas has increased, thus the agency has taken a step back into the shadows and outsourced its traditional activities to unmerciful private firms. A poll released by ORB (an independent polling agency based in London) estimates that over a million Iraqis have been killed since the 2003 US-led invasion. An article on the RT website states: "The US military's use of depleted uranium in Iraq has led to a sharp increase in leukemia and birth defects in the city of Najaf. Cancer is now more common than the flu."[lxxxi] The invasion of Iraq is undoubtedly one of the most cowardly and unjust wars ever fought, yet regardless of this, the US Educational and Cultural Affairs website pathetically states that projects such as the regeneration of Babylon "... manifests America's deep respect for the people of Iraq."[lxxxii] Imperialism isn't dead. We have witnessed the colonisation of the opium and oil-rich Middle-East and, by using the media as a propaganda machine, the invasion of foreign lands, the murder of civilians and the bankrupting of nations can each be justified. Terrorist franchises, such as the Taliban and al-Qaeda, are heavily financed by the opium trade – drug-dealing, organised crime and terrorism are completely integrated. So, with that in mind, consider the technical and scientific analyses of over 1,500 technical professionals of the world's *three* worst structural failures in history.

10. Anomalies of the
World Trade Center Disaster

In 2009, a peer-reviewed scientific paper titled *Active Thermitic Material Discovered in Dust from the 9/11 World Trade Centre Catastrophe* was published by the *Open Chemical Physics Journal*. This independent investigation demonstrated that explosive residue of specialised thermite (which can only be made in advanced military labs) was found in dust samples taken from the wreckage left at the Ground Zero site on 9/11. As stated by various engineers, scientists, architects and pilots, jet fuel *cannot* burn at temperatures hot enough to melt steel. Thermite, a mixture of iron-oxide and aluminium, once ignited, will burn at around 2,500 degrees Celsius and can instantly liquefy steel. The aforementioned peer-reviewed paper ends with this sentence: "Based on these observations, we conclude that the red layer of the red/gray chips we have discovered in the WTC dust is active, unreacted thermitic material, incorporating nanotechnology, and is a highly energetic pyrotechnic or explosive material."[lxxxiii] The use of explosives in the 9/11 disaster has been proven by a range of independent forensic investigations. Witnesses (including paramedics, firemen and policemen) reported hearing a series of explosions in the moments prior to the collapse and also to seeing molten steel around the destruction site – these reports have been verified by audio/video footage and photos. The prestigious architect, Jan Utzon (son of Jørn Utzon who designed the Sydney Opera House), has been dissatisfied with the official 9/11 story and stated: "It is in everyone's interest to have that event investigated to the extent that the subsequent explanation satisfies most people, including professionals at all levels."[lxxxiv] The use of explosives explains why the Twin Towers imploded and descended at almost free-fall speed through the path of greatest resistance – disintegrating in approximately ten seconds, they proved to be the worst structural failures in history. Due to the breaches in regulations and an overwhelming number of fallacies and anomalies presented in the official 9/11 report, members of the professional community subsequently created organisations such as Architects and Engineers for 9/11 Truth, which is now comprised of over 1,500 technical experts who have laid their reputations on the line to expose the falsehoods of 9/11 and reveal the truth – *whatever that truth may be*. The 9/11 conspiracy isn't the result of idle speculation on internet forums, but is instead the result of damning evidence and analyses. The evidence has been investigated by thousands of technical professionals comprised of:

- Engineers, scientists, architects, pilots, demolition experts and construction workers.
- Firemen, police and medical professionals.

As stated by the Medical Professionals for 9/11 Truth: "The official 9/11 Commission Report inadequately answered, and in numerous cases even failed to address, many of the most important questions that were called to its attention."[lxxxv]

Image 10.1 The Twin Towers and Building 7 (left of the Twin Towers). All three skyscrapers fell on September 11th 2001.

The Third Tower

Unbeknown to many, the skyscraper named Building 7 (7 World Trade Center) also collapsed on 9/11, yet it was *not* struck by an airplane. A total of three steel-frame skyscrapers were destroyed – the world's three worst structural failures occurred in a single day, yet the official 9/11 report does not provide sufficient reason as to why this third tower collapsed. As stated in a paper entitled *Can Physics Rewrite History?* by C Thurston: "The straight-down, vertical collapse of Building 7 could not have happened and with such perfect symmetry unless all 58 perimeter columns and all 25 core columns were somehow cut almost simultaneously at the foundation level."[lxxxvi] Imploding into its own footprint (in a similar fashion to the Twin Towers), it was reduced to rubble in less than seven seconds:

Image 10.2 From left to right, the image stills of Building 7 show how it collapsed in 6.5 seconds, imploding perfectly within its own footprint.

Astonishingly, for the third time in a single day, in less than seven seconds, an entire skyscraper was reduced to rubble – most people are not even aware of this third skyscraper falling on 9/11. As stated by physics instructor David Chandler: "Building 7 fell through itself for over 100 feet with zero resistance, an impossibility in any natural scenario. This period of free-fall is solid evidence that explosives had to be used to bring the building down."

Criticism of the 9/11 Investigation: Breaking the Code of Practice

With funding from the US Congress, the National Institute of Standards and Technology (NIST) undertook a completely inadequate investigation into the 9/11 World Trade Center (WTC) disasters. Both the 9/11 commission report and the National Institute of Standards and Technology report have been discredited by thousands of professionals. Crucial evidence was removed from the WTC site and disposed of – not only a violation of the code of conduct, but also of the law. In criticism of the official government investigation, the highly acclaimed scientist, Dr. Lynn Margulis, stated: "This is not science... it's trying to prove preconceived ideas."[lxxxvii] The following brief list of breaches in regulations has led to widespread criticism of the official 9/11 investigation:

- A vast amount of evidence was removed from Ground Zero and destroyed after 9/11, including the steel frames of the buildings (the aggressive destruction of crucial evidence is blatant).
- The official 9/11 investigation failed to conduct significant forensic analyses and didn't even test for explosives – an independent investigation later demonstrated that explosives were used on 9/11.
- The NIST investigation failed to conduct a full investigation into Building 7 and didn't follow the national standards.

The official 9/11 investigation was fraudulent and the government's verdict is irrational and not supported by the evidence. Due to the nature of the WTC collapses and the overwhelming evidence of explosives being used, the official investigation *should* have conducted testing to establish if explosives had been used, yet it did not do so. Firefighter Erik Lawyer, who is the founder of the Fire Fighters for 9/11 Truth organisation, stated: "With all these indicators, would you test for exotic accelerants/explosive residue/thermite? How could you confirm or rule out the possibility terrorists planted explosives in addition to the aircraft hits?"[lxxxviii] Considering that several thousand people were murdered that day, it is beyond absurd and also criminal that the official 9/11 investigation didn't test for such devices.

Conclusion

Former British Defence Secretary Denis Healey stated: "World events do not occur by accident. They are made to happen... most of them are staged and managed by those who hold the purse strings." To the average person, this information may seem implausible and audacious merely because it seems to be beyond the realms of possibility, but as the evidence demonstrates, 9/11 was a highly organised false-flag operation. In conclusion, the Twin Towers and Building 7 (a total of three skyscrapers) did not collapse due to the impact and explosion of two hijacked planes and the subsequent fires (a physical impossibility) but instead, the third skyscraper, Building 7, was the operations room from which the Twin Towers were flattened in controlled demolitions, before being demolished itself to destroy the evidence. The official investigation didn't test for explosives because the findings would have implicated a conspiracy from within the "US government".

Hegelian Dialectic

The Hegelian Dialectic is the simple yet extremely effective practice of "problem-reaction-solution" which a rogue government employs to achieve a desired objective – many major events of the past 100 years have followed this practice. In order to achieve a desired outcome, a rogue government must cause a problem intended to threaten, harm or kill the citizens (commonly referred to as a 'false-flag event'). Following the reaction from society in regards to this false-flag event, the rogue government will blame the problem on an enemy or a fault from within its own society. Next, the rogue government will provide a solution which, in usual circumstances, would not be accepted by the public but, in this manipulated situation (designed to distress, panic or harm the citizens), is accepted by the masses. Often the solution will be warfare against an enemy or the introduction of new regulations to further restrict individual freedom (it is an incremental descent into totalitarianism).

The Hegelian Dialectic – the three stages of 9/11:

- Problem: A false-flag terrorist act led to mass death and widespread panic.
- Reaction: After devastation set in, the citizens felt continuously threatened by the "terrorists" and submitted to the "solutions" proposed by the rogue government.

- Solution: The rogue government implemented new terrorism laws (the USA PATRIOT Act was composed by a professor from the Jesuit Georgetown University) to further restrict the rights of its own citizens and declared the ambiguous "war on terror". This was followed by an invasion of the Middle East (justified by the reaction in Stage 2), which has led to the murder of millions of Afghans and Iraqis.

Not only were the "US government" (specifically the Knights of Malta, the CIA, Israeli Mossad and British Intelligence who are under direction from the upper echelons of the Jesuit order) aware of the 9/11 ploy, but they helped to stage the entire event (George W Bush certainly wasn't the brains of this operation and it is possible that he had very little involvement, if any). It was a massive ritual, a sacrifice of almost 3,000 people which has subsequently allowed for the conquest of land in the Middle East and the regeneration of Babylon. The date of the disaster has disturbing synchronicity with the eerie announcement from George H Bush when, 11 years prior to this, on September 11th 1990, he famously declared: "Out of these troubled times, our fifth objective – a New World Order can emerge: a new era – freer from the threat of terror."lxxxix Of course, not by coincidence, the president's announcement of a New World Order was planned for this date, exactly 11 years to the day before the world was changed forever. Certain terrorist franchises were initially funded by American and British intelligence in the 1980s before later being framed for the 9/11 crimes they couldn't possibly have committed. Evidently, these psychopathic oligarchs will go to extreme lengths to achieve their objectives, and they thrive off the fact that society is ignorant and dismissive of their agenda. The events of 9/11 led to dramatic and controversial changes in domestic and foreign policies (such as the USA PATRIOT Act) and, by using the planet's most capable military power, the New World Order is being progressed whilst cunningly disguised behind the façade of a War on Terror. What's more, terms such as "environmentalism" and "sustainable development" are being used to further manipulate individuals into surrendering their liberties. Welcome to the New World Order.

11. The Confederacy

I am no fan of politics, which means the following chapter involved great effort and was extremely tedious to research. However, it does contain some extremely important information with regards to how the future is being shaped.

The Manifestation of Oligarch Ideologies

Various governments and non-government organisations are subordinate to a confederacy – the oligarchs' *Shadow Council*. Replete with greed, the sole objective of this highest-level executive body is full-spectrum dominance. An ex-British Intelligence officer at MI6 named Dr. John Coleman refers to this alliance as the Committee of 300. As an early whistle-blower, Coleman's work was met with resistance and hostility and critics often question his credibility, but today there can be no denial of this Shadow Council and their New World Order agenda. In his book *The Committee of 300*, Coleman summarises as follows: "There is an upper-echelon coordinating, controlling body that oversees the activities of the 'local level' agencies. There is a society behind the secret societies, an all-powerful group that knows no national boundaries, above the laws of all countries."ˣᶜ The framework for this agenda is the United Nations, established in 1945, which works with many philanthropic organisations and agencies in every sector, from finance to health, and is made up of over 190 member-states working to "promote international peace". Through ever-increasing global governance from non-elected bodies such as the Council on Foreign Relations, the Bilderberg Group and the Club of Rome, an increasing amount of aggressive policies, ranging from health to technology and the environment, are being coordinated centrally.

For a demonstration of the globalists' tactics and ideologies, refer to a report released by the Club of Rome titled *The First Global Revolution: A Report by the Council of the Club of Rome*: "In searching for a new enemy to unite us, we came up with the idea that pollution, the threat of global warming, water shortages, famine and the like would fit the bill. In their totality and in their interactions these phenomena do constitute a common threat which demands the solidarity of all peoples. But in designating them as the enemy, we fall into the trap about which we have already warned, namely mistaking systems for causes. All these dangers are caused by human intervention and it is only through changed attitudes and behaviour that they can be overcome. The real enemy, then, is humanity itself."[xci] A common ideology amongst the globalists (and typical of an oligarch), as confirmed by the writers of this report, is that they believe humanity (the "enemy") to be a burden to the planet. And make no mistake about it: this report by the Club of Rome clearly alludes to manufacturing threats and uniting the nations under a common cause. Evidently, some of the true policy-making positions and influential political-science department positions are filled by functional sociopaths and psychopaths and, through them, a totalitarian agenda is being progressed.

Tel-lie-vision

The founder of CNN, billionaire media mogul Ted Turner, felt so strongly about the cause of the United Nations that he made a significant donation – the largest gift ever given to any organisation. In 1997 he announced that he would donate $1 billion for UN agencies.[xcii] Since then, the same Ted Turner has made several alarming statements with regards to controlling the global population: "We're too many people. That's why we have global warming... We have got to stabilise the population." This disturbing statement coming from a super-wealthy "philanthropic" globalist is not unique. According to Ted Turner and his counterparts, the global population needs to be stabilised in order to save our planet from "global warming". He is a fan of China's forced abortion and sterilisation methods under their one-child policy.[xciii] Conservative billionaire Gina Rinehart called for the "sterilisation of the poor", claiming that the only way to alleviate poverty is to stop the "under-classes" from multiplying.[xciv] As we shall see in this chapter, culling the global population (referred to as the population surplus) is not only high on the New World Order agenda, it's considered imperative to achieve sustainable development in the 21st century. However, this short-sighted genocidal fury is totally irrational, as will also be demonstrated shortly. The media is a platform used to shape beliefs, define normality and set trends. By persistent repetition, news that is deemed beneficial for the New World Order agenda is used to form the people's opinion. We are conditioned to fear all potential threats, whether it is mass immigration, terrorism, pandemics or economic crises – through fear and manipulation, we wilfully submit our liberties to rogue governments. An oligopoly is when a few firms dominate an entire market and, throughout the 20th century, the media's influence on society saw an exponential growth. Today, a handful of corporations oversee the distribution of news around the world, and these media conglomerates have unprecedented power.

Objectives and Potential Implications of the New World Order

With vain attempts to rationalise the agenda, the globalists believe that success is inevitable. It's a calculated attack upon individual liberty and, based upon the statements, policies and proposals from the globalists, a New World Order has the following objectives:

- To implement a global government as a central authority and for it to be headed by one global leader.
- To control the flow of all information and resources (such as the media, internet, food cultivation and production, water and land).
- To implement one global electronic currency.
- To implement a global healthcare system and education system.
- To reduce the global population and to remove the middle class from society.
- To further suppress/control all scientific and technological developments and maintain our dependence upon the supposedly limited natural resources.

Although most individuals are oblivious to this gradual reconstitution of society, a world central authority will enforce policies for all local communities around the world, as is evident with Agenda 21 (which shall be reviewed shortly). All business transactions will eventually take place using a single global currency (which is likely to be issued electronically), and every child throughout the world will be vaccinated, fed genetically modified foods and taught an identical curriculum. In an era where citizens have been reduced to the status of mere consumers and useless eaters, a New World Order will be powered by an impersonal global government and the oligarchs' multinational corporations. It was the Italian dictator, Benito Mussolini, who once said: "Fascism should more appropriately be called corporatism because it is the merger of state and corporate power." In developed countries, local communities and jobs will be at risk as labour is further outsourced to the lesser developed countries. Over the past few decades, lesser developed countries have been increasingly exploited by multinational corporations who place no value on human life and take full advantage of slave labour to profit billions of pounds each year

– they are responsible for the inhumane treatment of their employees who hand-craft our shoes, clothes and electrical gadgets. The cost of living is increasing at a rate faster than that of the average income, and this will continue as the gap widens between rich and poor – the plan is to remove the middle-class from society. Through lack of competition in a closed market, a global government could further oppress its citizens through increasing legislation, restricting individual rights and governing their daily lives. The voice of individual representation and local communities could vanish as national sovereignty and "democracy" become subject to the authority of this informal global government. The loss of cultural identity and increased global inequality would cause civil unrest, increased drug dependency (both legal and illegal) and an increase in domestic terrorism and civil wars. Under the rule of a totalitarian global government will come a unified New Age religion, as was the aspiration of Robert Muller who was Assistant Secretary-General of the UN for 40 years. He became known as the "Philosopher" and the "Prophet of the UN" as his efforts were concerned with spirituality and politics. He called for a unified religion and a global dictator: "We must move as quickly as possible to a one-world government; a one-world religion; under a one-world leader".[xcv] Muller created the World Core Curriculum, helping to inspire the Global Education movement which earned him the UNESCO (United Nations Economic, Social and Cultural Organization) Prize for Peace Education. His vision (which is shared by his counterparts) is to implement a compulsive school curriculum and a New Age global religion which is to be headed by a global dictator. To give an example of the quest to unify spirituality, the Tony Blair Faith Foundation was established (by the war criminal Tony Blair) to promote "inter-faith" dialogue and help to unify the religions of the world. It appears that inter-faith dialogue and a New Age religion is high on the agenda, but why is this so, living in a secular society?

Political Correctness "Gone Mad"

In a 2009 UNESCO report were universal plans for teaching children sex education, recommending that children as young as five should be taught explicit sex acts.[xcvi] Unfortunately, these suggestions are becoming all too common – some of the suggestions are too grotesque to even repeat here. When such immoral and absurd policies are mentioned in the media, they are commonly passed off as liberalism or political correctness "gone mad", but these disturbing proposals are typical of the malevolent New Age agenda and may eventually be enforced. There is also talk of lowering the legal age of consent in Britain and, in the wake of Britain's most prolific paedophile, Sir Jimmy Savile, being exposed, a highly experienced barrister named Barbara Hewson called for the age of consent to be lowered to 13 in order to end the persecution of old men: "I'm not advocating either rape or compulsory sex, I'm just simply saying the age of consent in this country at the moment is too high."[xcvii] One clear objective is to continue the sexualisation of children and there are *many* examples of the state trying to involve itself in the most personal aspects of family life.

Ecological Methods of Genocide: the Depopulation Agenda

In a 1991 interview with the UNESCO Courier, Jacques Cousteau reluctantly stated: "It's terrible to have to say this. World population must be stabilized and to do that we must eliminate 350,000 people per day."[xcviii] Jonathon Porritt, an environmental advisor to ex-Prime Minister Gordon Brown, suggested that Britain needed to drastically reduce its population by up to 30 million if the country wanted to feed itself sustainably. According to the globalists, sustainable development primarily depends upon how many people live on Earth, thus a reduction in population is crucial to the success of a New World Order. Philosopher Bertrand Russell summarised the long-term optimistic ambition of the elites: "Gradually, by selective breeding, the congenital differences between rulers and ruled will increase until they become almost different species."[xcix] Hitler's "superior race" ideologies and ambitions were modest in comparison to those of the present-day elites.

Agenda 21 is a soft law designed for the "sustainable development" of the 21st century and has been adopted by almost every country on Earth. A genuine risk to our liberty is "environmentalism", and it is the radical ecologists (or eco-terrorists who hold the philosophy known as "deep ecology") who regard the environment as holding the legal right to live and flourish. The Earth Summit Strategy to Save Our Planet is summarised as follows: "Agenda 21 proposes an array of actions which are intended to be implemented by every person on Earth... it calls for specific changes in the activities of all people... unlike anything the world has ever experienced."[c] Agenda 21 is an example of a centrally coordinated global strategy that is being implemented at the local level in every community. Governments are increasing regulations over our property rights, as demonstrated by the *Recommendations from the*

Vancouver Plan of Action: "Land... cannot be treated as an ordinary asset, controlled by individuals... Public control of land use is therefore indispensable."[ci] We are seeing a growing list of aggressive proposals and policies which aim to govern our daily lives and take away our basic rights to own property and land. The economic and ecological methods of genocide are considerably more effective than any military means. To the globalists, the importance of population reduction is horrifyingly evident. Various methods which are being employed to keep the population "under control" are made justifiable and legal through the United Nations and its agencies, such as the World Health Organisation. In regards to overpopulation and reincarnation, it was Prince Philip (husband of Queen Elizabeth II) that once remorselessly stated: "I must confess that I am tempted to ask for reincarnation as a particularly deadly virus." This is an ideology common in an eco-terrorist and a typical prejudice of a neo-pagan oligarch. The prince's considerate offer isn't likely to be needed as the tactics for controlling the population are increasingly complex and effective. A 1994 report titled *The Coming Fall of the House of Windsor*, published by the Executive Intelligence Review, presents incriminating evidence of Prince Philip's involvement in genocide and is summarised as follows: "The most monstrous crimes committed in all known human history... since its founding in 1961... the World Wildlife Fund has engaged in wilful genocide against the nations and peoples of the sub-Sahara regions of East, West and South Africa... the 'kingpin' of this criminal conspiracy has been Prince Philip."

Short-Sighted Genocidal Fury

Advocates of population reduction include European royalty, members of the Vatican, Bill Gates, David Rockefeller, Henry Kissinger and Ted Turner. In 2009, a group of influential American billionaires met secretly in New York to discuss methods of preventing population growth.[cii] This discreet and informal meeting of philanthropists included Warren Buffet, Bill Gates, David Rockefeller and Ted Turner. In a presentation on climate change given at a TED convention (Technology, Education and Design) in February 2010, Bill Gates estimated: "The world today has 6.8 billion people. That's heading up to about 9 billion. Now if we do a really great job on new vaccines, health care, reproductive health services, we could lower that by perhaps 10 or 15 percent."[ciii] On the pretext of vaccinating the Third World, the Bill and Melinda Gates Foundation was established and now works alongside the World Health Organisation. After taking on the mission to "eradicate" polio in India, and after hiring some of Bollywood's top actors to promote his propaganda campaign, there have been some *extremely* disturbing statistics published by the Department of Paediatrics for St Stephen's Hospital in Delhi, India: "In 2011 there were an extra 47,500 new cases of NPAFP [non-polio acute flaccid paralysis]. Clinically indistinguishable from polio paralysis but twice as deadly, the incidence of NPAFP was directly proportional to doses of oral polio received."[civ] The report published by St Stephen's Hospital goes on to say: "In 2011, an additional 47,500 children were newly paralysed in the year, over and above the standard 2/100,000 non-polio AFP that is generally accepted as the norm [emphasis added]." The Oral Polio Vaccines (OPV) given to children have adverse effects and can leave children paralysed or dead, as it is evidently doing. It's not through ignorance that this is happening, but as Bill Gates stated himself, a really good job on vaccinations can help "reduce population growth". Under the guise of vaccine equality, the philanthropic Bill Gates and his entourage are manipulating parents; they nobly aim to vaccinate every child on Earth. As stated in an online article by William Engdahl, in reference to his book *Seeds of Destruction*: "Gates's interest in inducing population reduction among black and other minority populations is not new, unfortunately... since the 1920s the Rockefeller Foundation had funded the eugenics research in Germany through the Kaiser-Wilhelm Institutes in Berlin and Munich, including well into the Third Reich. They praised the forced sterilization of people by Hitler's Germany and the Nazi ideas on race 'purity'."[cv] Forced abortions, sterilisation and population reduction may have been familiar practices in Nazi Germany or communist China, but what place do such barbaric practices have in the "free world" of the 21st century? According to one popular health website, if vaccines were to be used in the population-reduction scheme, there are three general ways in which it could be done:[cvi]

- By accelerating degenerative diseases, killing people slowly in an unnoticeable way over the course of 10-30 years.
- To reduce fertility through efforts to reduce birth rates, a "soft kill", seems more ethical.
- An increased death rate in future pandemics – vaccination efforts could be followed by a deliberate release of a highly virulent flu strain with a high fatality rate. This "bio-weapon" approach could kill millions of people whose immune systems have been weakened by previous vaccines.[cvii]

When speaking out against the dangers of many of our foods and vaccines, board-certified neurosurgeon Dr. Russell Blaylock stated: "We're seeing a society that not only has a lot more people of lower IQ, but a lot fewer people of higher IQ. In other words: a dumbing down, a chemical dumbing down of society. So you can kind of piece it together as to why they [governments] are so insistent in spending so many hundreds of millions of dollars of propaganda money to dumb down society." [cviii]

The Alimentary Crisis

In 1970, Henry Kissinger stated: "Who controls the food supply controls the people; who controls the energy can control whole continents; who controls money can control the world." In 1995, this statement was echoed at the United Nations 4th World Conference on Women in Beijing when Catherine Bertini, Executive Director of the UN World Food Program, said: "Food is power. We use it to change behaviour. Some may call that bribery. We do not apologise." The alimentary crisis (the lack of nourishment and nutrition) sees, on average, one person starving to death every five seconds. The driving force behind this extreme poverty is the unequal and illegal distribution of wealth throughout the world. A 2004 study entitled *Social & Economic Injustice* estimated: "1.2 billion (20%) of the world population now lives on less than $1/day, another 1.8 billion (30%) lives on less than $2/day, and 30,000-60,000 die each day from hunger alone." [cix] Most of the people on this planet live in extreme poverty – global wealth is becoming more and more concentrated. Setting the obvious moral and ethical issues aside, is overpopulation a genuine threat to sustainable development in the 21st century?

Is the World Overpopulated?

No, the world is not overpopulated. New York City has a population density of approximately 27,500 people per square mile. [cx] Theoretically, everybody on Earth (seven billion people) could fit into the state of Texas at a density of approximately 26,500 people per square mile (that's a population density 1,000 less than New York City). [cxi] There are over 57 million square miles of land mass on Earth. Do not be fooled - there is plenty of room for growth and there are more than enough resources for the development of life on Earth. The world is not overpopulated, it's very poorly managed. As stated on the

Overpopulation is a Myth website for the Research Population Institute: "Overpopulation is a myth. This myth has caused human-rights abuses around the world, forced population control, denied medicines to the poor and targeted attacks on ethnic minorities and women."[cxii] Today, living conditions for the majority of the world's population are worse than at any other time in history. With over one billion people on the verge of starvation and around two to three billion earning just a few dollars a day, propaganda campaigns claim that the cause of such inequality is overpopulation and that sustainable development depends on a finite population density, thus, by their reasoning, depopulation is crucial to the success of a New World Order and global "equality". This is totally absurd, irrational and inhumane; the root cause of starvation and poverty is the following:

- Mismanagement of the planet (the illegal concentration of wealth) and the suppression of innovative technologies.
- Under-production.
- Resource under-utilisation.

Don't be fooled into thinking that overpopulation is a threat to sustainable development. Even with current technological capabilities the demographic potential of this planet is *vast*. The oligarchs have consolidated their wealth and they now control most of the natural resources and financial institutions on planet Earth – 1% of the global population is in control of more than half the world's wealth, and they won't stop until they have it *all*. The energy monopolies burden the population with ever-increasing bills each month and do not support new innovative techniques for energy. In 2011, an average British household energy bill cost £1,356 – this cost has doubled in just seven years![cxiii] One estimation stated that 20,000 old-age pensioners died from the cold in 2011, which is over 50 a day – it's the most vulnerable in society who are intentionally being targeted. In addition to the incalculable human cost, the financial cost to the National Health Service to treat the casualties of the cold each year is in excess of £1 billion.[cxiv]

12. New World Order Summary

With plans to halt population growth, the genocidal irrationalism and anti-human fanaticism of the ruling oligarchs is blindingly obvious: they aim to sacrifice millions of people in order to make way for a global totalitarian government. The question is: will they fully succeed, and to what extent will this impact on future generations? With thermonuclear warfare looming, we are fast approaching a turning point in human history, one which could potentially plunge mankind into a new Dark Age if the New World Order is successful. If it fails, according to Executive Intelligence Review, mankind could emerge from "... the 500-year cycle of history now coming to a close, into a new Renaissance."[cxv]

The Rise of the Phoenix

A giant phoenix has swept down upon humanity and is flying us back to Babylon. Within the Security Council Chamber in the United Nations Conference Building, we see the phoenix depicted on the oil-canvas mural (see Image 12.1).

Image 12.1 A depiction of the phoenix on the oil-canvas mural located in the Security Council Chamber in the United Nations Conference Building.

As stated by 33rd-degree Freemason Manly P Hall in his book *The Phoenix: An Illustrated Review of Occultism and Philosophy*: "The Phoenix is generally regarded as representing immortality and resurrection... The Phoenix is one sign of the secret orders of the ancient world and of the initiate of those orders." So where does the concept of the New World Order originate and what is the solution?

13. The Reformation and the Counter-Reformation

When tracing the origins of the New World Order, the first part of our journey takes us back to one of the most significant events of the last millennium. The 16th-century Protestant Reformation led England, Germany and various other European countries to break away from Roman Catholic rule. According to some conventional historians, the account of the Reformation is as follows...

The Reformation was initiated by Christians who exposed a conspiracy within the Roman Catholic Church. The early Protestants (those who "protested" against the church) revolted against Roman Catholic rituals, doctrines and overall ecclesiastical structure, and set out to abolish the authority of the papacy. The Reformation was one of the first media-led revolutions – the distribution of religious pamphlets and translations of the Bible sparked an enlightening amongst Christians throughout Europe, weakening the oppressive Roman Catholic superpower. Through study of the Bible, Christians began to learn of the absolutes of grace and salvation offered directly by God (according to the Gospels, salvation is not mediated by the Church). It was the collapse of the Eastern Roman Empire and the invention of the printing press that fuelled the success of the Protestant Reformation. Author and professor of theology Martin Luther (1483-1546) played an important role in the Reformation and published a revolutionary doctrine on salvation called *Justification by Faith Alone.* Following the split from Rome, the Tudor dissolution of monasteries was eagerly led by Henry VIII in England in 1538 – this resulted in the English monarch becoming the Supreme Governor of the church by "Royal Supremacy".

A Venetian Conspiracy...?

"Unconventional" historians claim that, from behind the scenes, intelligence agents of the Venetian oligarchs initiated this Reformation and that Martin Luther was merely a pawn on the Venetians' chess board. In order to destroy the ever-burdensome Venetian oligarchs, the League of Cambrai was formed in 1508 by what the Encyclopaedia Britannica states was: "... an alliance of Pope Julius II, the Holy Roman Emperor Maximilian I, Louis XII of France, and Ferdinand II of Aragon".[cxvi] A series of wars followed involving all the major European powers – Venice suffered the most catastrophic military assault in its thousand-year history and peace was not achieved until 1529.[cxvii]

Image 13.1 Battle of Agnadello, the League of Cambrai (Pierre-Jules Jollivet, 1794-1871).

Although the Venetians had accumulated incredible wealth since the founding of their city upon marshy lagoons some 1,000 years prior, they were growing ever weaker. Based on circumstantial evidence, some researchers claim that, through a sophisticated system of embassies and domestic and foreign intelligence networks, the Venetians played the game of geopolitics in order to instigate the Protestant Reformation and ignite spiritual passions throughout Europe (which led to some of the most violent wars of the last millennium). Somewhat controversially, historian Webster Tarpley claims that the Venetians' aim was to divert foreign aggression away from themselves, to divide the continent and thereby inevitably to control the religious beliefs of the peasants. Thus, Tarpley claims, Lutheranism, Anglicanism, Calvinism and the Enlightenment were born – this was the Venetians' "order out of chaos". Tarpley states: "It is therefore vital to the Venetians to control philosophy and especially science, the area where human powers of hypothesis and creative reason become a force for improvements in the order of nature. The Venetian Party is implacably hostile to scientific discovery. The Venetian Party has also created over the centuries a series of scientific frauds and hoaxes, which have been elevated to the status of incontrovertible and unchallengeable authorities. These have been used to usurp the rightful honour due to real scientists, whom the Venetians have done everything possible to destroy."[cxviii] Tarpley's outlook is somewhat pessimistic – it was the newly founded "freedom of conscience" and "freedom of the press" (which followed the Protestant Reformation and preaching of the "true" Gospel) which fuelled the scientific revolution. It also gave rise to individualism and secular humanism (a philosophy centred on man which replaces the need for God) – for better or for worse, man had now become the creator of his own destiny.

The Counter-Reformation and the Jesuit Agenda

In order to subdue the heretical Protestant revolution, led by Pope Paul III at the Council of Trent in 1545, the Catholic Church initiated the Counter-Reformation (the Council of Trent was held between 1545 and 1563). Prior to this, in 1536, a monastic order of the Roman Catholic Church called the Jesuits (the Society of Jesus) was founded in Paris by a Spanish nobleman, Ignatius of Loyola.[cxix] As a practitioner of mysticism and heretical Christianity, Ignatius was a member of Los Alumbrados (a 15th-century Spanish illuminised brotherhood). For centuries, various military (and quasi-military) orders and societies have been used as fronts by the Roman Catholic Church to protect the papacy from bad press. Headed by the Superior General (commonly known as the "black" pope), the Jesuits, a strict military-style order, devised plans for political subversion and set out to destroy the Protestant movement. The main objective of the Jesuit order was to gain world domination by seizing the authority of the pope and, ultimately, to suppress freedom of conscience. To cite one of their early endeavours, the failed assassination attempt against England's King James I in the early 17th century (also known as the Guy Fawkes Gunpowder Plot) was a conspiracy of the Jesuits which aimed to secure a Roman Catholic succession for the throne. To this day, the people of England still celebrate the failed Gunpowder Plot on November 5th, yet most are unaware that this conspiracy was a Roman Catholic Jesuit ploy.

Image 13.2 The Council of Trent – one of the Roman Catholic Church's most important ecumenical councils.

A brief search of the New York Times newspaper archives from the 19th and 20th centuries reveals how truly problematic the Jesuit order has been since its establishment. Portugal, Spain, Germany, Japan, Nicaragua and Guatemala are just a few of the countries that found good cause to expel the Jesuits. Canadian historian J E C Shepherd states: "Between 1555 and 1931 the Society of Jesus [the Jesuit order] was expelled from at least 83 countries, city states and cities, for engaging in political intrigue and subversion plots against the welfare of the State." As the New York Times bluntly stated back in 1880: "The one historical fact remains, that they [the Jesuits] did always, sooner or later, come into collision with every power under whose protection they lived."cxx The American physician and historian Emanuel Josephson states: "[Wherever] a totalitarian movement erupts, whether Communist or Nazi [Fascist], a Jesuit can be found in the role of 'adviser' or leader; in Cuba [it was] [Jesuit-trained] Castro's 'Father' Armando Llorente." Revealing how close Hitler and the Nazis were tied to the Roman Catholic Church, the American historian Leo Lehnmann stated: "It was a Jesuit priest, Father Staempfle, not Hitler, who really wrote Mein Kampf."cxxi Some have claimed that Hitler was a staunch Christian, but the claim is simply untrue – after all, why would a man who exterminated Jewish people worship a Jewish man (Jesus) as his God?

Furthermore, various researchers assert that modern communism was founded through the Jesuits and that they pioneered the French and Russian revolutions in order to remove various monarchs throughout Europe. The incalculable damage of the Jesuit order and their malevolent agenda should not be overlooked. A thorough investigation of the Jesuits would demonstrate that commonly during a revolution or tyrannical rule of a nation, a Jesuit advisor is to be found not far away.

Educators and Moulders of Theological and Secular Opinion

A former Jesuit priest turned critic of the institution, Malachi Martin, stated: "There was no continent Jesuits did not reach; no known language they did not speak and study, or, in scores of cases, develop; no culture they did not penetrate; no branch of learning and science they did not explore."[cxxii] Today, the Jesuits have divided the United States and Canada into nine provinces or regions – a provincial superior, appointed by the Superior General in Rome, heads each region (see Image 13.3). Throughout the US alone, they manage over 20 universities and, as stated on their website: "In the same way that the United States Assistancy is comprised of individual provinces, so too is the rest of the world, with other Assistancies and Jesuit Conferences representing each region."[cxxiii]

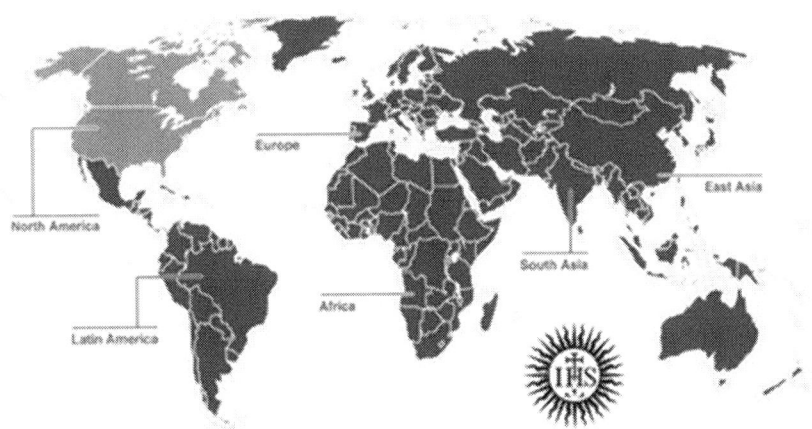

Image 13.3 Global Jesuit province map: in the same way that the US and Canada has been divided into provinces "...
so too is the rest of the world."[cxxiv]

Many Jesuits maintain positions as teachers, lawyers, archaeologists, astronomers, physicists, theologians and theoreticians. Located in

Washington DC alongside the White House and the Supreme Council or "House of the Temple" (the Freemasonic temple which acts as the headquarters of the Scottish Rite Southern Jurisdiction) is Georgetown University. Georgetown University is a private Jesuit university which has educated heads of state, heads of governments, ambassadors, members of the US Senate, White House staff, CEOs and royalty from all over the world. The following are just a few of the notable Jesuit Georgetown alumni:

- Bill Clinton – former US President.
- José Manuel Barroso – President of the European Commission and former Prime Minister of Portugal.
- Felipe VI – King of Spain.
- King Abdullah II of Jordan.

Viet Dinh, Roman Catholic and professor of law at Georgetown University, was the chief architect of the USA PATRIOT Act (as previously mentioned, following the Hegelian Dialectic, the USA PATRIOT Act was part of the pre-planned solution to the 9/11 terror attack). The House of the Temple Freemasonic lodge (see Image 13.4) stands approximately one mile north of the White House.

Image 13.4 The Supreme Council of the Temple of the Inspectors General Knights Commander of the House of the Temple of Solomon – Freemasonic lodge in Washington
(image credit AgnosticPreachersKid via Commons[cxxv]).

Summary

The history of the Jesuit order is far too extensive to cover in one chapter, but it should be noted that the role of the pope is merely symbolic – the Jesuit order and the Superior General maintain one of the highest concentrations of power on Earth. Intrinsic to their values, the Jesuit order has *always* covertly attacked freedom of conscience, freedom of the press and the right to bear arms, whilst eliminating people who it deems to be liberal or heretical. Although the traditions of the Jesuit order are centuries old, it continues its pursuit of "world domination" to this very day. The Jesuit order has been evicted from numerous cities and countries due to its countless illicit activities, yet despite this it eventually finds its way back inside a nation. As shall be reviewed later, the Jesuits have established and infiltrated various orders and societies, such as Freemasonry and the Illuminati, as a means to accomplish their goals. Author John Daniel states: "The truth is, the Jesuits of Rome have perfected Freemasonry to be their most magnificent and effective tool, accomplishing their purposes among Protestants."[cxxvi]

The Third Reich: Rise of the Nazis

In the 1920s, at a time when Germany's economy was in a state of ruin, the National Socialists (the Nazis) and the military elite, known as the SS, began rising to power with guidance from Rome and European royalty and nobility. Prescott Bush and the Union Banking Corporation, Prince Charles Edward (the Duke of Saxe-Coburg and Gotha, also known as Prince Charlie, who was born in Surrey, England), Averill Harriman (son of an American railroad baron) and Fritz Thyssen (whose autobiography was called "I Paid Hitler") acted as some of the financial backers of the vast military expansion of the Nazi war machine which attempted to conquer the world. Conventional historians often fail to mention the significance of the underlying motives and interests of the Nazis, including the philosophies of an occult order named the Thule Society. The Thule Society, whose members included Nazi elites, was greatly influenced by the founder of the Theosophical Society, Helena Blavatsky, who venerated the Aryan race – a master bloodline that is claimed to have originated in Atlantis and which, according to its adherents, is destined to rule over the Earth. Blavatsky stated: "The Semites, especially the Arabs, are later Aryans — degenerate in spirituality and perfected in materiality."[cxxvii] Obviously, this influenced some of the ideologies and subsequent atrocities of Nazi racism, race superiority and the extermination of Jews (a Semitic people). Theosophy is merely a consolidation of Eastern mysticism and blends Hinduism, Buddhism and Tao into one specific movement, also known as the New Age. Hitler was inspired by theosophy (and occultism in general), and the Nazi Swastika was adapted from an ancient esoteric symbol which was also incorporated in the logo of the Theosophical Society. This archetypal spiritual symbol is thought to have first appeared in the Indus valley approximately 3,000 years ago, but has been used by many cultures all over the globe – from China, Japan and throughout the Middle-East, to Europe and even North and South America.

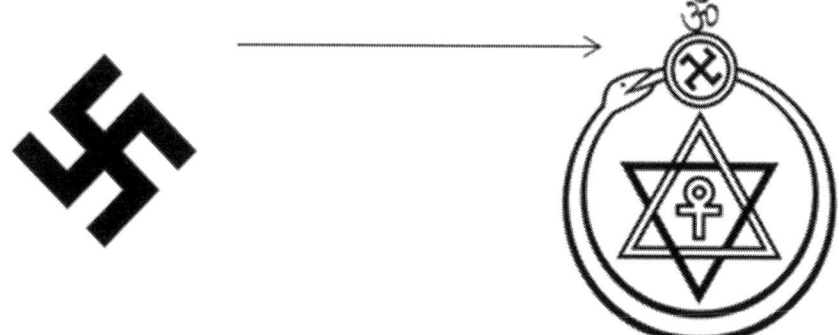

Image 13.5 The Nazi Swastika (left) and the Theosophical Society logo (right).

Image 13.6 Swastika on a Greek silver coin from Corinth, 6th century BC.

Image 13.7 5th or 6th century Anglo-Saxon cinerary urn with Swastika motifs, found in Norfolk, England.

Image 13.8 A Hindu statue with the Swastika on the chest.

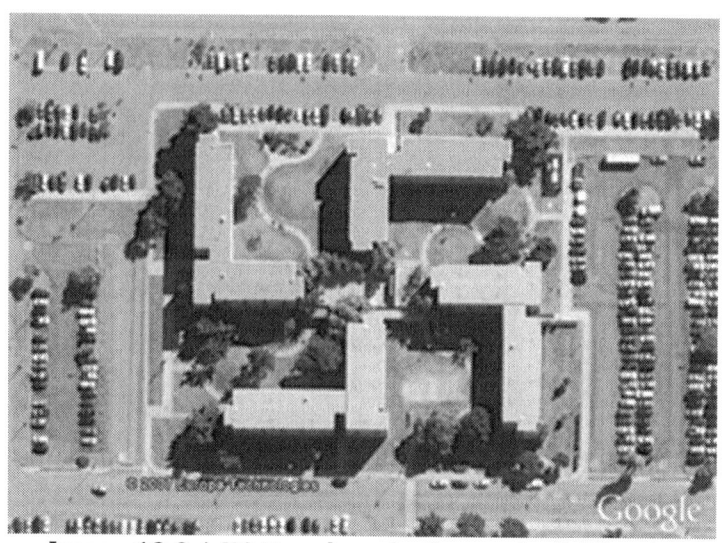
Image 13.9 A US Navy base in Coronado, California.

As Image 13.9 demonstrates, a US Navy base in California was designed to incorporate the ancient spiritual symbol of the swastika. Of course today, the Swastika has very negative connotations.

NASA and the Nazis

The Nazi occultists went on expeditions to Tibet, Iceland and Antarctica for technological and spiritual research and development. It was the Germans who developed the V1 and V2 rockets, military robots and a sub-orbital bomber aircraft, for which vast underground bases were constructed to develop the technologies. The sinister side to these developments saw Jews (and other prisoners) forced to work around the clock. Many slaves died of exhaustion and several public executions took place on a daily basis – to serve as an "incentive" for the other prisoners. Whilst many historians may claim that a secret space programme was non-existent, others argue that it was one of Hitler's top priorities and, today, the achievements of the US space programme stand on the shoulders of Nazi efforts. Following the death of Adolf Hitler, many of the intellectuals and financial investors behind the Nazi movement were not brought to trial, but instead, led by the US military, Operation Paper Clip saw hundreds of Nazi war criminals (such as engineers, eugenicists, scholars and military men) shipped over to America. Following a "cleansing" of their background, they were granted US citizenship and began work on various projects such as Area 51 and NASA's space programme. NASA was formed around a core of Nazis and occultists and, as a reflection of their esoteric beliefs, the NASA spacecraft-naming convention is derived from ancient pagan mythology. I have discovered that by arranging the names of the spacecraft and using some creativeness to fill in the blanks, a theme of the New Age objective is revealed (the spacecraft names are in bold italics):

Apollo's **Enterprise** called **Columbia** [mother goddess]
will **Endeavour** to **Discover** the lost city of **Atlantis**...
all **Challengers** will be destroyed.

Coincidently, the Challenger spacecraft was destroyed in January 1986 when it disintegrated after take-off, leading to the death of its seven crew members.

World War One, Two and Three

When discussing the New World Order, many researchers commonly reference a dubious letter supposedly written by the 33rd-degree Freemason and Sovereign Grand Commander of the Scottish Rite Southern Jurisdiction, Albert Pike, to Guiseppe Mazzini (an Italian politician). The letter, said to have been dated August 15th 1871, is likely to be a fraud or hoax. It is believed to have been held in the British Museum Library in London but has seemingly "disappeared" (and the Freemasons officially declare it to be a fabrication).cxxviii In the letter, Pike is said to have outlined his vision for three world wars which are required before the New World Order can be finalised. The reason for referencing the letter is because it provides an interesting perspective on three major wars. The letter outlines Pike's reasons for the wars and is summarised as follows:

- World War 1: To overthrow the Czars in Russia in order to build a communist nation and weaken or remove religion from society. To allow the British to gain control over Palestine.
- World War 2: The differences between the Fascists and political Zionists will be exploited before destroying Nazism whilst strengthening Zionism and establishing a sovereign state of Israel in the land of Palestine.
- World War 3: The differences between Zionism and Islam will ignite a final world war in which the two entities will mutually destroy one another.

Although this letter is a fraud, both World Wars One and Two achieved the objectives supposedly written by Pike – I do believe that these wars were mapped out long before they occurred. I also believe that the differences between Zionism and Islam will continue to be exploited – as tensions continuously rise in the Middle East, World War Three is on the horizon. Remarkably, the symbolic hostility between Muslims and Jews originated in antiquity, as will be investigated later in this work. After the establishment of the political Zionist movement (Zionism is a form of Jewish nationalism) in the 19th century, various Zionists campaigned for the re-establishment of Israel as a homeland for the Jewish people – generally speaking, the Jews preferred European life and didn't want to return to the Middle East, and therefore the early Zionist campaigns proved unsuccessful.

Ancient Israel

It was almost 2,000 years prior to this when, in 66 AD, the Israelites began a revolt against Roman rule in Judea. As tensions escalated, thousands of Jews and Roman citizens were slaughtered in battles. In a devastating blow to Jewish heritage and identity, an imperial Roman assault, led by Titus, destroyed the Jewish Second Temple in Jerusalem on Tisha B'Av in 70 AD (interestingly, the Babylonians destroyed the First Temple, the Temple of Solomon, on exactly the same day just a few hundred years prior, before the Israelites were sent into exile). After the Roman assault left Jerusalem in ruins, many survivors were sold into slavery, or once again displaced to "the four corners of the Earth", and their land was later renamed Palestine.

Image 13.10 The Second Jewish Temple: The Temple of Herod.

In 1917, during the First World War, the United Kingdom's Foreign Secretary, Arthur James Balfour, wrote a letter (known as the Balfour Declaration) to the Zionist Walter Rothschild, which publicly declared British support for a Jewish homeland in Palestine. From 1920 until 1947, the land was under British administration and, following the termination of the British Mandate of Palestine on Friday May 14th 1948, the independence of the State of Israel (Medinat Yisrael) was officially declared. After all the savageries of World War Two and widespread persecution, the Jews were more than convinced to leave Europe and return to their homeland. Within a matter of hours, this declaration was followed by an invasion of the former Palestinian mandate by the Arab armies from Lebanon, Syria, Iraq and Egypt[cxxix] – war between the Arabs and Israelis broke out and the dispute has never been resolved. It only requires a minimal amount of investigation to discover that both the Nazi movement and the Zionist (Israeli nationalist) movement were funded by the same families (which included the Saxe-Coburg and Gothas, the Rothschilds, the Rockefellers and the Warburgs) in order to justify the establishment of a Jewish homeland (with guidance from the "Mother Church" in Rome and the Jesuit order, it certainly goes deeper than being a purely "Jewish" conspiracy) – yet again we see a game of geopolitics: the Hegelian dialectic of thesis and anti-thesis results in synthesis. One focal point of the Arab-Israeli conflict is the site of Solomon's Temple, the Temple Mount on Mount Moriah. Following the Muslim conquest of Jerusalem in 691 AD, the Islamic Dome of the Rock was built over the site of Solomon's Temple and is now regarded as the third holiest site in Islam – it is one of the most contested pieces of land on Earth. What is obvious is that the tension has been, and will continue to be, exploited using the formula of the Hegelian dialectic. In other words, World Wars One and Two were planned well in advance, with the aims of legitimising the establishment of Israel (and to give the Jews a reason to return home), progressing the colonisation of the Middle East and ultimately provoking a Third World War in which the political Zionists and Islamic world will "mutually destroy" one another – from this, when the fearful and weary citizens of planet Earth are ready to submit, the New World Order will be finalised.

14. The Knights of the Temple and Jewish Mysticism

An ancient Hebrew teaching known as the Kabbalah is a core doctrine for various secret societies – it is Jewish mysticism which originates from the Sefer ha-Bahir. These mystical teachings are thought to have been transcribed by Rabbi Isaac the Blind in the south of France during the 12th century before the documents fell into the hands of nine French noblemen who were known as the Knights Templar. Founded on Christmas Day in 1119 and sanctioned by the pope in 1128cxxx, the Templars became an international order. Special privileges meant that they were exempt from certain laws and taxes and, amongst other jobs, they worked to protect pilgrims in the Holy Land of Jerusalem (the name Knights of the Temple is in reference to Solomon's Temple). As the first multinational bankers, their innovative financial techniques were a very successful form of banking and their networks ran from Egypt to the City of London. They built up a fleet of ships and constructed hundreds of churches and castles throughout Europe and the Middle East, many of which still stand today (their skills of masonry, the science of navigation and their fascination with the occult were evidently inherited by the Freemasons). The Templars embraced Kabbalism and Gnosticism and are rumoured to have participated in satanic rituals. Whilst in Israel, they embarked upon crusades on behalf of the papacy not only to regain control of the Holy Land, but also to discover more esoteric teachings and prevent the Muslims (who occupied Jerusalem) from gaining knowledge of Kabbalistic secrets.

The Darker Side of the Templars

Various researchers claim that some of the Templars were a group of brutal, bloodthirsty murderers and rapists, that they worshipped an idol of Satan in the form of a baphomet and that they participated in various other dark activities including demonic sex rituals. However, various other researchers contest this, claiming that the Templars were tortured into false confessions and that these satanic activities are merely urban legends. It appears that the perverse rituals made famous by the Templars are commonplace today – stories often make the headlines when politicians or, more commonly, priests and clergymen are ousted for sex scandals, specifically child abuse. According to the testimonies of various former satanists, one particular requirement for becoming a satanic priest is first to be ordained as a Catholic priest, thus a clear link can be drawn between satanism and paedophilia and it is one indication of why child abuse is so widespread within the church. The Vatican has recently been reported to have paid out over £1 billion in response to sexual abuse allegations.

The Normalisation Agenda

Amongst the oligarchs and their counterparts today, satanic rituals are common practice. Just one of *many* scandals to emerge in Britain is that of an old "national treasure" named Sir Jimmy Savile, who obtained a knighthood from Queen Elizabeth II and a papal knighthood from Pope John-Paul II, making him a Knight Commander of the Order of Saint Gregory the Great. Savile, now regarded as Britain's worst sex offender, rubbed shoulders with the elite (he was a great friend of Prince Charles, British ex-Prime Minister Margaret Thatcher and the British ex-Prime Minister Ted Heath) – he held a key position within their protective network and the details of his crimes were purposely suppressed until after he died in 2011. Although he abused hundreds of children over the course of five decades, Savile rightly considered himself as untouchable – the authorities and his employers at the BBC were aware of his crimes for many years. One particular case, which only recently came to light, involved a 12-year-old child in a hospital in which Savile had once worked as a voluntary porter. The terrified child was abused in a black mass ritual held in a room filled with candles and several adults wearing gowns and masks, in which she heard "ave Satanas" being chanted (which is Latin for "hail Satan") throughout the ordeal. What the British public have witnessed is just a fraction of what occurs within some Freemasonic and royal-political elite circles, the church and the entertainment industry. There are various worldwide paedophile networks in operation and many of the offenders (including priests, police, barristers, politicians and royalty) enjoy immunity from prosecution and exposure. Both the BBC and the Vatican have acted as conduits for child grooming and paedophilia, and they are also playing a key role in an agenda to normalise this grotesque culture. If that sounds absurd, take a look at the British justice system, which is extremely lenient towards paedophiles and punishes them with insufficiently brief prison sentences - if they get locked up at all. The people of Britain are living in a society where graffiti artists are getting longer jail sentences than child abusers. There is a clear link between satanism and paedophilia and it is a serious problem, not just within the church. With such dark spiritual characteristics, it certainly appears as though the New World Order is more than just a "political ideology".

The World's Financial Capital – the City of London Corporation

As the first multinational bankers, just how powerful were the Knights Templar? Consider the extremely powerful and unaccountable financial capital of the world, located in the heart of England. As one of the largest concentrations of financial powers the world has ever known, the plutocratic City of London is a sovereign state. Centuries of shady activity conducted within the confines of this financial island have seen governments continuously surrender their authority in exchange for City loans. If the Queen wishes to enter the City of London, a ceremony is held in which she wears a modest outfit and is met by the Lord Mayor (who is different from the Mayor of Greater London), dressed in his or her regalia. Many modern central banks are based on the Bank of England model and the City has been a prominent financial hub for several hundred years – ever since the construction of a 12th-century monastic complex named the Crown Temple Church built by none other than the Knights Templar.

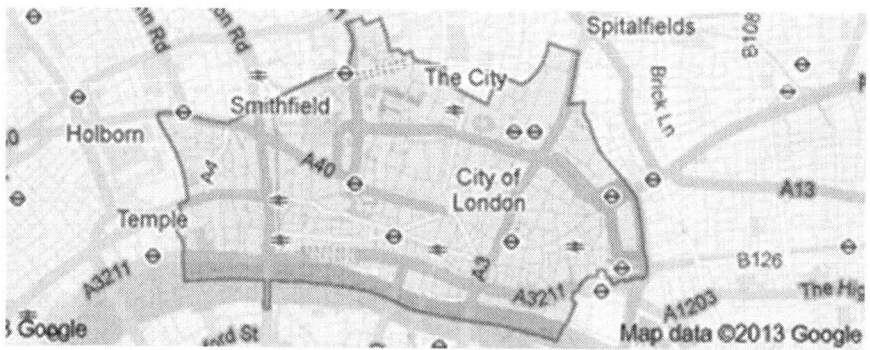
Image 14.1 The City.

The Crown Temple Church served as the Knights Templar headquarters in England and also as an early depository bank – the most prominent legal and financial institutions have been based here ever since. In this region sits the Bank of England, the London Stock Exchange and the Royal Courts of Justice. The symbol of the Knights Templar is the famous St George's Cross:

Image 14.2: The Symbol of the Knights Templar.

The City of London coat of arms still displays the Knights Templar cross (as do various other coats of arms and flags). This same cross was used on the sail flags of Christopher Columbus's ship when he travelled the Atlantic to "discover" North America. The flag of Switzerland also bears the Knights Templar cross. Switzerland is home to the Bank of International Settlements – over 50 of the world's central banks belong to this institution; it is the central bank for all central banks, it is immensely powerful and is not accountable to any national government. It is immune from tax and national laws and clearly undermines the concept of a constitution or democracy. Its meetings are shrouded in secrecy – officers and employees even enjoy a level of immunity from criminal and administrative jurisdiction: "…even after such persons have ceased to be Officials of the Bank."[cxxxi]

The End of the Templars

After years of terror and the accumulation of vast wealth and power, the Knights Templar began to unsettle both the pope and the king of France. On an unlucky Friday 13th October 1307, the French king, Philip IV, had the Templars arrested before charging them with various offences – many of them were tortured and executed. It was at this time of torture that the Templars confessed to participating in satanic activities and this is why various researchers dispute the credibility of the confessions. Some of the remaining Knights are said to have escaped to Scotland, Spain and Portugal, or even to have taken to the high seas to live a life of piracy. It was after the formation of the Knights of Christ in Portugal (a continuation of the Knights Templar) that an expert mariner and the Grand Master of the order, Henry "the Navigator", sailed with the Templar cross on his ships' sails (as did Christopher Columbus). Some of the Templars are also said to have fled to the island of Malta to establish trade routes with North America – their rituals and traditions lived on. By no coincidence, it was around this time that both Spain and Portugal became successful explorers of international waters and established power bases throughout South America where the Roman Catholic Church and the Jesuits still have great power today (and maintain involvement in political subversion, the drug trade, gun running and child abuse). The basic structure of the Knights Templar was as follows:

- The outer layer of the fraternity was comprised of the uninitiated members who were taught a separate doctrine to that of the "masters".
- The inner core was comprised of the elect (those who were truly initiated) in order to conceal the true secrets from the masses.

The 33rd-degree Freemason Albert Pike reveals: "The Templars, like all other secret orders and associations, had two doctrines, one concealed and reserved for the masters, which was Johannism; the other public, which was the Roman Catholic."[cxxxii]

The Knights of Malta

Founded in around 1048 AD, the Sovereign Military Hospitaller Order of St John of Jerusalem of Rhodes and of Malta (also known as the Sovereign Military Order of Malta or the Knights of Malta) are a chivalrous order which: "... has maintained the values of chivalry and nobility".[cxxxiii] Following the end of the Knights Templar, in 1312 Pope Clement V issued the Papal Bull, *Ad providam*, which transferred the Knights Templars' assets to the Knights of Malta! This ancient and mysterious order is today headquartered in Rome and although the Knights of Malta do not rule over any territory, they are regarded as a sovereign state and the *smallest country* in the world. Aside from issuing its own passports and postage stamps and holding permanent observer status at the United Nations, the order marks the intersection between the US elite and the Vatican.   According to author Martin Lee: "Nobility forms the backbone of the Sovereign Military Order of Malta; more than 40 percent of its 10,000 constituents are related to Europe's oldest and most powerful Catholic families. Wealth is a de facto prerequisite for a knightly candidate."

The Vatican and US Intelligence

Although the order was ejected from the island of Malta in 1798, they still retain sovereignty under international law and can offer diplomatic immunity to the Grand Master and members of the Sovereign Council – many of the knights demonstrate fidelity towards the order above any commitment to their own nation. In alliance with the Vatican and the Red Cross, the order helped many Nazi war criminals to escape Germany at the end of the Second World War, including around 8,000 Waffen-SS members who were taken in by Britain and Canada. From Europe to South America, members of the order have included European nobility, Nazis, high-ranking military personnel, secret service and intelligence agents, corporate elites, priests and politicians. General William ("Wild Bill") Donovan played a key role in the formation of the CIA (the Central Intelligence Agency) – he was a Knight of Malta and, according to author Martin Lee: "... there can be no doubt that Donovan earned his knighthood by virtue of the services he rendered to the Catholic hierarchy in World War II... Pope Pius's decoration of Wild Bill Donovan marked the beginning of a long-standing, intimate relationship between the Vatican and US intelligence that continues to the present day."[cxxxvi] Award-winning journalist Seymour Hersh confirms this by stating: "US military forces are directed and dominated [by the Knights of Malta]."

The Order of St. John

Queen Elizabeth II is the Sovereign Head of the Order of St John of Jerusalem (which is the Protestant arm of the Knights of Malta) – a role which essentially requires subordination to the pope. The St John Ambulance organisation operates worldwide and is dedicated to the teaching and practice of medical first aid through thousands of volunteers (who are mainly Protestants).

Image 14.3 Order of St John of Jerusalem.

It is difficult to associate anything esoteric or malevolent with philanthropic and hospitable organisations such as the Knights of Malta or St John's – they are therefore the perfect cloak of deception. Needless to say, a layer of protection hides the faces of the Roman Catholic Jesuits who have been continuously working behind the scenes towards a New World Order. Now that we have a little background on some of the Roman Catholic orders and their esoteric history, let's briefly review the origins and fundamentals of all secret societies.

15. Ancient Kabbalah and Modern Science

It's apparent that aspects of modern science have been adapted from ancient and occult teachings. Some things are undeniable; the mysteries of mankind and the esoteric sciences have been handed down throughout the ages within secret societies. A profound and sophisticated intelligence has filtered down from the ancient Sumerian, Babylonian and Egyptian mystery schools, although, even 3,000 years ago, this specialist knowledge was nothing new. With familiar names such as Nimrod of Babylon, King Solomon of Israel, Isaac Newton, George Washington, Benjamin Franklin, Aleister Crowley and celebrities such as Frank Sinatra, Madonna and Jay Z, an outstanding number of artists, liberators, scientists and those behind the scenes shaping history have dabbled in the occult. So why, with the advances in science and technology, are these practices still prevalent today? It is remarkable that some of these practices have aided revolutions in modern science, specifically the teachings of the Jewish Kabbalah. As stated on kabbalah.com: "... [Kabbalah is] an ancient wisdom that reveals how the universe and life work... Kabbalah is an ancient yet entirely new paradigm for living." 1,000 years ago Kabbalah was regarded as mysticism due to the advanced concepts contained within the ancient teaching. Today, it is *still* regarded as mysticism as it is claimed to conceal advanced information that will continue to be unlocked until the 25th century.[cxxxviii] Quantum physics, chaos theory and the concept of parallel universes all stem from the ancient occult discipline of Kabbalah.[cxxxix] As stated by world-famous theoretical physicist Michio Kaku: "The mysteries of both Superstring Theory and the Theory of Everything (ToE) are mirrored with the teachings of Kabbalah." Kabbalistic scientists helped usher in the nuclear age before detonating the first atomic bomb in World War Two (a major milestone for the occult warmongers). Armed with an Old Testament and the Kabbalah, a Jewish rabbi known as Nahmanides conducted his study in the 13th century and concluded that reality has ten dimensions, of which only four are "knowable". Today, in an active research framework called String Theory, physicists have also concluded that there are ten dimensions of reality, of which only four are measurable, thus modern scientists have aligned themselves with the ancient theory devised by rabbi Nahmanides. Those dimensions are:

- Three dimensions of space.
- One dimension of time.

- Six "curled" dimensions that are not accessible or measurable by direct methods (at 10^{-43} seconds after the Big Bang creation event, six of the nine space dimensions ceased expanding[cxl]).

Our reality is a four-dimensional, digital simulation and it was Pythagoras that apparently once said: "All things are numbers". The study of numbers is a religion in itself, integral to those rooted within the Mysteries. In the 18th century, through study of Kabbalah, Albrecht von Haller made a major biological breakthrough, discovering that the liver helps to digest fats. Seen by many as the father of modern physics, Albert Einstein also studied the Kabbalah and some researchers claim that it was from this study that Einstein was able to condense multiple complex equations into just five symbols: $E=MC^2$.

Philosophy

The nature of reality, the round Earth, the atomic structure of matter and instructions on how to invoke demonic entities can all be found within the broader spectrum of this mysterious and ancient teaching. Kabbalah is a truly esoteric science and, traditionally, potential students would have to deem themselves worthy of being taught its secrets through various stages of initiations and oaths, whilst today the teachings have gone mainstream. A very intriguing philosophy of Kabbalah teaches: *death is a mere illusion* and *immortality is the only true reality* – through a continued in-depth study of this mystical teaching, it is claimed that mankind will eventually find the key to unlock immortality. Some general Kabbalistic concepts teach that man can supplant God and redefine truth and that the concept of good and evil is relative. This is an interesting yet subtle twisting of what is taught in the Bible – the Bible claims that God is an absolute authority who predefined a moral code.

The Fundamentals of Secret Societies

Before investigating illuminised Freemasonry and the origins of the New World Order, the basic concept of every secret society must be understood. What are the underlying philosophies? What is at the root of deception and the driving force behind the dark New Age agenda? Without understanding the fundamentals, one will be trapped in a world of confusion and contradiction. After briefly reviewing some Kabbalastic mysteries, we now have a basic understanding of the significant and influential concepts that originate from this ancient teaching. We also have an understanding of how esoteric orders have dominated warfare, politics, trade and commerce (and why secrecy and brotherhood are so important). Surprisingly, the fundamentals of all secret societies can be unlocked with a little understanding of the Bible which, as previously mentioned, claims that morals are not relative and that man does not define good and evil, but that instead, these are defined by God and thus morality is "objective". Philosophically speaking, this does make sense; in a Godless world, man becomes the measure of all things and acts as the final authority.

A Snake...?

According to Genesis, God created Adam and Eve, placed them in the Garden of Eden and specified some basic rules before a character known as the "serpent" was introduced. The Hebrew word is "ha-nachash", for which his identity has commonly been translated as the "serpent". What was this mysterious character who spoke with such confidence and persuasion when tempting Eve to eat from the "Tree of Knowledge of Good and Evil"? Nacash has various interpretations depending upon the context. It can also be translated as "the shining one". As an expert on Semitic languages and the Hebrew Old Testament, Dr. Michael Heiser states: "... [Eve] was speaking to a manipulative, upright and bright being who might have been serpentine in appearance."[cxli] With subtlety, the "nachash" tempts Eve by playing upon her ego and deceiving her:

> "Ye shall not surely die... for God knows... Your eyes shall be opened, and ye shall be as gods knowing good and evil"
> (Genesis 3:4-5).

This implies that the nachash had hidden knowledge to which man did not have access. Rather than holding a presupposition that God was correct, Eve (clearly an evidentialist) decided to judge for herself and disobeyed God's original command by "eating" from the Tree of Knowledge. By contradicting God and claiming that man can define his own moral code, the nachash assisted mankind's descent into sin. In summary, the nachash promotes a secular humanist philosophy (by claiming that man can define good and evil) and makes three promises to Eve, which, in turn, are integral to *every* secret society and New Age spiritual movement:

- Ye shall not surely die: The Kabbalistic concept of immortality – man can overcome death.
- Your eyes shall be opened: The concept of an enlightenment which leads to salvation or a spiritual evolution (Gnosticism, New Ageism and Freemasonry).
- Ye shall be as gods: Man can reach the status of a god (New Ageism, Transhumanism and Freemasonry).

The origins and philosophies of all secret societies are rooted in the Genesis account of creation. Various secret brotherhoods have sought the sacred knowledge that was gained in the Garden of Eden. As will be reviewed in the remaining chapters, the Gnostics, the Kabbalists, the New Agers, the Freemasons and various other secret societies all share these basic ideologies which were promoted by the serpent. Both the Freemasons and the New Agers believe that man can undergo "modifications" in order to enhance divinity or come closer to the status of a god ("As above, so below"). Darwin's theory of evolution claims that man is a naturally evolving species which is growing in sophistication and, from an atheistic perspective, one has to wonder what the next stage of evolution for mankind is. The transhumanist movement aims to use technology to enhance man's ability and to assist the evolutionary process, as will be reviewed later. From Theosophy comes the New Age, a movement that is concerned with divine knowledge, spiritualism and Luciferianism or "light". As one of the fastest-growing religions throughout the world, New Ageism seems to be the prime candidate for the chosen religion of the New World Order. With both the Kabbalah and the Bible giving insight into the nature of reality, let us explore further.

16. The Nature of Reality

Space-Time

"Space-time" is a term used to describe the three dimensions of space (height, width and depth) combined with the notion of time (which is regarded as the fourth dimension). Both space and time exist in relation to one another, and the concept of them being interwoven is quite ancient. An old saying amongst the 16th-century Jewish scholars went: "HaMakom V'HaZman Echad Hu" which translates to: "Time and space are one". Merging the concepts of space and time into a single continuum has simplified various physical theories and provided a logical understanding of how the universe works at either the subatomic (microscale) or supergalactic (macroscale) level. So what about a reality that is not measurable or directly accessible? Is our world but a sub-set of a larger reality? Both the Bible and Kabbalah claim it is and, today, physicists accept that it is. Whilst physical life is confined to the dimensions of space-time and bound by the laws of physics, our reality is but a sub-set of a larger reality. If the universe is the result of random and unguided events, how do we justify morality, the laws of logic and the uniformity in nature (the preconditions of intelligibility[cxlii])? If the universe was merely a cosmic accident, why are the laws of nature consistent?

The Microscale

The concept of atoms has been discussed in philosophy for thousands of years. Scientific theories about atoms began with the advances in chemistry around 250 years ago. Since the discovery of particles, scientists have been consistently flummoxed. Everything in the known universe is made of atoms, yet these atoms are more than 99% "empty space". From the platform of human consciousness to the glorious wonders of the natural world and the sophisticated manmade structures in every town and city – all matter is an assembly of atoms. Atoms are made up of three particles (namely protons, electrons and neutrons), which are governed by the rules of quantum theory. It is quite the mystery as to how this underlying simplicity creates such a diverse and complex universe. As Dr. Brian Cox and Jeff Forshaw stated: "Quantum theory is perhaps the prime example of the infinitely esoteric becoming the profoundly useful."[cxliii] One of the more profound scientific discoveries demonstrates that a single atom can exist in more than one place at the same time. According to Heisenberg's Uncertainty Principle, it is impossible to simultaneously measure the position and the momentum of a particle. Furthermore, a particle is not only a particle; it also behaves as a wave, until a conscious observation acknowledges it – this is called "wave-particle duality". So, the most solid of brick walls and pavements (and tables, chairs and human skeletons) are actually made up of more than 99% "empty space" and particles are actually waves, that is, until somebody is looking. The discoveries in quantum physics defy common sense and the philosophical implications are quite outlandish (which is why this particular branch of physics is so intriguing). Apparently, humans are more than just observers in this reality; to a limited extent, our consciousness creates a reality – observation is creation.

Quantum Philosophy

One thing is for certain - the study of quantum physics reveals a joining of modern science with the truly ancient and esoteric teaching of Kabbalah. Quantum physics says that *nothing* is certain and that a particle can be in more than one place at the same time. Conscious observation not only affects the outcome of a test scenario; on the quantum level, it *creates* the scenario. The average person may believe the substance of the universe to be physical matter. A philosopher may believe the substance of the universe to be consciousness – consciousness precipitates matter. Theoretical physicist Fred Alan Wolf describes quantum physics as: "Probabilities for which actualities manifest." Our brains behave as a filter and render a three-dimensional model of reality *inside* our heads, including the appearance of all objects (textures, colours and shades) – in one sense, these objects are not solid and don't actually exist. In the quantum world, the terms "object" and "separation" become redundant. Replace these words with the term "relationship", as everything is connected – on the microscale, there are no objects and there is no separation. This can be demonstrated by looking at the smallest measurable unit of matter called the Planck length – attempting to divide a Planck length causes it to lose locality, indicating that everything in our world is quantised – our physical reality, the fabric of the universe itself, is made up of quanta or indivisible units. The subatomic nature of reality remains quite the mystery and the discovery of "non-locality" (the fact that "dividing" reality has a limitation) is one indication that we live in a hologram (hologram is a Greek term that translates to "whole message"). The term hologram used in this scenario is an abstract description and the theory of a holographic universe implies that reality is more like an image or a software program rather than a piece of hardware or something that is solid. The human body is a biological computer and consciousness is like a low-level programming language of reality. Using tools such as the media, the human mind is targeted and exploited (by influencing emotions and attempting to unify/modulate the human thought process) because we are more than observers of this universe; to an extremely limited extent, we are the creators of reality.

A Simulation: Virtual Reality

Is reality but a persistent illusion? Do we exist within a virtual environment? The nature of reality is something we can barely fathom. If our universe can be considered as a physical effect, then what is its cause? Advances in the understanding of this "physical effect" suggest that a "non-physical cause" brought the universe into existence, independent of all matter, energy, space, time, information and life – but is this primary cause a transcendent intelligence (God)? Consider a home computer (Image 16.1). On a piece of physical hardware (which consists of a motherboard, processor, memory and hard drive) sits a piece of software called the operating system (such as Microsoft Windows or Mac OS X) which handles the input requests via a mouse or keyboard.

Image 16.1 A typical home computer.

The purpose of the operating system is to govern the interaction between the end-user and the computer hardware by allocating resources, scheduling tasks and reading or writing to and from the memory. This enables a user to browse the internet, stream a video or create a word document. Commonly, the operating system is interwoven with the hardware, as is demonstrated in the following abstract representation (Image 16.2):

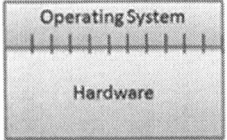

Image 16.2 An abstract representation of a typical computer – the operating system is interwoven with the underlying hardware.

The act of virtualising an operating system is essentially separating it from the underlying hardware, and today this practice is common within the IT industry, specifically in the cloud computing sector. Virtualising operating systems is highly efficient as it allows for consolidation and cost reduction – multiple instances of an operating system can run off a single computer. A virtual operating system (which is referred to as a virtual machine or an instance) does not use dedicated hardware, but instead it sits on a "hypervisor" that is responsible for governing the interaction between the operating system and the hardware. Image 16.3 is an abstract representation of multiple virtual operating systems which are separated from the underlying hardware:

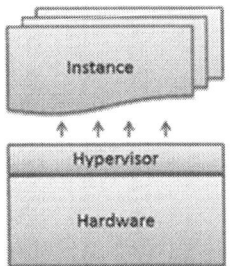

Image 16.3 An abstract representation of virtual machines. The instance of the operating system is separated from the underlying hardware.

After briefly considering the concept of virtualisation within the IT industry, apply this understanding to our physical reality. Our physical reality is similar to a piece of software that is governed by fixed laws. Reality has a persistent illusion of solidity when, in actual fact, nothing is solid. There appears to be an underlying, governing hardware (or a non-physical, transcendent reality that is independent of space-time) off of which our virtual reality "runs". We can't directly access this underlying non-physical "hardware", but we do have definite evidence of its existence and also evidence of "entities" that access our space-time (see Chapter 23 – The UFO Phenomenon). The concepts of both paranormal and supernatural activity have always been met with great resistance by the scientific community and worldviews have not accounted for such activities, which is obviously understandable. But today we can no longer consider science as a field that doesn't account for the "super" natural – it was demonstrated by the Hawking-Penrose singularity theorem: the Big Bang creation event was not subject to the laws of nature, thus it was the result of a supernatural or "above nature" occurrence. One viable explanation for supernatural activity within this reality, such as UFO sightings (if such sightings could be proved genuine), is that they are "trans-dimensional" episodes (entities moving across dimensions but still within the 10 dimensions of space-time) or "extra-dimensional" episodes (occurrences that descend from outside the 10 dimensions of space-time).

Summary

Matter, energy, information and life exist within the boundaries of space-time:

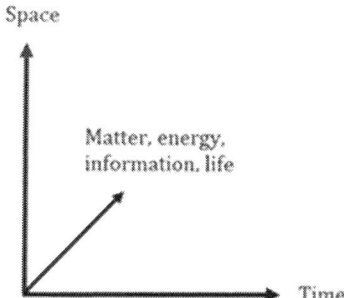

Figure 16.4 Space, time, matter, energy, information and life.

The universe is not infinite in time or in space. The universe had a beginning and it will inevitably have an end. It begs the question: is the universe the effect of random and unguided events, or is our reality transcended by a Creator? If there is a Creator, how could we discover His existence and identify Him? To answer these questions indefinitely, we must briefly define some of the laws of nature, gain an understanding of good science and investigate the smallest unit of life, the cell.

17. Bioinformatics and the Principle of Necessary Inference

An End to the Dispute

Every theory has a variety of interpretations and implications. An assumption of truth, for the reason that a theory can't be proven false, is something that we are all guilty of, but what is truth? Your version of truth may be different to my version of truth, which, in turn, may contradict absolute truth. Depending upon the scenario, truth can be subjective and relative (biased and opinion based) or it can be objective and absolute (factual, unbiased and unchanging). You can accept only one of two beliefs:

- The universe and all life within it are the result of natural, random and unguided events (the naturalist, materialist and atheist worldview).
- The universe and all life within it are part of an intelligent design (the creationist, deist and theist worldview).

People's worldviews are shaped from birth and influenced by factors such as family, education, society, media and religion. Every scientist, archaeologist and historian has access to the same data, but it's the interpretation of that data which can vary. Evidence does not talk for itself and to claim that "the evidence speaks for itself" is the fallacy of reification – evidence *always* requires an interpreter. Scientists are by no means prejudice-free and typically a scientific theory is constructed based on the investigator's worldview (the atheist and theist worldviews are diametrically opposed). For example, a presupposition or a particular worldview can determine how an investigator interprets the fossil record or the evidence for the Big Bang theory. Debates between the atheist and the theist (between a "believer" and a "non-believer") can become circular and often contain mistakes in reasoning (a mistake in reasoning is called a logical fallacy), and can result in hostile disputes. However, there is a simple and efficient way to avoid hostile disputes and to identify the *most plausible* and *logically coherent* explanation.

Modus Operandi: The Origin of Information

Using the scientific method, we can draw a reasonable conclusion about the mysterious origin of life and the universe – one that does not contain logical fallacies or contradict known facts. First, we must determine what science actually is. Second, we must determine what the laws of nature are and the implications in this particular scenario. The scientist's dilemma was perfectly summarised by Albert Einstein who said: "No amount of experimentation can ever prove me right; a single experiment can prove me wrong". A theory is a system of ideas usually built upon a foundation of evidence, observations or practices. Theories can never be considered absolute truth. A good scientific investigation aims to find failures in a theory, not just successes. The empirical method defines 4 stages for deriving a theory:

1) Observe the phenomenon.
2) Discover patterns and measures from within the observation.
3) Draw a conclusion based on those measures and patterns.
4) Use independent data to challenge the theory (in an attempt to falsify it).

This is empirical science. Perhaps a fifth stage should include preparation for ridicule upon the revelation of your discovery.

A Falsifiable Statement

Consider a good scientific theory:

- All lizards are cold-blooded.

Using the empirical method, this statement can be put to the test and potentially proven false (hence why it is falsifiable). Through a series of observations, a scientist could observe all the known lizards in the world to determine if they were cold-blooded. After all the data has been gathered, the result of the investigation would determine the validity of the initial statement and would also allow for reasonable predictions to be made. For example, if 100 different species of lizards were investigated and they were all found to be cold-blooded, it would be reasonable to *assume* that all undiscovered species of lizard are also cold-blooded.

A Non-falsifiable Statement

A non-falsifiable statement is one that is impossible to prove false; it is non-scientific, misleading and quite dishonest. Both history and science are full of non-falsifiable statements and, as Chuck Missler says: "Society is quite vulnerable to intellectual illusions."

Summary

Good scientific theories should:

- Be falsifiable and easy to test (tests should be repeatable).
- Be clear and concise.
- Be used to make accurate predictions.
- Not contradict the known laws of nature.

The Laws of Nature

The universe adheres to rules or "laws of nature". Whilst theories are used to examine a particular occurrence and hopefully explain how or why it happens, laws are basic facts or formulas that tell us what actually happens. The laws of nature are universally valid, precise and simple to understand and, from them, accurate predictions can be made. Mankind depends upon uniformity in nature; for example, gravity keeps the planets in orbit and allows people to walk around in their daily lives. Although it is taken for granted and given little consideration, empirical science and all human activity is dependent upon this uniformity in nature.

Summary

The laws of nature are based on experience, are universally valid and are *assumed* to be immutable (unchanged over time). The laws of nature are simple to understand and can be divided into the following two categories:

1) Material (matter and energy).
2) Non-material (information).

In terms of matter or material entities, the laws of nature have been well-defined in the fields of physics and chemistry. In the field of information science, the laws of nature are a relatively new discovery. Information is a familiar term, but what is information and how is it relevant in this scenario? Information has a concise definition but first, to understand the relevance and nature of information, let us look at some brief examples.

Information Systems

Consider an information-based system such as the dexterous robot hand:

Image 17.1 The Dexterous Robot Hand
(courtesy of Shadow Robot Company 2008: www.shadowrobot.com).

Just like a human hand, it is a material entity (composed of matter). A complex set of instructions (a software program) controls the robot hand and allows it to operate in a similar fashion to a human hand. The software (designed by a human) is essential to the functioning of the hand – the hand is dependent upon this information. If the information were to be deleted, the robotic hand would be useless, thus it is an information-based system. Now consider a CD or DVD that contains information similar to the robotic hand:

Image 17.2 CD/DVD.

The weight of the CD/DVD does not increase or decrease based upon the volume of information it contains. Filling a CD with media files does not generally increase the weight of the disc and deleting the information does not decrease the weight of the disc. The same is true for the robotic hand; the weight of the hand would remain the same regardless of how much information it contains. One observation to be made at this stage is: information is a *non-material* entity (it has no mass or spatial extension); it is *not* a property of matter, but it can control matter and is *essential* to functionality. On the subject of the nature of information, the father of cybernetics and National Medal of Science recipient Norbert Wiener stated: "Information is information, neither matter nor energy." So then, what exactly is information? To avoid any equivocation or ambiguity, we must define the term information.

What is Information?

The Universal Definition of Information: "An encoded, symbolically represented message conveying expected action and intended purpose". A clear distinction can be made between matter (material entities) and information – information is *not* a material entity. After an extensive study of the information conveyed within natural human languages and abstract/artificial languages (such as machine languages), leading expert Professor Dr. Werner Gitt identified five attributes of information:

- Statistics (occurrence of symbols).
- Syntax (set of symbols or grammar).
- Semantics (meaning).
- Pragmatics (expected and implemented action).
- Apobetics (intended purpose or result).

This is a clear and concise definition domain that can be used to discover whether an unfamiliar system is an information-based system.

Laws of Nature

There are several laws of nature observed in all information systems[cxliv]. They include:

1) Material entities cannot create non-material entities.
2) Information is not a property of matter, information is non-material.

3) Information requires a medium for storage or transmission.
4) Information cannot originate in statistical processes.
5) Information requires a coding system.
6) Coding systems are an intentional choice, the agreement between a sender and recipient.
7) The definition of a set of symbols is a process that requires consciousness or intelligence.
8) All given chains of information can be traced back to an intelligent source.

These statements were derived from extensive testing and have never been contradicted. On the subject of codes, sequence complexity and biopolymeric information, a publication listed on the *National Center for Biotechnology Information* website recognises: "One of the requirements of any semantic/semiotic system is that the selection of alphanumeric characters/units be 'arbitrary'."[cxlv] Essentially, this means that a coding system is a formalism based on "personal choice", and is not the product of "causal determinism". Now that we are familiar with the nature of information, let us briefly investigate the most complex information systems known to man.

Bioinformatics and Cybernetics

A synthesis of computer science, information theory, chemistry and molecular biology has provided a greater understanding of the nature and complexity of living systems. Bioinformatics is an interdisciplinary study of the information present within biological systems – during this past century, biology has become an information science. The science of cybernetics is concerned with "control and communication in animal and machine".[cxlvi]

Man and Machine

Bioengineers are now able to encode audio and text on to synthesized DNA. In today's Information Age, computer data growth has exploded – doubling every two years, the demand for reliable data storage is growing. Remarkably, the stability, durability and density of DNA make it a perfectly viable solution to the problems surrounding present data storage technologies within the world of IT. One estimation suggests: "A device the size of your thumb could store as much information as the whole Internet".[cxlvii] This clearly demonstrates that a living cell is literally (not metaphorically) an information-based system and DNA an "information molecule". Professor Hubert Yockey notes: "It is astonishing that the technology of information theory and coding theory has been in place in biology for at least 3.850 billion years."[cxlviii] The structural and functional units of all living systems are cells. Contained within every living cell is DNA, which contains the most complex code in the known universe. The DNA molecules contain the highest density of information known to man – they contain the instructions to make living organisms. A human body is comprised of approximately 100-300 trillion cells that work in harmony with one another as a highly complex integration of components and subsystems. It is the coding systems and processing of algorithms, not blind chemical reactions, which govern life to achieve metabolism for the continuation of life on earth. Dr. Don Johnson notes: "[a cell is]...viewed as a complete computational machine in terms that are akin to a multi-core computer cluster, where there is a centralised memory and instruction set."[cxlix] The human genome project (which was the process of sequencing the 3 billion chemical-base pairs that make up human DNA) was not so much a job for biologists as a job for information scientists and computer programmers who worked to sequence the most complex codes known to man. DNA is like an architect's blueprint for molecular robots to follow, but who coordinates the robots in each individual cell? In fact, comparing DNA (or the genome) to an architect's blueprint is an extremely weak analogy. A blueprint is merely a two-dimensional static diagram. The genome is multi-dimensional, dynamic and contains poly-functional nucleotides – there is no human engineering achievement that could serve as a sufficient analogy for the complexity of a living cell. The genome has a meaningful language convention. Cells contain complex error-detecting and error-correcting codes, but where does this coding system come from? As a computer science graduate, I can testify as to how challenging these kinds of mechanisms are to design. Let's briefly consider the basic functions of a living cell.

Choreography of the Chromosomes

A single living cell is now understood to be the most complex information system known to man – more complex than any city on Earth or any space shuttle ever designed. The embedded genetic algorithms within the cell are highly optimised, goal-oriented and far beyond anything man can conceivably design. Contained within the microscopic city of a living cell are various power stations which serve as energy sources for the molecular robots who work in harmony with the processing units, the central memory bank (which stores information), and the various assembly plants. The city has various packaging and shipping centres with thousands of different robot machines. Made of protein, these machines are arranged in a 3-dimensional configuration and from a functional and structural perspective, they are the most complex molecules in nature. The cell contains complex communication systems (most of which exceed our level of understanding) which use digital languages and decoding systems and which are governed by a control system with proofreading and adaptive coding that serve as a "quality control" system. The cell is surrounded by a membrane border, full of gateways and security guards to regulate entry or exit from the cellular city. This entire city can self-replicate within a matter of hours, but from where does the information of the cell originate? In a paper by *the Open Cybernetics & Systemics Journal*, Dr. David Abel asks: "How did inanimate nature give rise to an algorithmically organised, semiotic and cybernetic life?"[cl]

A Brief Conclusion

A cell is a biosemiotic and biocybernetic system. Based on the definition domain, cells truly are information-based systems, and thus a profound conclusion can be made:

All life forms are information-based systems containing a DNA code. DNA contains the highest density and complexity of information known to man. Within the field of information science, it has been determined that coding systems do not originate in material processes and that inanimate objects do not produce non-material entities (such as prescriptive algorithmic information), thus the information contained within every living system and all given chains of information can be traced back to an intelligent source – "a Sender"[cli] – and this conclusion aligns with the law of biogenesis which states that "life always produces life". As I stated in the opening chapter of this work: "If an attempt to demonstrate the existence of God were to be successful, scientific naturalism and materialism would need to be falsified... If it could be demonstrated that the prescriptive algorithmic information present within living systems is not reducible to nature, it would rule out a naturalistic origin of life." We now know that information and cybernetic systems are not reducible to nature, thus scientific naturalism has been falsified.

Fundamental Questions

For the naturalist, the question still stands – how did the first three-dimensional cellular architecture assign formal meaning to each physical symbol before processing a dynamic prescription to produce an output that allowed for replication which gave rise to life on Earth? In reality, the material world cannot dynamically assign meaning to symbols before creating and processing a prescription to achieve biofunctionality. What rational justification does an investigator have if they are to claim that coding systems, formal prescriptions and sophisticated biofunctionality can arise from non-agent mediated mass/energy interactions? Can DNA originate by itself through unguided natural events? No, it isn't what is observed in nature. A coding system is a formalism based on "personal choice" – it is not the product of causal determinism. The formalisation and application of dynamic coding systems (such as DNA or the Latin alphabet) is totally arbitrary – whilst physical laws act as constraints, these physical laws do not create coding systems and protocols or force agents into using them. Can an unguided cell mutation (the fundamental Darwinian mechanism) or natural selection (the "post-mutation" sorting process) add new functionality to a living system? The field of evolutionary biology lacks unambiguous examples of true gain-of-function mutations – most examples demonstrate that mutations do *not* add functionality but, instead, reduce complexity or rearrange existing information. The same is obviously true in the world of electronic computers and software engineering: "Such a random net increase in non-trivial functionality has never been documented in computer science."[clii] Dr. Lee Spetner states: "All point mutations that have been studied on the molecular level turn out to reduce the genetic information and not increase it."[cliii] As proposed by biochemist Michael Behe, the irreducible complexity of cellular design refutes the claim that a cell was a "creation of pure chance" which evolved over time. The numerous interacting components of a cell (such as the bacterial flagellum) contribute to an overall function, so that if a single function were to be removed, the entire system could not operate – the overall system is dependent upon complex subsystems.[cliv] The functioning of a living cell (such as the bacterial flagellum) depends upon every mutually interconnected aspect within it and the embedded digital information demonstrates an intelligent, pre-planned design.[clv]

Applying the Principle of Necessary Inference

In a publication in *Biocybernetics*, dual-PhD-wielding scientist Dr. Don Johnson asks: "How could nature create multi-level encryption and multiple semiotic coding systems?"[clvi] Furthermore, how could nature create the multiple operating systems and specialised communication networks that are present within living cells? Endless hypothetical scenarios can be argued which aim to provide a purely naturalistic explanation for the origin of life. However, the laws of chemistry and physics do not generate prescriptive algorithmic information. If information is *not* produced by inanimate matter through chemical or physical processes, then living systems *must* be the product of design – this is the "necessary inference" based on an evaluation of the available data. Considering that the Designer has the ability to encode such complex information on to a molecule, He is quite the engineer. Based on the highest level of science, I have personally concluded that the naturalist worldview (atheism) is not a viable belief – it's not based on empirical science, it contains erroneous presuppositions and is falsified by the evidence. In his book *Programming of Life*, Dr. Don Johnson asks: "How did nature defy computer science principles by avoiding software engineering's top-down approach?" With a PhD in both chemistry and computer science, Johnson spent 10 years as a senior research scientist in the pharmaceutical and medical fields. He states: "Maybe it's time to leave the 'flat-earth' mentality that views things only from a particular limited perspective."[clvii] From a scientific standpoint, the naturalist must refrain from dogmatism and provide a rational theory (which consists of a plausible mechanism, a level of prediction and empirical evidence) to illustrate how life and information systems can originate through natural processes (or simply accept that their worldview has been operationally falsified). Some say a faith in God is nothing more than "filling in the gaps" of that which we don't understand but actually, due to some of the greatest achievements in science and engineering, recognising that life is the product of an Intelligent Designer is the most plausible and coherent explanation. For the time being, a naturalistic origin of information (and life) scenario has been ruled out and there is also a means for falsifying this "creationist" worldview should new evidence arise. Today, the common belief is that "chance, time and necessity" caused life to evolve from inanimate matter and that life is nothing more than a cosmic accident. In light of the current evidence, any rational thinker should refuse to believe that man (and every biological system on Earth) evolved from inanimate pond-scum. As previously quoted in the opening chapter of this book, Professor Antony Flew once stated: "The burden of proof is on those who believe God exists." After falsifying the naturalist worldview, the burden of proof now lies on the naturalist who must provide a rational explanation of how information and life can originate through material processes. As a highly acclaimed academic, Antony Flew was one of the world's most famous atheists, but some years before he died, his atheistic view took a complete change in direction when he became a deist; a major reason for this radical change in belief was the advances in the understanding of DNA.

What is Biological Evolution?

On the topic of evolution, philosopher David Berlinski states: "Before you can ask 'Is Darwinian theory correct or not?', you have to ask the preliminary question 'Is it clear enough so that it could be correct?'. That's a very different question. Nothing in the theory is precisely, clearly, carefully defined or delineated." The term evolution is ill-defined, misused and misunderstood. The general theory of evolution is a framework from which "sub-theories" can be tested. The level at which Darwinism works empirically is the "micro-level" – it gives a valid scientific explanation of why dogs can be crossbred to produce a new breed of dog (in other words, it's a legitimate explanation of why there is variation *within* a species). The evidence for macro-evolution (which, in this context, is the initial chemical evolution in which life and information is presupposed to have originated from inanimate matter and the notion that one kind of animal can evolve into another – "from molecules to man") is non-existent, yet the naturalist will often equivocate on the term "evolution" and use examples of micro-evolution in an attempt to demonstrate the validity of their naturalist worldview. Those who believe in God are also guilty of equivocating on the term (or blindly denying the notion of) evolution, and this is why observing a debate between an atheist and a theist (between a "believer" and a "non-believer") can become extremely tedious. The theory of evolution gained publicity during the more primitive era of modern science when, in 1859, Charles Darwin published the compelling yet controversial book *On the Origin of Species*, which has since become the foundation of evolutionary biology. As a true scientist, Darwin set a test for his theory: "If it could be demonstrated that any complex organ existed which could not possibly have been formed by numerous, successive, slight modifications, my theory would absolutely break down". Today, we can confirm that certain organisms do not form by "numerous, successive, slight modifications" and thus, by his own standards, his theory has "broken down". Darwin was unaware of the true complexity of biological systems and the nature of coding theory and cybernetics.

The Missing Link

The fossil record is far from complete and the media are often reporting on possible discoveries of the "missing link". It seems as though society is under the impression that there is one piece of evidence missing from the theory of evolution, when in fact it's more like a missing chain. The fossil record is merely a subjective interpretation, not evidence of macro-evolution (and remember, evidence cannot talk for itself, it requires an interpreter). Here is a brief summary of the non-trivial issues surrounding the naturalist worldview:

- In the fields of semiotics and information science, it has been demonstrated that information and coding systems do not originate through unintelligent/material processes.
- Semiotic and cybernetic systems are not the product of causal determinism – how could nature defy the fundamental principles of semiotics, coding and information theory?
- Cells have never been observed to self-originate and self-program radical new functionality.
- The cosmic beginning *implies* a transcendent, non-physical causal agent ("cause and effect").

Is Darwinism just an answer to the questions that society doesn't want to ask? The advances in science over the past century have seen a dramatic increase in challenges surrounding the naturalist worldview. Furthermore, in respects to the origin of life and the universe, natural processes cannot be used to explain the origin of natural processes. Intelligent design is not taught in the school curriculum and it is obvious that man's rational thinking has been exploited. In alignment with the oligarchs' New World Order, it is evident that children are taught what to think, not *how* to think.

The Anthropic Principle

There are, throughout the entire universe, tightly bound relationships that cannot be altered without making the development of life impossible – life on Earth is dependent upon a vast number of environmental specifications. The amount of finely tuned, life-supporting ratios is quite astounding. As stated by astrophysicist Dr. Hugh Ross: "... [the more scientists explore] the more severe the limitations they find governing the structure and development of the universe to accommodate those requirements."[clviii] The anthropic principle is the impression that the universe was designed to precise specifications on which advanced life depends – it has led many "non-religious" or secular scientists to acknowledge the theory of intelligent design. Sir Fred Hoyle was one of Britain's best-known mathematicians and astronomers during the 20th century. Spending decades searching for answers to the questions plaguing the origins of life and the age of the cosmos, Hoyle coined the term "big bang". Although he was not a Christian or creationist, he understood the problems surrounding the naturalist worldview and recognised the fine-tuning of the universe was evidence for a creator: "A common sense interpretation of the facts suggests that a superintellect has monkeyed with physics... The numbers one calculates from the facts seem to me so overwhelming as to put this conclusion almost beyond question." On this subject, Oxford professor Dr. John Lennox stated: "The more we get to know about our universe, the more the hypothesis that there is a Creator... gains in credibility as the best explanation of why we are here."

According to Dr. Ross's calculations, there is a minimum of 147 finely tuned characteristics throughout the entire universe, crucial to the support of physical life. A modification to any one of these life-supporting conditions would render the development of physical life impossible. The chance of all these requirements being met is one in 10^{186}. The precision of this finely tuned cosmos is trillions of times greater than any human engineering achievement and, statistically speaking, the chances of this reality being nothing more than a cosmic accident are so remote that naturalism should be regarded as irrational.

Conclusion: Recognising the Boundaries of Science

As a former atheist, I now recognise that the most plausible and logically coherent worldview is the creationist worldview. The causal-agent responsible for this level of design and accuracy transcends space-time and, for reasons unknown, He clearly went to great effort to ensure that life could develop here on Earth. Today, various schools of thought have been created and controlled, ones which aim to guide the spiritual and philosophical outlook of the masses. Darwinism has shaped the worldview of millions of people worldwide, convincing them that macro-evolution is an incontrovertible fact which eliminates the need for a Creator. Due to the level of design of the universe and the complexity and diversity of all life within it, our Creator *appears* to be both personal and intimate and potentially possesses infinite power – it would be difficult to place an upper limit on the ability of this Super Intelligence. In an attempt to identify God and gain an understanding of man's purpose, the boundaries of science have been reached – other methods of investigation are now required. The most obvious objection to accepting the reality of a Creator God is His absence – where is God? However, this should not prevent us from searching for Him. It also begs the question: who created God? However, it is a logical contradiction for the cause of space and time to be dependent on space or time – either the primary cause (God) of the universe was *always there* or *never was*.

18. A Review of the Scriptures

Objective

The primary objective of this chapter is to discover the potentially unique attributes of a set-apart faith and the source identification of a message which may be of "extra-dimensional" origin. Given the scenario, God would oversee and protect the distribution of His message – His credibility and integrity would depend upon it. For source identification, this message should have unique attributes, to set it aside from other doctrines and to encourage man to put it to the test. A good starting point would be the Abrahamic faiths.

The World's Most Predominant Faiths

The Abrahamic faiths (Judaism, Christianity and Islam) are monotheistic belief systems. As a collective, they have in excess of 3.6 billion adherents worldwide (which is over 50% of the global population). As shall be reviewed shortly, all three faiths identify Abraham as the patriarch. Whilst the similarities between these religions are relatively superficial, it should be recognised that their differences are fundamental. Essentially, the foundation of these three faiths is the Hebrew Tanakh, a collection of 24 books composed by various authors – these are the books of law, poetry, history, wisdom and prophecy which are known as the "Old Testament" of the Bible. During the reign of Ptolemy Philadelphus in the 3rd century BC, the Old Testament was translated from Hebrew into Greek by 70 interpreters; this translation is referred to as the Septuagint or "the Seventy".

Textual Criticism

With regards to matters of doctrinal significance, has the Bible undergone various revisions and alterations? The Bible is the most famous and widely distributed book on Earth – it is a universal text. It has over 5,000 predictive verses and 1,500 direct predictions on over 700 separate issues. In order for the Bible to be evaluated, it is crucial to have ample evidence that it has not been modified. The Dead Sea Scrolls were the most important manuscript discovery of all time. Hidden in a cave at Qumran were hundreds of manuscripts and manuscript fragments, some of which are over 2,000 years old. They help verify that the content within the Old Testament has not been modified – at least not since it was translated into Greek some 250 years before Jesus was born. Aside from the Dead Sea Scrolls, there are tens of thousands of ancient manuscripts, manuscript fragments and early church writings which can be cross-referenced to verify the accuracy of the modern Bible. After corroborating all the available data, the conclusion is practically unanimous: with regards to matters of doctrinal significance, the Bible has not undergone revisions and alterations – it has been carefully preserved and transmitted throughout the ages. The abundance of evidence has been extensively scrutinised and competent scholars don't generally dispute the integrity of the modern text – the debate is over whether it's "divinely inspired". The Old Testament, and the Bible as a whole, is one of the most well-preserved texts of the ancient world.

A Brief Analysis

Astrophysicist Dr. Hugh Ross states: "Of all the philosophical and theological works of the past several thousand years which talk of a non-physical reality, the only message which is consistent with the discoveries of modern physics and astronomy comes from the Bible."[clix] Thousands of years ago, Isaiah, Moses, Job and various other Israelite prophets and kings accurately and repeatedly described cosmic dynamics: a beginning in finite time, a transcendent non-physical cause *and* an expanding universe – all of which perfectly align with the modern understanding of cosmology. Philosophy, morality, science and spirituality (the foundations of society) are each rooted in the Genesis account of creation, as are the laws of logic, the sanctity of marriage, the origins of secret societies and a prophetic template for the New World Order. Logically speaking, the Bible *appears* to validate every aspect of our existence. In the Bible, God promises to uphold the universe in a consistent manner – God alone accounts for the preconditions of intelligibility (a "random-chance" universe in which man evolved from pond-scum has no rational basis when attempting to account for these preconditions).

Questions about Jesus

Christianity is considered the least integral of all the Abrahamic faiths. It's oriented around the Brit Chadashah (New Testament) revelation of Yehoshua (Jesus Christ) as not only the Messiah, but the incarnate "Son of God" (a claim which many Jews and all Muslims reject). Critics (usually Jews, Muslims and the secularists) consider the New Testament to be heretical and regard the Christian faith as idolatrous, blasphemous or repackaged paganism. Throughout this chapter and the next, various passages, prophecies and key words from the Bible will be evaluated in order to unlock some of the mysteries that have been presented in this work and provide a framework for the remaining chapters; however, the New Testament shall initially be sidestepped to avoid circular reasoning. Christianity, Islam and Judaism each claim to be exclusive, thus one of my primary objectives when researching for this work was to identify which one of these faiths, if any, was unique and could be set apart from false doctrine and paganism. In my early stages of coming to faith in a Creator, I wondered if the elevation of Jesus to the "Son of God" was the inevitable separation from Jewish monotheism. Jesus was raised as an authentic Jew and ministered to authentic 1st-century Israelites, so how did so many of those Jews who followed Jesus, and were the foundations of the Christian church, justify such a heresy? Or did this elevation of Jesus to the status of God come centuries after His death (as Dan Brown, author of *The Da Vinci Code*, claims)?

Divine Plurality within the Old Testament

The God of Israel revealed His name as YHWH to Moses (pronounced Yahweh, His name translates to "I am"). According to the Hebrew Old Testament, YHWH is the unique identifier of the Most High God who works in fellowship with a divine council. A phenomenon unique to the Old Testament known as a theophany was a visible or auditory manifestation of YHWH – there are various accounts in which God took on physical forms, sometimes anthropomorphic (human), and sometimes as a supernatural manifestation within a "natural" object (such as a burning bush or the clouds) so as to interact with humans. Our English translation of the Bible obscures some of the original Hebrew vocabulary. The Old Testament continuously makes statements of "divine plurality" by using terms such as "Elohim" and "Bene Ha Elohim" [clx] (refer to Table 1):

Hebrew Term:	Used in Reference to:
YHWH	The Most High God
Elohim	God, gods, divine messengers
Bene Ha Elohim	Sons of God
Ruach	Spirit, Wind, Breath

Table 1: Hebrew references.

Whether talking about messengers (angels), the "sons of God" or God Himself, the Old Testament makes reference to various divine beings (the term "divine" can be applied to any entity outside of physical reality – humans and animals are not divine). Referring to Jesus (or any other man) as a "son of God", in the figurative/spiritual sense, is not a violation of Jewish monotheism. But why did a group of Israelites elevate Jesus to the status of the Most High God (the "I am") and regard them as both one and the same? Why did Jesus claim to be the "I am"? Why do Christians find the hypostatic union (Jesus being simultaneously man and God) logically coherent and not a contradiction of monotheism? It is a supernatural paradox. The Old Testament is the subject of much controversy; one reason is due to the many verses of Genesis which refer to God in a plural context:

Then Yah (God) said, "Let *us* make mankind in *our* image,
in *our* likeness." (Genesis 1:26).

Verses such as these are known as the "Genesis Plurals" and the reason for the plural context of these statements is fiercely debated. However, the following scripture illustrates that, in the Old Testament, God has "components" or a "composite nature":

The Ruach (spirit) of Yah (God) was hovering over
the surface of the waters (Genesis 1:2).

Whilst the Bible (and possibly our intuition) states that God is a singular, transcendent being (outside of space-time), independent of space-time and neither temporally nor spatially restricted, it is reasonable to conclude that He can partially enter into His creation, *if He so chooses.*

Binitarian Monotheism

Binitarian monotheism (i.e. two personae, two individuals or two aspects within a single God, a concept also known as the "Godhead") was a Jewish rabbinical concept until approximately the 2nd century AD. My research has found that tension between the concept of a "singular divine transcendence" and "anthropomorphism" (the embodiment of God in human form), wasn't present in ancient Israel prior to Jesus. To claim that the Jews did not believe in a "Godhead" before the 1st century AD, or that their understanding of God was contradictory to the Christian worldview, is refuted by study of the Old Testament, an understanding of ancient Jewish theology and culture *and* the emergence of new evidence. Dr. Michael Heiser states: "Just over thirty years ago, rabbinical scholar Alan Segal produced what is still the major work on the idea of two powers in heaven in Jewish thought: *Two Powers in Heaven: Early Rabbinic Reports About Christianity and Gnosticism* (Brill, 1977). Segal argued that the two powers idea was not deemed heretical in Jewish theology until the second century AD."clxi The Israelite concept of the "Godhead" was not Roman, Christian or Gnostic – it was Jewish and already ancient before Jesus was born on Earth. One particular scripture in the Hebrew Old Testament which illustrates this concept of the Godhead is a scene in the Book of Daniel, which involves a heavenly enthronement and the manifestation of two divine beings. The first being is the "Ancient of Days" (which is another name of YHWH or the Most High God). The second being is named "the Son of Man". In his book, *Two Powers in Heaven*, Jewish scholar Alan Segal admits that this passage is problematic for the modern Jewish worldview: "... the passage seems to describe more a danger than a solution." The Hebrew Old Testament scripture reads as follows:

I watched till thrones were put in place, and the **Ancient of Days** was seated... I was watching in the night visions, and behold, One like the **Son of Man**, coming with the clouds of heaven! He came to the **Ancient of Days**, and they brought **Him** near before **Him**. **Then to Him was given dominion** and glory and a kingdom, that all peoples, nations, and languages should serve Him. **His dominion** is an everlasting dominion, which shall not pass away, and **His kingdom** the one which shall not be destroyed.
(Daniel 7).

In the New Testament, Jesus claims the title "Son of Man" and states that His life will be given as a ransom. Recognising the obvious complexity of the Most High God, through a firm understanding of the Old Testament narratives and the witnessing of Jesus, thousands of Israelites accepted Him as the long-awaited Messiah and the embodiment of YHWH or "second" member of the Godhead. Dr. Michael Heiser states: "This explains why these Jews, the first converts to following Jesus the Christ, could simultaneously worship the God of Israel and Jesus, and yet refuse to acknowledge any other god."[clxii] The "composite" or "multi-personal" nature of God (which many Christians now articulate as the "Trinity") is undoubtedly a complex and supernatural paradox. However, acceptance of this matter shouldn't be restricted by the finite limitations of man's understanding. I now recognise that Christianity was born as the natural successor to Judaism – the early Messianic or "Nazarene" Jews (those who followed Jesus of Nazareth) could continue to worship in the synagogue and observe the Torah alongside their orthodox brethren. During the 2nd century, the number of non-Jewish followers of Christ outnumbered the Jewish followers and, through divine guidance, His message spread throughout the Middle East, Africa and Europe (despite widespread persecution from the Romans) to become the largest religion on Earth. Today, the greatest paradox seems to be that Christianity is so isolated from the Torah and the Jewish loyalty to the King of the Jews. There is a definite integration, coherence and continuity between the Old and New Testament. Jesus Christ fulfils the Messianic requirements beyond competent dispute and it is erroneous to claim that the Council of Nicaea or the Gnostic gospels were responsible for elevating Jesus to the status of God (as various uniformed critics and Dan Brown's *Da Vinci Code* claim), as this can be falsified by a critical analysis of the evidence (evidence which Dan Brown was either unaware of or failed to mention because it contradicted the narrative of his mystery-detective adventure).

Hear, O Israel! Yahweh our Elohim, Yahweh is One!
(Deuteronomy 6:4).

An Integrated Message

Chuck Missler is an engineer who has worked on the board of directors for many public companies, including Western Digital and Cybernetics Corporation. After a lifetime of investigation, he concludes: "The Bible is an integrated message, 66 books penned by 40 different authors over the course of almost 2,000 years, not just thematically but the design of the message itself demonstrates integration, implying the origin of this message came from outside the dimensionality of our space-time."[clxiii] That is a bold but interesting analysis coming from an engineer, but what evidence does he have to support this claim? "It wrote history in advance,"[clxiv] he says. Missler states that he came to the realisation that every name, number and detail in the Bible is there by deliberate design: "Firstly, discover the integrity of the design. Secondly, every section points to one person, the Messiah. Once you realise who he is, he authenticates the package. That's the epistemological cycle." One particular attribute which the God of the Bible uses to authenticate His message and set it apart from all other doctrines is the ability to accurately write history before it happens – the Bible contains the largest collection of prophecies on Earth. Given that God is neither spatially nor temporally restricted, prophecy must be His source identification or "fingerprint".

Progressive Revelation

The sheer volume of unambiguous prophecy within the Bible is one of its many advantages over any other religious text on Earth. Commonly, when people (myself once included) interpret a statement to be a possible contradiction or absurdity within the Bible, they conclude the entire scripture to be unreliable and discredit its validity rather than investigating the underlying meaning. Those who hold a faith in God can be accused of helping to self-fulfil prophecies; although living in the post-Christian era, the "end-times" prophecies are evidently being fulfilled by non-Christian-anti-human-fanatics (the Luciferians, Satanists and New Age occultists). What is compelling is that the current geopolitical climate runs parallel with the "end times" scenario as spoken of in the Bible – remarkably, we have been forewarned about these *exact* circumstances and also instructed on what to do. Over 40 different authors contributed to the compilation of the Bible, including Moses, King David, King Solomon and Paul the Apostle. It was written over the course of almost 2,000 years and many of the authors did not know or directly communicate with each other. Despite this, every book of the Bible complements the other and creation theology is consistent with *every* book in the Bible.

The Messiah and the Wise Men

The common thread of many of the world's religions and cults is that of a Messiah or "God" on Earth – does this discredit the story of Jesus? Why has the concept of a Messiah been around since the beginning of time? We shall later explore these questions but first, with regards to correctly identifying the Biblical Messiah, the prophet Daniel (who was held captive in Babylon by Nebuchadnezzar II in the 6th century BC) provides us with one of the most astounding Old Testament prophecies. The "70-week prophecy" promises an "everlasting righteousness" and allows for Jesus (the most influential man to ever live) to be identified as Messiah. So profound were Daniel's insights that even King Nebuchadnezzar II turned from his pagan beliefs and humbled himself before the Most High God. The birth of the Messiah is today surrounded by myth and tradition and has been completely trivialised. It's the story of the magi, also known as the wise men, who came from the East and bought gifts to Jesus sometime after His birth (the term "magic" is derived from the Latin "magi" or the Greek term "mageia"). In antiquity, there were various types of magi who consisted of intellectuals and specialists in various disciplines such as astrology, astronomy, magic and divination (there was a fine line, if any at all, between occult experiments and legitimate science). The prophet Daniel was counted amongst the "wise men" of Babylon under the reign of Nebuchadnezzar. Through inspiration from Daniel, many of the magi turned from paganism and Zoroastrianism to worship the Most High God of Israel. Daniel's prophecies were spoken of throughout countless generations in the Middle East, thus many of the magi were aware of a coming Messiah and their intention would have been to seek Him out. Following Daniel's "70-week prophecy", the wise men that travelled to Jesus after His birth (as recorded in the Gospel) *could* have been from Babylon or Persia. According to the scriptures, the birth of Messiah was a momentous event which marked the beginning of the end of man's rule over the Earth.

The Pagan Influence

Three hundred years after the death of Christ, His message had spread throughout the Middle East, Africa and Europe. Although Christianity had flourished, there was still a widespread persecution of Jews and Christians. Their refusal to participate in the imperial cults was considered treason. By the early 4th century AD, Emperor Constantine's position of power was insecure; he made the political move to legalise Christianity and implement it as the official state religion. Interestingly, the remnants of the ancient religion of Mithraism, the cult of Saturn and the cult of Sol Invictus are still felt in the modern day. Mithraism was one particular mystery religion of the Indian, Persian and Roman empires which incorporated various rituals and initiations. In the Roman pantheon, the Sun God was known as Sol Invictus (the Unconquerable Sun), and some researchers claim that his birthday was celebrated on the winter solstice, December 25th (although this claim is still debated). From a modern perspective, it can be argued that the celebratory customs of Mithra, Saturn and Sol Invictus were gradually Christianised and cunningly disguised behind complex Roman Catholic theology. After Constantine became the first "Christian" emperor, Christianity gradually became separated from its Hebrew roots and mixed with secular and pagan traditions. Today, headed by the pope (and shadowed by the Jesuits and various oligarchs), the Roman Catholic Church is possibly the most powerful and wealthiest institution on Earth (its property and investment portfolio is vast) and it declares itself as the "Mother Church". Along with failed attempts at destroying the Bible, the Roman Catholic Church established its own traditions and enforced them as being equal to, or above, the Bible (which helped fuel the 16th-century Protestant Reformation, as previously discussed). Some of the pagan traditions and themes include:

- The celebration of the winter solstice, which is now regarded as Christ's birthday (Christmas) on December 25th.
- The celebration of the spring equinox, which is celebrated as Easter.
- Appointing a pope or "holy father" as God's authority on Earth.
- Elevating the Virgin Mary to the status of a goddess (the "Queen of Heaven" or the "mother of God").

As will be explored further, these traditions of apostate Christianity are foreign to the Bible. Throughout the ages, critics have often claimed that the story of Jesus is a mythological amalgamation of ancient pagan myths. However, this requires a manipulation of accounts, selective and superficial descriptions and an ignorance of Biblical theology (for example, the birth date of Jesus is not mentioned in the Bible, nor are any of the aforementioned man-made traditions). This hypothesis which suggests that the story of Jesus is a retelling of more primitive religions has been labelled "parallelomania" and various academics discount the mythical parallels between Christianity and the sun-worshipping religions. Samuel Sandmel describes it as: "...apparent similarities and construct parallels and analogies without historical basis."[clxv]

A Brief Overview of Christianity

Throughout Brazil, Africa, India and China and within the ancient Greek and Roman empires, various practices have been commonplace:

- Cannibalism and death sports.
- Infanticide (the killing of infants) and child sacrifice, in which children were abused, burnt and slaughtered in rituals for the gods.
- Child abandonment was common throughout the Greek and Roman empires.

Early Christians, such as Clement of Alexandria and Tertullian, criticised abortion, infanticide and the lack of morals within the pagan empire. It was the early Christians who began proactively caring for neglected children, providing them with food and clothes, setting up orphanages and shelters and campaigning against such atrocities. These actions were revolutionary and eventually led to the outlawing of abortion, sacrifice and abandonment. After the death of Jesus, a distinction between pagan culture/morals and the Christian culture became apparent. The primary reason for this was Jesus's demonstration of love and His teachings of equality – to Him, all life is precious, regardless of gender, age, belief, disability or sinful nature. Early Christians also began to boycott gladiatorial sports where humans and animals fought to the death while being watched by thousands of cheering spectators. The historian, William Edward Hartpole Lecky, stated: "There is scarcely any other single reform so important in the moral history of mankind as the suppression of the gladiatorial shows, and this feat must be almost exclusively ascribed to the Christian Church." Jesus didn't own slaves, he never raised a raised sword and he didn't even put pen to paper, yet despite this, his teachings have directly influenced billions of people who have worked throughout the ages to increase the moral standards of society both home and abroad. It was Christians who worked to bring about:

- Charity and nursing.
- Education for children.
- Orphanages, shelters and elderly care homes.

Summary

As the most intimate of faiths, Christianity is truly unique. According to the Bible, the true nature of God was revealed to us through His human incarnation. This is why Christianity flourished; early conversions from Jewish, pagan and atheistic beliefs to Christianity came from the witnessing of good nature, faith, compassion and the integrity of God's word. Christianity is not a faith that involves "good works" or the appeasing of God as a *prerequisite* for salvation. Any faith or belief system which requires good works (to outweigh past sins) or the appeasing of God in order to *achieve* salvation is a form of mysticism or paganism. This is what sets Christianity apart: the only prerequisite for salvation is to receive Jesus through faith – *salvation comes through faith*. According to the scriptures, He lived a sinless life (achieving that which man cannot) before being crucified in our place as a "blood atonement" – but why does our salvation depend upon His blood atonement? It is evident that one objective of the New World Order is to remove the basic ideology that man is made in the image of God. We have entered into an age of which the Bible speaks more than any other – with the story of the Bible drawing to a close, it is time to take heed.

"What God's justice demanded, His love provided."
– Unknown.

19. Rejecting the Seed of Abraham: The Arab-Israeli Conflict

Before tracing the origins of the New World Order, we must understand the profound significance of the story of Abraham. He was the patriarch of the Jewish faith and founder of the Jewish nation. The symbolic yet bizarre story of Abraham and his two sons, Isaac and Ishmael, is the key to understanding all the Abrahamic faiths, the modern Arab-Israeli conflict and the destiny of every human being on Earth. The Jewish Israelites descend from Isaac and the Arabic Muslims descend from Ishmael. Isaac and Ishmael were brothers and their father, Abraham, was a descendant of Noah's son, Shem, and thus Arabs and Israelites are a Semitic people with a shared genetic heritage. Today, the renowned hostility between many Arabic/Muslim and Jewish people in the Middle East appears to be based upon the denial, or presumed inaccuracy, of scriptural authority – but what both peoples are missing is the prophetic and symbolic significance of Abraham's story. A sibling rivalry born in antiquity is today being exploited with the aim of initiating World War Three, in order for these two groups to "mutually destroy" one another and to pave the way for a global leader or "peacemaker" who will finalise the New World Order. The Bible maps out some of the major events leading up to the implementation of a final empire, including a cataclysmic war, the building of the Jewish Third Temple and a global peacemaker who, according to Revelation 13:7: "…was given authority to rule over every tribe and people and language and nation." The ancient books of the Bible reveal deep insights into events long before they take place, serving us a reminder that we are in the possession of a unique series of messages that originate from outside of space-time. clxvi

Born of the Slave

Abraham was a man of great faith and obedience; he was also inquisitive and even challenged God's pending judgement of Sodom and Gomorrah. The story begins when Abraham enters into a covenant with God and is commanded to migrate from his birthplace of Ur in Babylonia to the chosen nation of Israel. According to Genesis 12:2, God promised to make him a great nation: "I will make you into a great nation, I will bless you and make your name great; and all people on Earth will be blessed through you". Genesis 18:18 states: "…all nations on Earth will be blessed through him". From a critical perspective, these promises are compelling – Abraham is revered by over 3.6 billion people alive today. With divine authority, Abraham was promised descendants, land, redemption and a relationship with God. The most significant aspect of this covenant was the promise of the offspring or the "seed" from which a blessing for all mankind would come. By the time Abraham and his wife Sarah had settled in Israel, many years had passed; they were both growing old and Sarah was barren. Perhaps the feeling of uncertainty grew unbearable for Abraham and he began to question God's promise as, with the blessing of Sarah, he took Hagar, his slave woman, and impregnated her in an attempt to produce an offspring and save the covenant – in other words, Abraham attempted to save the covenant through his own works. Hagar gave birth to Abraham's firstborn son, a boy whom they named Ishmael – he was a child "born of the flesh" and "born of the slave" woman (the significance of this shall soon be obvious). Following the birth of Ishmael came the miraculous pregnancy of Sarah, just as God had promised. Sarah gave birth to Abraham's second son whom they named Isaac – he was the son "born of the promise" and "born of the spirit".

Although Ishmael was the firstborn, he was "born of the slave", thus he was not due to inherit the promises of God's covenant with Abraham (the blessing, the nation or the offspring). Tension between Hagar and Sarah and Isaac and Ishmael (between the "slave" and the "free", or the "flesh" and the "spirit") grew and, after years of conflict, Ishmael wanted to kill Isaac. With guidance from God, Abraham reluctantly expelled Ishmael and Hagar from the household. Evidently, God wanted to protect the child born according to the promise, but why would God allow for this? As the descendants of Isaac and Ishmael, both the Jew and the Muslim might argue over who the rightful inheritor of the Abrahamic covenant is, but instead, they should recognise the symbolic meaning of this story. Like Ishmael, our first birth, regardless of whether we are Jew or Gentile (non-Jew), is characterised by the slave nature: we are *all* born of the *flesh* and born into slavery.

Salvation, Solution and Destiny

The story gets all the more bizarre when God tests Abraham's faith by commanding him to climb Mount Moriah and offer Isaac as a sacrifice. This devotion and willingness to pay a price for God's love was characteristic of Abraham, yet the act itself would have been truly barbaric. Under the impression that God could resurrect Isaac from the dead, Abraham bound Isaac to an altar and was ready to slay him. Before the killing could take place, a divine messenger of God intervened and stopped the human sacrifice. After Abraham demonstrated his level of faith, it was affirmed that the one and *only* human sacrifice would come from the line of Abraham, Isaac and his son, Jacob (Jacob was later renamed "Israel"). It is easy to focus one's attention on Israel as the "chosen nation", or the Jews as the "chosen people", and get caught up in the modern political issues, but what was the reason for God choosing a nation and a race? Why did God test Abraham's faith in this bizarre way? From a critical perspective, the conflict, or sibling rivalry, which was born in antiquity, has been inherited by the modern descendants of Abraham's sons. Both the Muslim and Jew may claim to be the rightful heir of the Abrahamic covenant (and, subsequently, the holy site on which the Temple of Solomon once stood) and accuse one another of being "born of the slave", yet both peoples are missing the point. We all must focus our attention on the prophetic significance of the story of Abraham, Isaac and Ishmael – it was setting the stage for Jesus the Messiah, the most influential Rabbi ever to live. He was the promised blessing for all nations. He has introduced billions of Gentiles (non-Jews) to the Almighty God (YHWH). Without Jesus, there would be no blessing for all nations, the Abrahamic covenant wouldn't have been fulfilled and mankind would still be in slavery. In all His wisdom, Jesus declared: "... you shall know the truth, and the truth shall make you free." The reason for God choosing a nation and a race was to deliver our Messiah who was a son "born of the promise" and "born of the spirit" through a virgin birth. Thus, only after accepting Jesus can *we* become "born again", be "born of the spirit", inherit the promises of God and truly be freed from the enslavement of sin. Hundreds of years before Jesus was born and endured the crucifixion, it was foretold in the Old Testament by the prophet Isaiah: "He [Jesus] is despised and rejected of men. But He was wounded for our transgressions; He was bruised for our iniquities: the chastisement of our peace was upon Him; and with His stripes we are healed." (Isaiah 53:3-6).

Mutual Enrichment

The crucifixion of Jesus and the concept of sin may seem confusing but is well summarised by Professor Walter Veith: "The Jewish Encyclopaedia states that the husband could represent his wife and help the judge defend her if the verdict involved his personal rights. Here we have a glorious parallel with the heavenly judgment. Christ the Bridegroom purchased His people, His bride, with His own blood. He serves as our court-appointed advocate to help the Father defend us against the accusations of Satan and He also defends His own right to grant us salvation and to ultimately take us up to heaven."clxvii

It begs the question, why did Jesus have to "die for our sins"? To understand this, consider the following:

A man breaks a criminal law and is arrested before being sent to court where he stands before a judge. If the crime were to go unpunished due to a conflict of interests, and the criminal was released, would the judge become an accessory to the crime?

God is a Righteous Judge. Man has clearly transgressed His law and rejected His authority – if sin were to go unpunished, God would become an accessory to the crimes of mankind. As the Creator of all life, God predefined a standard of goodness and it is upon His authority that we should base our morality; otherwise, morality becomes a subjective, arbitrary opinion. The law was designed to protect the vulnerable and to allow for man to live in a mutually enriching relationship with God. All human ancestry is interconnected, everybody on Earth shares a common ancestor and we are all related to Jesus by blood. After He lived a perfect life and accomplished that which we couldn't, He qualified to atone for our transgressions. At the cost of His conviction, we can be saved through faith in Him and deemed as righteous in the eyes of God. Jesus accepted punishment on our behalf, He willingly paid the price for His family and, under His guidance, we can share His inheritance with Him in the Kingdom of God. In the same way that Abraham attempted to save God's promise through his own works, we are reminded that our own works will never qualify us for salvation – salvation is a gift. Man can only be saved through God's grace or "unearned merit" (from a Christian perspective, good works are a sign of salvation, not the method to "earn" salvation). In the same way that Abraham's firstborn son was born of the slave, we are reminded that, through our first birth, we are born into slavery. In the same way that Abraham was prepared to sacrifice his own son, we are reminded that God *did* make that sacrifice. Spiritually speaking, those who wilfully reject Jesus are the children of the slave and born of the flesh. Those who accept Jesus through faith become born again and are children of the Spirit. Galatians 3:28-29 states: "There is neither Jew nor Greek, slave nor free, male nor female, for you are all one in Christ Jesus. If you belong to Christ, then you are Abraham's seed, and heirs according to the promise". According to John 15:13, God's amazing love for mankind was manifested through Jesus: "Greater love has no one than this: to lay down one's life for one's friends". The realisation of what God has done for us is truly astounding and life-changing. Jesus bought an end to man-made legalisms, called us to pray for and forgive our enemies, and demonstrated that love for God is the greatest of all commandments. Although we often fall short of God's glory by failing to keep His commandments, His commandments will be written on our hearts – this is inner righteousness. Not only is God willing to forgive mankind's wrongdoings, according to Hebrews 8:12, He promised that He will: "… remember their sins no more". As it was foretold in the Bible, many of the Israelites rejected Jesus Christ (who was the seed of their ancestor, Abraham), as do the Muslims. Through mutual rejection of the seed of Abraham, the Middle East will descend into further chaos until World War Three begins – potentially, a war to end all wars. The only way to establish world peace (if neither Jew nor Muslim will receive Jesus and become born again) is for Jesus to return and reveal Himself as the King of Kings.

Zionism, the Third Temple and the Signs of the Times

One of the more pre-eminent and unmistakeable "signs of the times" was the restoration of the Jewish people to the land of Israel, an event which was foretold over 2,500 years ago by the prophet Ezekiel and various other Israelites. The Temple Mount is the very site where Abraham prepared to offer his son, Isaac, as a sacrifice on Mount Moriah. This location was chosen for the construction of Solomon's Temple – a site which once signified the physical presence of God on Earth, before He arrived as the Son of Man. Simon Sebag Montefiore's book, *Jerusalem: The Biography* states: "The anointed King Solomon was a charismatic king whose intellect produced some 3,000 proverbs and 1,000 songs, his army grew in excess of 10,000 cavalry and over 1,000 chariots".[clxviii] Constructed in approximately the 10th century BC, the Temple of Solomon housed the Ark of the Covenant – a chest constructed out of gold and wood, which contained the Ten Commandments. The First Temple of Jerusalem was an early milestone in the story of Israel before it was destroyed by the Babylonians.

The 4th Reich and the Times of the Gentiles

The Second Temple was rebuilt in the same location before it was destroyed by the Romans on exactly the same day, Tisha B'Av, in the year 70 AD. Before His death, Jesus had forewarned of Israel's destruction; He commanded the Jews and Gentiles to go forth and make disciples of all nations and to spread the Good News of salvation before "… the times of the Gentiles is fulfilled." (Luke 21:24). To align with His prophecy which foretold of Israel's destruction by the Roman Empire, the prophet Daniel foretold, a few hundred years prior, that a false prophet would come from the people who destroyed Israel – the *Romans* (Daniel 9:26-27). A common eschatological interpretation suggests that either the false prophet or the anti-Christ (or perhaps both) will hold political positions within a rebuilt Roman Empire. Since the 1950s, following the signing of the *Treaties of Rome*, we have seen the attempted revival of the Roman Empire in the form of a European super-state – this is the 4th Reich. With guidance from the Jesuits, the "Mother Church" of Rome and various noble families and papal-court Jews, all nations on Earth are now working towards a "common purpose". On-going efforts have achieved an economic and political unification (through establishment of a European Commission, a European Council, a European Parliament and court, a European Central Bank and a currency) which shall eventually come under the protection of one military force. The European Commission justifies this by stating: "… [it is] clearly the only credible answer to the hazards and opportunities posed by the increasing globalisation of the world economy." In one sense, the Holy Roman Empire is a continuation of the Roman Empire and various attempts at a revival have not yet fully succeeded (such as the 1st, 2nd and 3rd Reichs). Tisha B'Av has become a symbolic day of mourning for the Jewish people. Today, the Jews are ready to rebuild their final temple, the Third Temple, as prophesied over two thousand years ago. Failing to recognise Jesus as the true Messiah, many Jews believe that their Messiah will not arrive until the Third Temple is built. Gershon Salomon, of the Israeli Temple Mount Faithful movement, states: "As foretold thousands of years ago by the prophets of Israel, the signs of the end-times are more apparent than ever. This is the foremost period of the end-time redemption of the people and land of Israel that has ever occurred. This special time has outstanding significance for the future of all the nations and all of mankind."[clxix]

The Zionist Agenda

Today, for many people of Jewish (and even non-Jewish) heritage, Zionism (Jewish nationalism) has replaced the Torah (the first five books of the Bible), thus they have rejected the authority of God. During the past century, society has undergone stringent social engineering to remove aspects of religion and morality, whilst shallow, self-indulgent lifestyles and false spiritualism have been promoted. I believe that one particular ambition of the Jesuit-influenced Masonic-Zionist agenda is to replace Jesus Christ with a humanist philosophy and for all nations to worship "god" by serving the Latin Kingdom of Israel or "new Jerusalem". The cultural Marxist, New Age and Masonic cultures are very sophisticated and are blinding people of all nations. Today, society rejects the need for absolutes and replaces objective truth with relativism, unity, inter-faith and compromise. The oligarchs and banking cartels may be rife with Zionism, but their radical and satanic agenda is far from Jewish. Generally speaking, society has a worryingly short attention span and the self-obsessed, superficial, consumer-based lifestyle is now all too common. Recorded in 2 Timothy 3, the Bible forewarns us of this age: "In the last days perilous times shall come. For men shall be lovers of themselves, covetous, boasters, proud, blasphemers, disobedient to parents, unthankful, unholy, without natural affection, trucebreakers, false accusers, incontinent, fierce, despisers of those that are good, traitors, heady, high-minded, lovers of pleasures more than lovers of God; having a form of godliness, but denying the power thereof. Ever learning, and never able to come to the knowledge of the truth."

On the flip-side, Neturei-Karta is the name of a movement of orthodox Jews in Jerusalem who refuse to recognise the existence of the State of Israel and actively challenge the Zionists. As stated on their website: "Neturei Karta opposes the so-called "State of Israel" not because it operates secularly, but because the entire concept of a sovereign Jewish state is contrary to Jewish Law. The true Jews remain faithful to Jewish belief and are not contaminated with Zionism." Thus, not all Jews are Zionists and not all Zionists are Jews. A total of 4,000 years of conflict has seen the Assyrians, Hittites, Egyptians, Babylonians, Persians, Greeks, Romans and Muslims all in turn attempt to conquer the "City of Peace". The Jewish people (just a few million in number) have a truly unique and supernatural history. They have undergone many attempts to be wiped out of existence, yet despite this, they have maintained their

Hebrew language and identity throughout the millennia as the safe keepers of God's word. Considering their relatively small population, their contributions to the fields of mathematics, engineering, science, technology and the arts is truly remarkable.

A Peacemaker..?

Many centuries ago, the Bible forewarned that Jerusalem would be a "burden on the world" and, since it was established just over 60 years ago, it has been central to diplomatic crises, calls for war and various UN resolutions – every decision surrounding this tiny Israeli nation and its people has the potential to evoke World War Three. Following the formalisation of Islam and the Islamic conquest of Jerusalem, the Dome of the Rock was constructed in 691 AD on Mount Moriah where it stands to this day under strict Islamic control. The Dome of the Rock shall not be willingly surrendered by the Muslims and thus, at present, construction of the Jewish Third Temple is not possible – drastic topographical changes will be required before its construction (in other words, the Dome of the Rock will be destroyed before the Jews construct their final temple). The legacy of both Islam and Judaism depend upon this region of land, but as prophecy indicates, a Jewish Third Temple will be built on Mount Moriah. Prophecy indicates that the Temple Mount will be secured and a treaty will be formed (Daniel 9:27). World Wars One, Two and Three were long mapped out by the upper-echelon of the esoteric brotherhoods. It's reasonable (yet deeply saddening) to conclude that the Zionists and fundamental Islamists will "mutually destroy" one another. I can only assume that an all-out war will surround the destruction of the Dome of the Rock before the Third Temple is built. But what changes will ensure this coming treaty and also allow for the building of the Third Temple? A sibling rivalry born in antiquity could be put to rest by a new "prince" who takes to the global political stage. Who will he be? In whose name will he come? Paul-Henri Spaak, former Belgian Prime Minister and President of the Consultative Assembly of the Council of Europe, said: "We do not want another committee. We have too many already. What we want is a man of sufficient stature to hold the allegiance of all people. Send us such a man and, be he God or the devil, we will receive him." This modern trend for globalisation and the desire for a single world ruler is the fulfilment of ancient prophecy – this is the Babylonian anti-Christ system.

Summary

As the prophets of Israel foretold many centuries ago, an anti-Christ system will rise to worldwide power before a tyrannical leader is due to step forth on to the global stage to deceive the world and desecrate the Third Temple – all before the Messiah returns to take His throne. Led by the satanic elite, the geopolitical climate has aligned so perfectly with what the Bible forewarned us of thousands of years ago – it takes the most stubborn of men to deny its authority. In Matthew 24:4-7, Jesus said: "Watch out that no one deceives you. For many will come in my name, claiming 'I am the Messiah' and will deceive many. You will hear of wars and rumours of wars, but see to it that you are not alarmed. Nation will rise against nation, and kingdom against kingdom. There will be famines and earthquakes in various places." In the past three centuries, the conflicts between nations and subsequent death tolls have been increasing in frequency and devastation and today nuclear warfare is looming. The last century was the bloodiest century in human history and the 21st century shows no signs of being any better. We are seeing wars, deaths, famines and natural disasters on a scale like never before, for which we are told: "When you see all these things, you can know his return is very near." (Matthew 24:33). We are living in the most challenging of times, but it shall also be the most rewarding. As we continue to see God's amazing words come to life, we must be proactive and do what we can to help one another through these life-changing tribulations. There is so much to learn from the Bible and this chapter has barely scratched the surface. The New World Order is the manifestation of a satanic agenda and is being implemented by the most powerful anti-Christian powers on Earth. Whilst many battles are being waged in the physical realm, the New World Order goes much deeper than a simple political ideology – this is spiritual warfare:

"For we wrestle not against flesh and blood, but against principalities, against powers, against the rulers of the darkness of this world, against spiritual wickedness in high places." (Ephesians 6:12).

Historically speaking, God's integrity has rested upon three things: the Israelites, Israel and the Bible (His people, His nation and His word) and an unjustified attack upon any of these is an attack upon God's absolute authority (but please don't assume the agenda of the modern Zionist-Israeli nation is synonymous with God's will, as it certainly isn't). Maybe you can recognise Jesus as a good teacher, a prophet or perhaps a fraud. Although His existence is no longer disputed by competent scholars, His ministry is scrutinised, His actions are legendary and His bold claims are more bewildering than anybody else in history. He claimed to be the *only* path for fallen man to receive salvation. Through His teachings and miracles, He demonstrated His authority over all of creation. Either accept Him for who He is or just reject Him – there is no middle ground, a compromise isn't possible. With over two billion followers alive today, Jesus's legacy is like no other. With over one billion Muslims who also await His return (but don't accept that He was crucified, resurrected or that He was the incarnate God), over three billion people are waiting for the second coming of Jesus, the most influential man to walk the Earth – correctly identifying who He is and what He has done for mankind is crucial: "That whosoever believeth in Him should not perish, but have eternal life." (John 3:15). If Jesus Christ, our Redeemer, died for us, the least we can do is live for Him. Now we have an understanding of the Arab-Israeli conflict, let us explore the origins of civilisation, false religions and the resurrection of Babylon.

20. The Origins of Civilisation

Time begins in Sumer

Various archaeologists, such as Dr. David Neiman, trace the cradles of civilisation to three particular fertile regions:

- The valleys of the Tigris and Euphrates rivers (modern-day Iraq).
- The valley of the River Nile in Egypt.
- The valley of the Jordan River.

Many archaeologists believe that within these regions, post-diluvian agriculture, metalwork and urbanisation first took place. By approximately 3,500 BC (before the beginning of recorded history), numerous cities had already been established in the region of Sumer (present-day Iraq). Along the River Nile in Africa, the Egyptian civilisation soon followed, as did the Phoenician civilisation (the land of Phoenicia was also known as Canaan) which was located along the Mediterranean coast in Israel and Lebanon. Evoking images of majesty, these early cultures developed their own writing, languages, traditions and religious and spiritual systems (although it is the early Sumerians who are considered to have influenced many of the neighbouring civilisations). The Bible confirms that, after the great floods receded, Noah and his three sons, Ham, Shem and Japheth (with each of their wives), began to rebuild civilisation in these Middle Eastern regions after descending from Mount Ararat in Turkey. This chapter is concerned with the region of present-day Iraq, once known as Sumer and later known as Babylonia (or Mesopotamia in Greek culture).

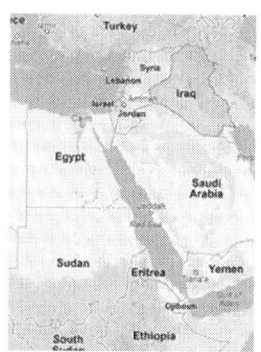

Image 20.1 The region of Sumer is modern-day Iraq.

History of Sumer

From ancient Sumer came the first written language, which is when, approximately 5,000 years ago, recorded history began. The Sumerians' script, known as cuneiform, is credited with having produced some of the greatest literary works in history (as previously mentioned, the Epic of Gilgamesh is just one of these works). It was on clay tablets that the Sumerians recorded many aspects of their lives, including commercial transactions, administrative procedures and laws – the discovery of over 250,000 of these clay tablets has allowed for a deeper insight into their advanced culture. From Sumer came the first urban centres, the first high-rise buildings, the first widespread road systems, the first schools, libraries, jails, courts, laws and even an advanced mathematical system. The ancient Sumerians have a truly exceptional history, with over 100 "firsts" as testimony to their sophistication. The region of Sumer served as a centre for culture, education and innovation for many centuries. Many modern researchers and academics are left baffled with regards to why there was such a sudden explosion of culture, but of course the reason is obvious: the people of Sumer were influenced by an older generation who had lived in the advanced pre-diluvian world, one where the inhabitants were capable of building sophisticated monuments, such as the Great Pyramid. As demonstrated in the earlier chapters of this work, before it was wiped out by a global cataclysm, the pre-diluvian culture was highly sophisticated – it is evident that the Sumerians (and other cultures during "rebirth" of civilisation) inherited, or were able to revive, some of the skills necessary to build and maintain a civilisation.

Birth of Babylon

Although the birth of the city and the Kingdom of Babylon is quite obscure, the processes for development were firmly established and various neighbouring regions were already thriving when Babylon began rising to world power. The political structure was headed by an absolute monarch who exercised a divine authority over judicial, legislative and executive matters. Working beneath the divinely-appointed king were priests, administrators and governors. Not only did the people believe the king to be appointed by the gods, they believed him to be a god (the tradition of the "divine right of kings" has trickled down to the present day). The earliest civilisations throughout the Middle East were full of vigorous social and religious activity. The rulers of each kingdom desired urban expansion and dominion over neighbouring regions, but the historical and archaeological records are too fragmented to give an accurate account of these battles for local supremacy.

Mystery Babylon

"Woe, woe, the great city, Babylon, the strong city!
For in one hour your judgment has come." (Revelation 18:3).

Throughout human history there have been just two systems of worship, which are diametrically opposed to one another. In the Bible, these systems are represented by two cities. The most frequently mentioned city is Jerusalem, "the City of God", and second to Jerusalem is Babylon, "the City of man", which is mentioned over 250 times. It was approximately 500 to 1,000 years after the floods receded that an infamous and mighty warrior named Nimrod (a descendant of Noah's son, Ham) travelled up from his birthplace of Ethiopia to Babylonia. With his army, he successfully conquered several cities within the region and established for himself a legendary empire. Nimrod is regarded as a tyrant and the world's first dictator (here we see another similarity between the Epic of Gilgamesh and the Genesis account from the Bible – is it possible that both accounts of these legendary tyrants are talking of the same warrior?). The Bible states:

"And Cush begat Nimrod: he began to be a mighty one
in the Earth. He was a mighty hunter before the LORD.
And the beginning of his kingdom was Babel, and Erech, and
Accad, and Calneh, in the land of Shinar." (Genesis 10:8-10)

The name Nimrod literally means rebel or tyrant, and some researchers speculate that he travelled northward from Ethiopia in search of the Garden of Eden, where the fall of man occurred – perhaps he was attempting to establish himself a new Eden, in rebellion against God. Titus Flavius Josephus (a 1st-century Romano-Jewish historian) states: "Now it was Nimrod who excited them to such an affront and contempt of God... a bold man, and of great strength of hand. He persuaded them not to ascribe it to God."[clxx] As legend states, in order to consolidate his power, Nimrod implemented a state religion and elevated himself to the status of a god whilst his wife, Semiramis, was elevated to the status of a goddess and the queen of heaven. Through these self-appointed deities, Babylon descended into the worst kinds of idolatry, wickedness, widespread corruption and human sacrifice. Spreading to foreign lands, the legends of false gods permeated antiquity and rained down throughout the ages – some researchers trace all false religions and spiritualism (the Mystery Religions or "the Mysteries") back to Sumer and Babylon. The Mysteries each had their own secret council which came under the rule of a supreme council – this was the Illuminati of antiquity. It was the ancestors of these council members who lived in the sophisticated pre-diluvian culture – the Illuminati of Sumer and Babylon would have striven to keep the knowledge of their ancestors alive in order to achieve the standard of living that their forefathers had enjoyed.

The Counterfeit System

Nimrod and deities such as Baal or Bel are associated with fire worship and idolatry. They are commonly identified with the Sun, which is the mightiest fire in the solar system – fire is the Sun's earthly counterpart. Shamefully, the Beltane Fire Festival is still celebrated throughout England and Scotland, on or around May 1st (May Day is an important pagan and druid holiday) and, in times gone by, animals and humans would be offered up as a sacrifice. As the mythology of ancient Sumer and Babylon evolved, it appears to have spread to Egypt and Phoenicia and as far east as India. To the Egyptians, deities with similar characteristics were known as Ra, Osiris and Horus, and to the Greeks, as Helios or Apollo. For the Canaanites, there was a god known as Molech – a giant statue of Molech was worshipped whilst babies and young children were sacrificed in a fire. Worryingly, a re-enactment of the worship of Molech takes place to this day when various elites (including US presidents) gather once a year at Bohemian Grove to re-enact the druidic styled ritual in front of a forty-foot effigy of an owl. The former presidential advisor David Gregen (who served during the administrations of Nixon, Ford, Reagan and Clinton) was confronted on camera by reporter Alex Jones to be asked some very awkward questions regarding his participation in the shady ritual at Bohemian Grove – Gregen was clearly caught off guard and his reaction was cringeworthy.

In antiquity, the practice of human sacrifice became customary. In the Bible, God commanded: "Do not give any of your children to be sacrificed to Molech." (Leviticus 18:21). The origins of paganism (the worship of the planets), polytheism (the worship of multiple gods) and pantheism (the belief that the universe and every object of creation embodies a divine nature) originated in Sumer – in fact, these belief systems are *counterfeits* and *distortions* of the original relationship man had with the Most High God (YHWH) in the Garden of Eden. Today, Sun and Mother Earth worship are still widespread and the Bible states: "They exchanged the truth about God for a lie and worshipped and served the creature rather than the Creator." (Romans 1:25). Paganism is tangible and alluring to the senses, but as we marvel at God's amazing creation, we must remember to worship Him, not His creation. Whilst Babylon was a literal city (which is today undergoing a regeneration), Mystery Babylon represents corruption; it's an extremely sophisticated counterfeit system that attempts to sell itself as an original. Author Charles Dyer states: "As the mother of all false religions, Babylon is the source from which arises false Christianity in our own day and certainly during the tribulation. All the streams of apostate Christianity — will converge into ecclesiastical Babylon (Revelation 17) during the tribulation."[clxxi] Today, Mystery Babylon is a universal religion; it takes the form of apostate Christianity and *every* other false belief system external to the Bible which does not acknowledge Jesus as our God incarnate and the unique saviour of mankind. As the modern-day globalists work towards a "common purpose" in defiance of God and attempt to undermine His word, we are witnessing the rise of eastern mysticism and the New Age – Babylon is manifesting itself like never before.

"Mystery, Babylon the Great, the mother of harlots and abominations of the Earth" (Revelation 17:5).

Consider Al Gore and Ted Turner (who share the worldview of Prince Philip and other elites): they call for worldwide worship of Mother Earth. Ted Turner even created a children's cartoon to promote this pagan propaganda called 'Captain Planet and the Planeteers'. It was themed on Gaia (the Greek-goddess personification of the Earth) who was awakened from a long sleep. As David Stewart rightfully states, mass-marketed false spiritualism, also known as the New Age movement, is: "... an expansive idea cantered around the birth of a new world 'consciousness'. As a religion of monism (all is one), New Agers aim to accomplish what the builders of the Tower of Babel failed to do — unify the masses of the world under a single religious umbrella, and, at the macro level, harmonically converge the world's energies with the power of Gaia. To promote such goals, New Agers claim that God is pantheistic (God is all and all is God) and that humans are divine members of the whole 'that God is'."[clxxii] Seductive, mass-marketed false spirituality is appealing to those who wish to find meaning in whatever suits their taste, rather than search out the truth.

The Tower of Babylon

Nimrod's intention was to build a sacred mountain from which he could reign from the heavens, keep watch over his empire and be seen for miles around. From this purpose-built sacred mountain, or "gateway to god", he could be worshipped not as a man but as God. With ambitions to unify the political and religious systems into a conglomerate and unite the world under his tyrannical authority, Nimrod's plan was foiled when God intervened and confused their language. This confusion of the language caused the inhabitants of Babylon to spread out and populate new lands, thus Nimrod's plan was never completed (the phrase "talking babel", or "babbling", originates from this confusion of tongues). One reason for God's intervention was to destroy this system prone to corruption, idolatry and satanism. Depictions of the Tower of Babel commonly show it as incomplete, such as we see with the 16th-century rendering by Pieter Bruegel the Elder (Image 20.2).

Image 20.2: The Tower of Babel (Pieter Bruegel the Elder).

Artists commonly depict the Tower of Babel as an actual tower, but it was almost certainly a ziggurat or pyramid (refer to Image 20.3), similar to those found in Africa, Egypt and South America. The craftsmen of the Tower of Babel were taught the secrets of Masonry. The apron worn by modern-day Freemasons is said to represent the fig leaves worn by Adam and Eve in the Garden of Eden and some of the esoteric knowledge that Adam and Eve gained from Satan survived the flood and was inherited by Nimrod. After God had confused their language, many of the inhabitants were forced to move abroad and their esoteric knowledge is considered to have become fragmented or partially lost.

As Above, So Below

Image 20.3 A Ziggurat.

Conceptually, the ziggurat or pyramid is a stairway to heaven and symbolic of a joining of heaven and Earth – this connection is a very familiar theme (Stairway to Heaven is also a famous song by Led Zeppelin). The ancient Hermetic philosophy "As above, so below" signifies a connection between the microcosm and macrocosm or, specifically, between oneself and the universe. As we have seen, the fusion of heaven and Earth is represented in esoteric art and architecture all over the world. There is actually a much more profound meaning to this concept, the origins of which will be revealed in the final chapters of this work. The pyramid symbolises the concept that man himself can become a god and be worshipped like the Most High – once again, we trace the origins of this philosophy back to the promises of Satan in the Garden of Eden. It is the manipulation of man's ego, leading him to believe that he can reach salvation or enlightenment based upon his own work or merit. On the physical plane, Nimrod acted as a proxy for the serpent by diverting worship away from God to himself. Nimrod became the dominant physical ruler on Earth, but the spiritual driving force was Satan.

Pyramid Symbology

Manly P Hall, 33rd-degree Mason and Masonry's greatest philosopher, states: "The mysteries taught that the divine energies from the gods descended upon the top of the pyramid. Man is taken from the quarry and by the secret culture of the mysteries gradually transformed into a true and perfect pyramid capstone. The temple is complete only when the initiate himself becomes the living apex through which the divine power is focused into the diverging structure below."clxxiii This pseudo-intellectual New Age drivel is refuted by the Bible, which tells us that these "gods" did not descend but were cast out of heaven (as will be reviewed later). As prophesied in Psalms 118:22, Jesus was the "rejected cornerstone" and the "chief cornerstone" – He is the cornerstone of the church itself. In no way can man become a cornerstone like Jesus or undergo a transformation to obtain divinity, yet this is the central (and false) philosophy of the Freemasonic and New Age movement. If man is not a servant of the Most High God, by default he is a *slave to sin*. Thus paganism, polytheism, atheism and *all* other false religions are the ways of Babylon. Satan cares not if you worship him directly and, as the famous quote goes: "The greatest trick the devil ever pulled was convincing the world that he didn't exist". Manly P Hall states: "Symbolism is the language of the Mysteries... by symbols men have ever sought to communicate to each other those thoughts which transcend the limitations of language."clxxiv A pyramid represents the global satanic system of control. Initiates of the Mysteries can progress roles and responsibilities within, but only the true elect will reach the top of the pyramid. The pyramid is layered and each layer of the pyramid corresponds to a stage of initiation or a degree. This structure is an incremental desensitisation for its members – the dark and satanic nature of the highest levels of the Mysteries would deter many new initiates (and, as briefly discussed, there are many dark activities at the higher levels). Only those who sit at the top of the pyramid (like Nimrod) are truly "enlightened" and embody "divine" power. The bottom layer, the base of the pyramid, is comprised of people (approximately 98% of the global population) referred to as the masses, sheep or cattle. It is now that we have an understanding of the pervasive centrepiece of the world's most iconic currency (which is similar to the British MI5 logo) which is the pyramid and the illuminated All-Seeing Eye:

Image 20.4 A US one-dollar bill with an unfinished pyramid and the Eye of Providence.

Image 20.5 A close-up of the All-Seeing Eye on the one – dollar bill and the Eye of Horus, Osiris or Ra.

Embedded within the psyche of the average American citizen is the All-Seeing Eye (also known as the Eye of Providence or the eye of Horus, Osiris, Ra or Lucifer), yet very few people understand its significance – it is rooted within the occult and it is satanic. The capstone of the incomplete pyramid is beaming with illuminating rays of light, a concept that resonates with the unfinished Tower of Babel.

> "And no wonder, for Satan himself masquerades
> as an angel of light." (2 Corinthians 11:14).

The illuminated eye also represents a New Age awakening and, as 33rd-degree Freemason Albert Pike revealed: "... to the Egyptian initiates was the emblem of Osiris, the Creator." And "His [Osiris's] power was symbolised by an Eye over a Sceptre. The Sun was termed by the Greeks the Eye of Jupiter, and the Eye of the World; and his is the All-Seeing Eye in our Lodges."[clxxv] Author John Daniel says: "This singular 'eye' is called the 'third eye' of clairvoyance in the Hindu religion, the eye of Osiris in Egypt, and the All-Seeing Eye in Freemasonry".[clxxvi] Both the pyramid and eye symbology has become widespread within popular culture, especially the music industry.

21. The Resurrection of Babylon

It was back in the 1990s, when Europe began to push for a "common future" and closer integration amongst member-states, that the Council of Europe issued a poster to promote the EU parliamentary agenda (Image 21.1). It displayed the unfinished Tower of Babel below inverted satanic pentagrams and a slogan that reads: "Many Tongues, One Voice". The five-sided satanic pentagram (in Greek, "pente" means five) has been used for many centuries by magicians to invoke demons and manifest the kingdom of darkness.

Image 21.1 The Council of Europe poster –
Europe: Many Tongues, One Voice.

Of course, this is the glorification of man's defiance against God and the manifestation of a satanic agenda born in antiquity. The slogan "Many Tongues, One Voice" is perhaps a subtle reference to the inhabitants of Babylon who spoke in one tongue before God confused their language.

The poster presents the people of Europe rebuilding the tower – the workers appear to be shaped like robots, and robots can only do what they are programmed to do. The baby located in the bottom left corner still has a round-shaped human head – this young mind has not yet been programmed. Today, Babylon is rising to power once again. This ancient city has come to represent a satanic government establishment which is seeking to obtain global control, as it did many thousands of years ago – the powers and principalities are rebuilding Babylon. Image 21.2 is of the EU Parliament building; its design has raised questions ever since it was completed in 1999. Is the "unfinished" look a representation of the Tower of Babylon? Merging it with Pieter Bruegel's rendering may give you an insight:

Image 21.2 The EU Parliament building (left)
merged with the Tower of Babylon (right).

Mother and Child Worship and the Son of God

Upon creation, Adam and Eve walked in harmony with God. Following their rebellion, they became separated from God due to their sin. Eventually, the objective reality of monotheism (a relationship with the Most High God) became distant and fragmented, thus paganism, pantheism, polytheism, monism, materialism, naturalism and atheism have all evolved from monotheism or the original relationship with the Most High God. An intriguing myth of antiquity is that of the *pagan trio*: Sun worship was in the form of the father, the mother and the son – Isis, Osiris, Horus. Many sceptics erroneously claim that the Biblical Trinity is a counterfeit of this ancient pagan trio. However, Isis, Osiris and Horus were three separate gods who existed independent of one another – tritheistic theology is distinct from Trinitarian Christianity and was deemed heresy by the early church. The Biblical Trinity is a truly unique theological concept which cannot be compared or mirrored with any man-made construct. Satan and his army are divine in nature; they reside in the spiritual realm and they know the true nature of the "composite" Godhead (Father, Son and Holy Spirit). Permeating myths through false belief systems discredits the absolute truth – this is why Babylon is such a sophisticated counterfeit. The mother goddess religion permeated ancient culture from Europe to the Far East and still continues to this day in the form of apostate Christianity, which elevates the Virgin Mary to the status of a deity, the queen of heaven and the mother of god (we shall explore the origins of the veneration of the virgin in the final chapters). A female deity, known as Ishtar, Diana, Athtar or Astarte throughout the ancient Near and Middle East, was commonly associated with sex and fertility, and it was during spring (Easter time) and early summer that rituals and sacrifices took place. Celebrated by pagans/wiccans, the festival of Diana still takes place to this day in England. In ancient Egypt, the mother goddess was Isis, her brother-husband was Osiris and they produced the offspring Horus. Image 21.3 shows this mythological family tree:

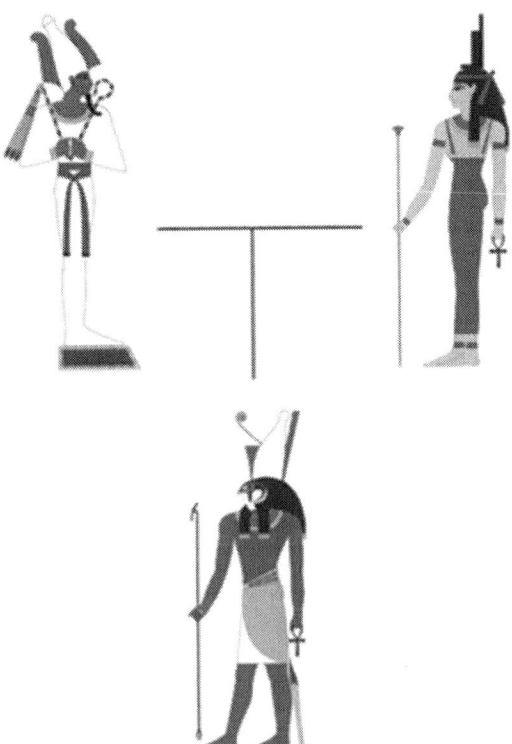

Image 21.3 Osiris, Isis and their offspring Horus.

Isis, Osiris and Horus

According to one version of the Osiris myth, Osiris was killed before his corpse was dissected into 14 pieces and scattered throughout the land. This shattering of Osiris, before the pieces of his corpse were scattered, is symbolic of God's intervention in Babylon when He confused the languages and caused the people to scatter abroad and inhabit new lands. Isis worked to place all the pieces of Osiris back together, but his genitals were never found. She replaced the lost organ with a facsimile and reconstructed him before impregnating herself to produce an offspring. Thenceforth, Osiris was known as the *god of the dead* (similar to the Babylonian god, Ereshkigal, and the Greek god, Hades) and their offspring, a son named Horus, became known as "god of the living" or the "son of god". Image 21.4 is an ancient representation of the Egyptian trio: Osiris, Isis and their offspring Horus.

Image 21.4 The Egyptian trio: Osiris, Isis and Horus.

The Pharaohs of Egypt were considered the sons of god (of the Sun god Ra). Image 21.5 is an ancient representation of mother and child in the form of Isis and Horus.

Image 21:5 Mother and Child: Isis and Horus
(statue housed in the Louvre – the image is licensed under
Creative Commons, courtesy of Guillaume Blanchard, July 2004).

Image 21.6 is a pagan representation of mother and child in the form of Mary and Jesus – note the similarity between the two depictions.

Image 21:6 Mother and Child: A depiction of Mary and Baby Jesus with pagan Sun discs, or "halos", behind their heads (Fra Angelico, 1395–1455).

Image 21.7 depicts an ancient Indian mother goddess and her child belonging to the Hindu pantheon – the mother and child theme was very common in various ancient civilisations:

Image 21.7 Ancient Hindu mother goddess and child.

Babylon Resurrected

I propose three aspects to the resurrection of Babylon:

1) Temporal or physical: a literal rebuilding of the ancient city and kingdom in the Middle East.
2) Spiritual and religious: Mystery Babylon, in all its variety, is the universal religion of fallen man.
3) Ideological or political: this is the building of a one-world fascist government which has been centuries in the making (and is driven by the spiritual realm).

In the same way that Isis worked to reassemble the pieces of Osiris and produce a divine offspring, the New World Order is the resemblance of Babylon and will produce a divine offspring – the anti-Christ who will come to rule over all nations. Symbolic of the resurrection of Osiris, the modern resurrection of Babylon aims to unite all the Mystery Religions under one rule of Osiris (Satan), the *god of the dead*. In the Gospel accounts, Jesus tells us that He is the "God of the living". Since World War One and Two, the royal-political elites have been obsessed with uniting the world under a single geopolitical system. Their UN logo displays a grid of 33 segments placed over the Earth (the importance of the number 33 will be discussed in Chapter 22 – Illuminated Fraternities) enclosed within two olive branches:

Image 21.7 The United Nations logo.

On this logo, each olive branch has 14 leaves – the number 14 resonates with the mythological story of Osiris who was cut into 14 pieces. After Nimrod's original plan to conquer the world was thwarted, it has taken over 4,000 years to come close to what he almost achieved. In 2009, construction of the largest and most expensive embassy *ever* built was completed, in close proximity to Babylon, near the present-day city of Baghdad. Ongoing efforts are being made to resurrect the ancient "City of Man". As stated on the Embassy's website: "Our second largest grant is the Future of Babylon Project, which is funded by the United States Government."[clxxvii]

22. Illuminated Fraternities

Freemasonry

Following the Protestant Reformation in England, the Jesuits revived Freemasonry in 1717 in order to infiltrate/supress Protestantism and restore the Catholic House of Stuart to the throne. According to 32nd-Degree Freemason William Peterson, 25 degrees of the Scottish Rite were written in the College of Jesuits of Clermont, in Paris, in 1754[clxxviii], thus high-level Freemasonry has *always* been a tool of the Jesuits. Manly P Hall states in his book, *The Lost Keys of Masonry*: "Masonry is a university, teaching the liberal arts and sciences of the soul to all who will attend to its words." Masons around the world include royalty, judges, barristers, police officers, members of secret services (CIA, MI5 and MI6), lawyers, politicians and celebrities. The age-old tradition of enrolling police officers, judges and lawyers meant that fellow Masons could become immune from prosecution and avoid unwanted attention during sinister business transactions or illicit activities – each Freemason is bound by oath to honour fellow brothers. Despite the criticism and hostility towards the Freemasons, not every Masonic lodge is necessarily a "nest of corruption". The organisation officially claims that it is not a religion, although one requirement for joining the fraternity states that initiates must hold a belief in a "supreme being" known as the "great" or "grand" architect of the universe.

Rebuilding the Temple

Nimrod, the great grandson of Noah, is considered the founder of the Freemason fraternity and is known as the first and most excellent master. The Freemasons are a tool used to progress the agenda of Nimrod. Islamic anti-Masonry claims that the organisation promotes the interests of the Jews, one of which includes the rebuilding of Solomon's Temple (the Third Jewish Temple). A key philosophy of Freemasonry demonstrates that man in his current form is incomplete and, whilst the organisation is associated with the reconstruction of a temple, this philosophy has a dual meaning, one of which is merely symbolic. The New Encyclopaedia of Freemasonry states: "He who considers the [rebuilding] story solely from its historical angle will never clear away the rubbish that covers the secret vaults". This Freemasonic concept of "rebuilding" the temple is symbolic of the transition to enlightenment and divinity. The temple is a representation of man and, although the Freemasons keep the true meaning of the temple concealed, the Bible reveals that the symbol of God's temple is man's body:

> "Know ye not that ye are the temple of God, and that
> the Spirit of God dwelleth in you?" (Corinthians 3:16).

When a man becomes born again in the name of Jesus, the spirit of God resides within him and this is God's "temple". Since the destruction of the Jewish Temple in Israel, the spirit of God no longer dwells within any man-made structure.

The Symbols and Structure of Freemasonry

Illuminised Freemasonry is a society within a society. The first body is "visible" within the public domain, occupying the lodges and participating in community and charity works. The second body is hidden, or "invisible", and the lower-level Masons do not learn of its secrets. Manly P Hall states: "An outer organisation conceals an inner brotherhood of elect."[clxxix] Albert Pike stated that lower-level, or visible, Masons are given: "... false explanations and misinterpretations of symbols" in order to mislead those who are truly uninitiated. Symbolism and numerology are integral to those who are rooted in the occult, for to them, it is a language. There are various reasons for the use of numbers, symbols and key words, but primarily it is to conceal their activities from the masses whilst at the same time reveal their activities to one another. Prophetic research pastor Mike Hoggard states that Masonic symbols can generally be arranged into 3 categories:

1) The transition from man to godhood.
2) The coming of a New Age and New World Order.
3) The rise and revelation of the anti-Christ.

As Above, So Below: Square and Compass

The most basic representation of the "As above, so below" concept is a triangle pointing upward to the heavens whilst a second triangle points downwards (Image 22.1):

Image 22.1 As Above, So Below.

In the natural world this principle can be found in any body of water (such as a lake) where a mountain or tree reflects off the water's surface. This concept is demonstrated in Washington DC where a lake of water reflects the US Capitol building, the Lincoln Memorial and also the Washington Monument (which is an ancient Egyptian obelisk). By merging the two triangles (Image 22.2), a hexagram (also known as the Star of David) is created; it is symbolic of a connection between oneself and the heavens ("As above, so below"). The Star of David (also known as the Seal of Solomon) is a widely used occult symbol which has been used by magicians, druids, witches and Satanists for many centuries. Since 1948, it has been used on the flag of Israel (but it is not a legitimate Jewish symbol):

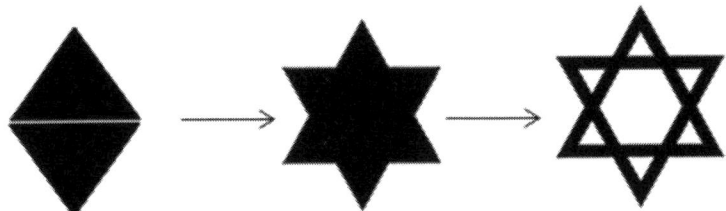

Image 22.2 From left to right: "As Above, So Below" represented by two triangles (left). Merging both the triangles (centre) creates the Star of David (right).

As shown in Image 22.3, upon removing the base of merged triangles, the outline of a square and compass is created – this is the logo of Freemasonry. The square and compass are the most basic tools of an architect, navigator and cartographer. In Freemasonic symbolism, the compass positioned above the square represents the Sun (male) impregnating the passive Earth (female) with its life-generating beams – it represents a fusion of heaven and Earth (As above, so below).

Image 22.3 By removing the bases of the hexagram (left) the Masonic square and compass is formed (right).

Navigation and the Curious Case of the Number 33

The compass (Image 22.3) is used to draw a circle from which a Compass Rose can be created. Image 22.4 shows a Compass Rose in the making:

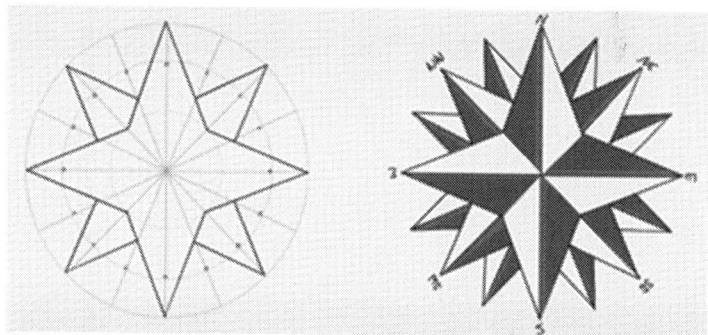

Image 22.4 16-point Compass Rose (courtesy of Wikihow: www.wikihow.com/Draw-a-Compass-Rose).

Triangulation is a process of determining the location of a point by measuring angles. The use of triangles for estimating distances dates back to the 6th century BC when Thales, an ancient Greek philosopher, made use of this technique.[clxxx] In the 13th century AD, before the invention of the magnetic compass, the Compass Rose (adapted from the ancient wind rose) was refined in Italy and has appeared on maps and charts ever since – the device is now regarded as an early achievement in navigational superpowers. There are a total of 32 points on a contemporary Compass Rose and "boxing the compass" is a term used by seafarers to describe the action of reciting all 32 points from memory (it was one of the first lessons taught to apprentice seamen). Researcher David Flynn suggests that, after boxing the compass: "... the final point is 0 and 33", suggesting that the Compass Rose has an esoteric 33rd point which is of importance when measuring or travelling the Earth."[clxxxi] The Ancient and Accepted Scottish Rite of Freemasonry has a total of 33 degrees and, upon reaching the highest level, the graduate becomes fully enlightened and an honorary member of the Supreme Council. In spiritual numerology, the number 33 symbolises the highest level of spiritual consciousness attainable by man, and this number resonates with the human spine, which is comprised of 33 bones. "Enlightenment" can also be achieved through the practice of Kundalini, which claims that an unconscious force, or "serpent", lies at the base of man's spine – through rituals and practices, the serpent progressively uncoils up through the 33 bones of the human spine before reaching the pineal gland (referred to as the 3rd eye) to cause an "awakening". The UN logo (displayed in the previous chapter) has 33 segments placed over the globe to symbolise global unification and a New Age awakening. Other esoteric and intriguing references to 33 include:

- London is a city with 33 small "cities" within it.[clxxxii]
- NASA's runway at Kennedy Space Centre in Florida is called runway 33.
- Researchers at the Brookhaven National Laboratory in New York found that the Sun's core rotates once every 33 days.[clxxxiii]
- Jesus was aged 33 when He was crucified.
- The Earth vibrates at 7.83 Hz due to lightning discharges and this is called the Schumann resonance. The human scale resonates at 33 harmonics or 32 overtones above this frequency. This is the range where our ears hear and where we make music.[clxxxiv]

It is now we begin to understand the significance of the number 33 in the esoteric world.

Illuminati: The New Age of Babylon

The Illuminati enigma is surrounded by plenty of controversy, hysteria and disinformation. Specialising in the dark arts, the Mystery Schools of antiquity were governed by individual councils who, in turn, were governed by a Supreme Council. Today, the Illuminati is a name used in reference to the collective of the wealthiest and most powerful families on Earth. Many of these royal, religious and political elites (the oligarchs) are generational Satanists with dark histories and extremely savage tendencies. The Illuminati is comprised of:

- A Supreme Grand Council.
- Secret societies (networks of magicians and druids, sacred bloodlines, astrologers/astronomers, witch covens, Satanists and higher-order members of secret societies such as the Skull and Bones).

Various members of the Illuminati trace their own genealogy, in an unbroken continuity, right back to antiquity. The modern ambition of full-spectrum dominance is nothing new. Everybody on Earth can be categorised as follows:

- The illuminated – the oligarchs and their counterparts account for 1% of the global population.
- The initiates – partially aware of, or working for, the agenda.
- The masses – approximately 98% of the global population are manipulated by the agenda.

In his book *Bloodlines of the Illuminati*, Fritz Springmeier attempts to identify the top 13 Illuminati bloodlines and names some of them as the Astors, the Du Ponts, the Rothschilds and the Merovingians (European royal families). Other researchers identify more arcane families as the "true Illuminati bloodlines", such as the Orsinis, the Aldobrandinis and the Borghese (the Black Nobility and papal bloodlines). These dynasties don't just own corporations; they control cities, countries and continents. The Illuminati have designed the current economic system to cause instability and perpetual debt – it must be unstable to the point of collapse (which it evidently is) before ushering in the New Age of Babylon. The undermining and annihilation of the current system is essential in order for the masses to surrender willingly. Perpetual famines, plagues and wars are all a part of this agenda which aims to cull the global population.

A Brief History

> "It is necessary to establish a universal regime over the whole world." Adam Weishaupt, Writings of the Illuminati, 1780.

The Jesuit Adam Weishaupt was a Professor of Canon Law at the University of Ingolstadt. He has been labelled as everything from a socialist to a philanthropist, a mystic to a Kabbalist, an alchemist and a Satanist. With guidance from his Jesuit brethren and funding from

European oligarchs, Adam Weishaupt formalised the Bavarian Illuminati (the Illuminated Ones) on May 1st 1776 in Bavaria, Germany (as previously mentioned, May Day is an important day of Druidic worship and Hitler committed suicide on April 30th, thus the Third Reich informally ended in time for May Day 1945). As stated by Leonard Ulrich, the maker of the documentary *NWO: Secret Societies and Biblical Prophecies Vol. 1*, every major war (from the French Revolution onwards) has been financed by the Illuminati bankers in order to conquer nations and progress a one-world government.[clxxxv] The following list is a section of the Illuminati's original agenda (which partially mirrors the communist and cultural Marxist ideology):

- The abolition of all monarchical government (on a global scale).
- The elimination of private property and inheritance.
- The destruction of the traditional family.
- The eradication of all religions and the enforcement of a new global religion.

America was seen as the new Atlantis and, upon its colonisation, a "Columbian faction" of the Illuminati was formed. Today the murder-management capital of planet Earth, the Pentagon, is based in the District of Columbia. Other ventures of the "Columbian faction" which brandish the name include: Columbia Records, Columbia Pictures, the Columbia Space Shuttle, and Columbia Broadcasting System (for which the logo is the All Seeing Eye of Horus). The three main Illuminati city-states are sovereign corporate entities working to control warfare, religion and finance on a global scale:

- City of London – the financial capital of the world.
- Vatican City – the religious capital of the world.
- Washington DC – the military capital of the world.

Image 22.5 London, the Vatican and Washington DC
each have an Egyptian obelisk.

Both Washington and Rome are Jesuit-controlled entities. As demonstrated in Image 22.5, present within the three aforementioned sovereign states is an ancient Egyptian obelisk which glorifies the Egyptian sun god, Ra, and also represents the missing phallus of Osiris (which Isis used to impregnate herself and give birth to Horus). These profane pagan fertility idols represent the generative principle – it's a covert mockery of a society totally unaware of the perverse Illuminati "fertility" cult and their global networks. Just as Isis produced an offspring after she replaced the lost organ of Osiris with a facsimile, these idols located in the city-states are symbolically aiding the New World Order and the production of a divine offspring – the anti-Christ. Today, the monument of the obelisk is present within many of the major cities on Earth.

Project Lucifer and the Coming Mass Deception

Founded in 1987 with involvement from the Jesuits, the Vatican Observatory Foundation is a little over 20 years old. The Vatican Observatory itself is one of the oldest astronomical institutions in the world. The Vatican Advanced Technology Telescope (VATT) is conducting research from Mount Graham International Observatory in Arizona. According to the Vatican Observatory: "Utilising the most advanced optics, electronics and mechanics, the Vatican is at the forefront of astronomy".[clxxxvi] The state-of-the-art near-infrared camera, known as the Large Binocular Telescope Near-infrared Utility with Camera and Integral Field Unit for Extragalactic Research, has been abbreviated to LUCIFER. Why is a religious institution so concerned with watching the skies? There are many curious utterances coming from the Vatican regarding alien life – the Catholic theologian, Monsignor Corrado Balducci claimed that alien visitations were real but not demonic. Father Malachi Martin stated on a Coast to Coast AM radio interview that the "... highest levels of Vatican administration and geopolitics know that, now, knowledge of what's going on in space, and what's approaching us, could be of great importance in the next five years, ten years." What could Malachi Martin be implying? As the Jesuit scientists continue to search the heavens using an instrument named LUCIFER, we are entering into a new phase of the Jesuit-led Illuminati agenda. In terms of eschatology, we are entering into a phase of mass deception – a deception unlike any the world has ever known.

23. The UFO Phenomenon

The Unidentified Flying Object phenomenon manifested in the 1940s after a number of high-profile, bizarre incidents (the incident at Roswell, New Mexico, became the most famous in history). Authors, film producers and journalists alike were all quick to respond, helping to shape UFO mythology within the media (which climaxed during the 1950s but is still as popular today as it was back then). A survey published in 2012, taken by the National Geographic Channel, found that 80 million Americans believed in the existence of UFOs.[clxxxvii] Undoubtedly, Hollywood and the media have greatly influenced society's views on the existence of alien life. In the run-up to 2012, a major milestone was reached for ufologists when, for the first time in history, authorities in the UK (and various other countries excluding the USA) declassified thousands of documented UFO reports, many of which come from competent witnesses (including military personnel, pilots, air traffic controllers and police officers). Firstly, what type of data is available to evaluate the possible existence of UFOs? The practical data comes in the form of:

- Thousands of authenticated photos and videos (vast amounts are still officially classified).
- Witness accounts (a high volume of reports come from the professional community, including astronauts, pilots and military personnel).
- Encounters and physical traces (ranging from highly complex crop circles to the more sinister nature of animal mutilations, abductions, impregnations, device implants and foetus harvesting).

All of this data can be categorised into one of the following groups:

- The Hoaxes.
- The Unreliable: Identifiable Flying Objects.
- The Genuine: Residual Unidentified Flying Objects.

After removing all the forgeries and unreliable data (which account for approximately 95% of all the reports), there is still a substantial amount of evidence to demonstrate that UFOs are a genuine phenomenon. NASA's Apollo 14 astronaut, Edgar Mitchell, stated: "We all know that UFOs are real; now the question is where they come from." In 2004 he told the *St Petersburg Times* that a "cabal of insiders" in the US government was studying recovered alien bodies and that this group had stopped briefing US presidents after John F Kennedy. There has been a dramatic increase in sightings and supernatural experiences in the past decade alone – hundreds of sightings and encounters are being reported every month throughout the world. In regard to the "alien visitors"', it's not a question of if they exist, but who they are, what their agenda is and where they come from. Has there ever been an open, objective and scientific investigation conducted into these phenomena? If not, why not? In this chapter, we shall look at some of the bizarre incidents surrounding UFOs and gain an understanding of why secrecy abounds.

Life on Another Planet: What are the Chances?

Due to the complexity of DNA and the fact that the origin of life cannot be explained by the atheist, a theory known as "directed panspermia" was proposed. It claims that aliens were responsible for bringing life here to Earth. The deliberate transport of micro-organisms across space was spoken of by various experts such as astrophysicist Carl Sagan and molecular biologist Francis Crick. The beginning of life is still a great mystery in the atheist movement and many speculate that the causal agent which is responsible for life on Earth originates from within space-time. Biochemists have established that the only elements other than carbon from which adequately complex molecules can be constructed (which are required for basic structural and metabolic functions) are silicon and boron, both of which have been generally ruled out as alternatives to carbon for advanced life; thus, *physical life forms must be carbon*. Scientists have compiled a list of the conditions and planetary characteristics needed to support carbon life and have ruled out a vast number of possible planets for where life could exist in the universe (the anthropic principle reveals how many conditions are required to permit advanced life to exist and how finely tuned these conditions must be – it also places a number of constraints on life travelling vast distances through space).[clxxxviii] Whilst the universe contains a gigantic number of planets, astronomers have been able to determine a number in the observable universe as being 10^{22}. Subtracting this number of planets (10^{22}) from the chances of all finely tuned life-supporting ratios being met (10^{186}) means the chances of life naturally originating on another planet are equal to 1 in 10^{164} or, in plain English, equivalent to winning the lottery a million times.[clxxxix]

The Nature of UFOs

Ufologists often speculate that these visitors come in peace and can offer mankind solutions to the many troubles here on Earth. UFOs and their alien pilots are portrayed as visitors from other planets (hence the name "extra-terrestrial"). If these entities were from another part of the universe, they would have to conform with the laws of physics. The distance between Earth and the nearest possible life-supporting environment is hundreds of light years away – biological creatures are not designed for extensive space travel. The chances of advanced life originating in other parts of the galaxy are *extremely* remote.

The observations of UFOs are as follows:

- They can make right-angled turns whilst travelling at thousands of miles per hour.
- They can travel faster than the speed of sound without creating a sonic boom.
- They can change shape and colour.
- They can materialise and dematerialise at random (and can go undetected on sophisticated monitoring equipment).
- A single flying object can separate into multiple objects and then re-integrate.
- They can light up the night sky and shoot finite beams of light.

After studying the characteristics of UFOs, various scientists have debunked the impractical extra-terrestrial hypothesis.

Inter-Dimensional or Extra-Dimensional?

In consideration of the universal physical limitations, alien craft can't be expected to traverse huge distances in space. UFOs appear to violate and manipulate the fundamental laws of physics and it is reasonable to conclude that they are non-physical in nature.[cxc] Astronomer Jacques Vallée proposed an alternative theory known as the inter-dimensional hypothesis. Vallée suggests that these entities exist within other dimensions of space-time and have the ability to manifest within our space-time. Whilst UFOs do exhibit typically physical behaviour, their manifestations are not consistent with the laws of physics, they have the ability to manipulate the laws of space-time and this suggests that they are *non-physical* entities descending from a *non-physical* reality. Based on these observations, another hypothesis has been proposed: the extra-dimensional hypothesis. The extra-dimensional hypothesis suggests that these entities are from *beyond* matter-energy and *above* the 10 dimensions of space-time – astrophysicist Dr. Hugh Ross favours this hypothesis.[cxci] So, are these entities here to help?

UFO-Related Crimes

A lesser known but severely sinister phenomenon relating to UFOs has been widespread throughout the world for decades (perhaps even centuries or millennia) and, since it was first reported in America in the 1970s, many identical cases have been documented throughout England and the rest of the world. Animal mutilations are extremely brutal yet very mysterious crimes which demonstrate a unique surgical precision when removing the limbs and organs of cows, sheep and various other kinds of animals (both domestic and wild). Typically, all the blood is drained from the animal with absolutely no spillage on the ground or the carcass itself, and organs are removed through tiny holes made on the body. These remarkably intricate procedures always have a "laser-like" accuracy and show a level of great sophistication – top medical professionals would struggle to carry out similar procedures. In relation to this subject, there are many satanic cults which perform ritualistic sacrifices of animals. However, these "amateur" satanic killings are often distinct from those which demonstrate a "laser-like" precision.

The Animal Pathology Field Unit

When talking to BBC News in June 2010, Mike Freebury of the Animal Pathology Field Unit (the APFU) in England said: "If you've seen some of the bodies that I've seen, it's just absolutely incredible. The flesh appears to have been cauterised, indicating some sort of thermic lance or micro-sonic wand has been used. We're talking incredible technology. There is never any blood. We were never able to catch the perpetrators in the act, but we have seen some very strange craft of unknown origin. We have them on film. We've managed to get frame-by-frame analysis of them done. It appears that these things were appearing literally within a second and then gone."[cxcii] Due to the bizarre nature of these crimes, the police often advise animal owners not to go public as media reports often get caught up in wild accusations and contradictions (which cause further distress for the owners of the animal). In England, the authorities (consisting of the local police, the Royal Society for the Prevention of Cruelty to Animals and the Animal Pathology Field Unit) investigate the crime scene with the aim of finding traces of the perpetrators (looking for footprints, signs of a break-in, vehicle tracks, causes of death and blood or entrails). The APFU recognises that in some of the mutilation attacks on hill farms around the UK, there are no possible routes for access in conventional vehicles and, in some instances: "The only way to access the particular field in question would be by air".cxciii A lack of evidence has prevented the police from drawing any credible conclusions and, through speculation, they quickly point the finger at local satanic cults. The crimes often appear isolated and it is difficult to associate them with any known local satanic cults or ritual dates. Even so, holding a local cult responsible would leave many unanswered questions with regards to the methods, technology and skills involved. The predators are clearly ruthless, subjecting the animals to extreme cruelty and leaving panic and fear amongst farmers and animal owners. These bizarre animal mutilations are a global phenomenon and happen frequently all over the world.

Case Study: Animal Mutilation in Scotland

In July 2008, a typically bizarre case was documented by the APFU in Scotland. A farmer had reported the discovery of a sheep's carcass, clean of blood, guts and organs. A precise parting through the spine had cut the sheep in half, leaving just the head end of the sheep with its lungs in place – the tail end was never found. The farmer stated that the mutilated sheep was found in a different field to the rest of its flock and the two fields were parted by a fence with no gate. It is a mystery as to how the animal was moved (either before or after it was killed) and why the surrounding area and the sheep's carcass were clean of blood – as usual, there was absolutely no spillage.

Summary

Due to the frequency and nature of these events, one could speculate that these killings were blood sacrifices, organ harvesting or performed simply for testing and analysis. Further to my initial research, I discovered that, from January 2012 onwards, there were many sheep, horse and pony mutilations (which saw the removal of eyes, tongues and genitals) recorded throughout England. It isn't only land animals, but a large number of seals, porpoises and dolphins have also been discovered after being mutilated in typically bizarre ways. Whilst these crimes are still occurring frequently throughout the UK, the APFU is no longer conducting any investigations and, at its request, I will not be using any of their photographs in this work.

Case Study: Device Implants

A surgeon named Dr. Roger Leir has become a trustworthy source of facts surrounding the controversial accounts of UFO abductions, implants and devices. Some years ago, Dr. Leir tended to a patient who was complaining of a tiny object lodged in his hand, beneath the skin. After x-rays revealed a small unidentified object, Dr. Leir decided to operate in order to remove the object, which turned out to be a small metallic implant. What immediately grabbed the attention of Dr. Leir was the surrounding tissue of the implant – it didn't show any signs of rejection or inflammation (which is unseen in the medical community). Research and analysis revealed that within the implant (which was made of rare elements) were carbon nanotubes (a new technology that scientists have only just begun working with). What is also remarkable is that Dr. Leir found that the implant was actually a nanotechnological device transmitting a radio frequency – it was some kind of advanced transmission device relaying information to an unknown receiver.

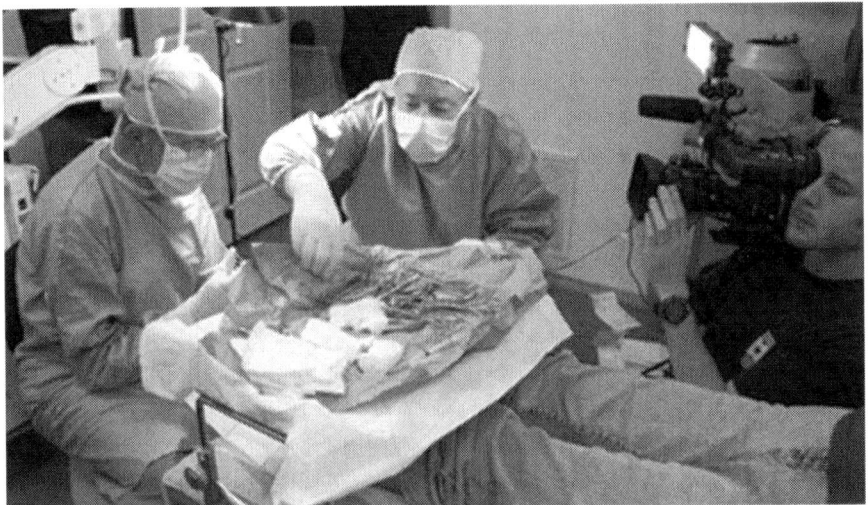

Image 23.1 Dr. Leir removing a device implant from a patient's foot (courtesy of www.alienscalpel.com).

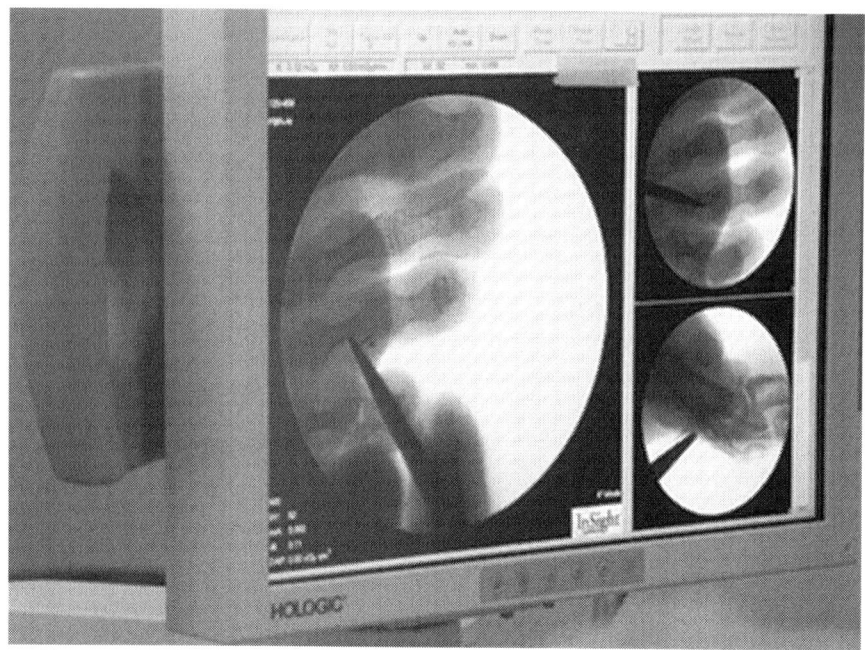

Image 23.2 An x-ray of the device implanted in the patient's foot
(courtesy of www.alienscalpel.com).

Dr. Leir has since gone on to perform over 10 more of these operations to remove similar devices from victims. Once removed, the devices undergo scrutiny by some of the most prestigious laboratories in the world. In one particular instance, the device was broken into several pieces upon being removed from the victim's hand before being placed into a vial of the victim's blood. Amazingly, the fragmented device reassembled itself, demonstrating a level of technology beyond anything the public has access to. When questioned on what he thought the implant might do, Dr. Leir said that although the function was unclear, it could be a genetic device: "... to change a person's DNA." It is worthy of mention that victims are often traumatised and wish to keep their identities private to avoid any media attention or accusations. Throughout this past century, there have also been many cases of abductions, including horrific cases of women being taken on board UFOs and artificially inseminated by the entities before being returned home. Months later, they are re-abducted to have their foetus harvested. Most competent researchers of this subject now recognise that these encounters are not "extra-terrestrial", but instead supernatural and demonic – clearly, these mysterious entities are malevolent and ruthless.

Satanism and Science Non-Fiction

There is a definite link between occult practices and the supernatural UFO phenomenon. Of course, this is the fusion of unconventional subjects – a strange blend of Satanism and science fiction (or non-fiction as the case may be). However, there is very real connection and, for those who are involved in the occult, such practices appear to be effective. Former Satanist Bill Schnoebelen stated: "There is a disturbing synchronicity between the rise of the modern UFO era and the convergence of spiritual forces which include the Theosophical Society, spiritualism (the re-emergence of the "New Age" belief system which is rooted in mystery Babylon), along with Aleister Crowley's influence on Masonry and witchcraft and Lovecraft's popularising the concept of star gods. This synergy between the occult and UFOs is growing." Close encounters with the entities are of a severely traumatic nature. Whether it is abductions, implants, testing, impregnation, the harvesting of organs or the killing of animals and humans, encounters with these supernatural entities have very negative impacts on people's lives and leave them emotionally, spiritually and psychologically traumatised. Similar to spiritual mediums, "galactic channellers" are in communication with the entities who deceptively claim to be from Sirius B and other giant star systems. With the aim of gaining power, guidance and divine knowledge, ceremonial magicians and Satanists perform rituals to open portals or windows to other dimensions and hold masses (holy ceremonies) to these entities that they refer to as "star gods". The Bible is clear when saying that no person should have involvement with the occult due to the dangers and deceptive nature of these demonic entities. Some of the naive ufologists and New Agers may speculate that a distinction can be made between bad and good entities. However, only the word of God can be trusted.

The Cosmic Christ

Addressing the United Nations in the 1980s, the Jesuit-favoured American president Ronald Reagan made a bewildering statement with regards to an alien threat: "Perhaps we need some outside, universal threat to make us recognise this common bond. I occasionally think how quickly our differences worldwide would vanish if we were facing an alien threat from outside this world." As more people begin to question the conventional theories on the origins of life and eventually realise that an advanced civilisation once ruled the Earth (as was discussed in the earlier chapters of this work), the UFO and extra-terrestrial phenomenon *could* be used as an explanation. The architects of the New World Order could be planning a cosmic deception. What kind of event would be required for us to surrender our few remaining liberties and accept a false saviour? The Jesuit priest José Funes is the current director of the Vatican Observatory and the pope's chief astronomer. Funes speculated that alien life could be: "… free from original sin" and that we should "… consider alien life as an extra-terrestrial brother."cxciv Vatican Astronomer Guy Consolmagno said he would be happy to baptise an alien. The acceptance of alien life appears to be becoming orthodoxy for the Roman Catholic institution, leaving little room for contrary beliefs. In light of all the statements coming from the Vatican, prophetic researcher and author Tom Horn has questioned whether the Vatican will make a claim that the virgin birth of Jesus was due to Mary being abducted and impregnated by aliens, thus making Him a "star-child" or human-hybrid. Approaching this subject from a critical perspective, there are a number of issues in hand:

- Why are the most well-funded Roman Catholic astronomers professing a belief in extra-terrestrial life and associating it with the widespread demonic UFO phenomena?
- From brief sightings to close encounters, why has there always been so much secrecy and ignorance surrounding these phenomena?
- Hollywood and the media has fed society with endless images of alien encounters and supermen. Today, many people profess a belief in aliens – have we been conditioned and subconsciously prepared for alien intervention?

Barbara Marciniak is an internationally acclaimed "trance channel" (intergalactic channeller) and a best-selling author. For over 20 years she has been channelling messages from entities who claim they are from the Pleiades (an open star cluster located in the constellation of Taurus) and states: "The Pleiadians are here to assist humanity with the process of spiritual transformation." She often talks of a coming "change in frequency", an "awakening" and a "shift in consciousness", and advises people of the steps that humanity must take to reach enlightenment.

Riddled with Luciferian philosophy, these New Age belief systems are full of pseudo-intellectual drivel which stems from the demonic realm – without realising, many people are led into false belief systems which are contrived by demonic entities. The common denominator between the pseudo-intellectual New Age movement and atheism is that both groups of people have the potential to be deceived by the coming "alien" intervention.

As Above, So Below

Messages that are channelled from these entities often speak of enlightenment and spiritual evolution. What is more intriguing is that the first religious figure they mention is Jesus Christ before they proceed to twist Biblical theology. Why is it that these supposed "extra-terrestrial" entities from other planets will always take time to reinterpret the Bible? Why do they try to convince people that they can obtain a divine status like Jesus? Why are their messages so similar to Freemasonic philosophy? It is the alluring language of the serpent which plays upon man's ego in an attempt to convince him that he "shall be as gods". Jesus has warned us: "Watch out that no one deceives you. For many will come in my name, claiming 'I am the Messiah' and will deceive many" (Matthew 24:4). It was foretold many centuries ago that a mass deception would occur: "For false Christs and Prophets will arise and show signs and wonders, to deceive the very elect, if it were possible" (Mark 13:22). The signs and wonders of UFOs are certainly occurring today and increasing in frequency. Satan has been described as the prince of the power of the air, an angel of light and the star that fell from the sky. Jesus said he was seen to: "... fall like lightning from heaven." Society is being prepared for a mass deception on a scale larger than 9/11. The nations of the Earth are going to be subjected to a sophisticated alien intervention, causing the secular world to reassess their worldview. Perhaps a technologically simulated "second coming" will be staged and a "cosmic Christ" will be presented, in order to cause the religious world to reassess their own doctrines. Will a cosmic Christ figure take to the global political stage as a religious leader of the New World Order? Just how close is the integration between the extra-dimensional entities and the "Illuminati" shadow government?

"Take no part in the unfruitful works of darkness, but instead expose them." (Ephesians 5:11).

24. The Hybrid Age

We are living in the Post-Information Age, an era in which scientists have begun blurring the distinction between humans and animals (and between man and machine). This is an area of science which is highly controversial, but serves as a reminder that ethics should regulate the secular world. So what is a hybrid? Daniel Engber, for *Slate.com*, states: "The word HYBRID, in the scientific sense, describes an organism that carries DNA from different species in each of its cells. Human-animal combos of this kind have indeed been created by several different labs — though only at the very early stages of development."[cxcv]

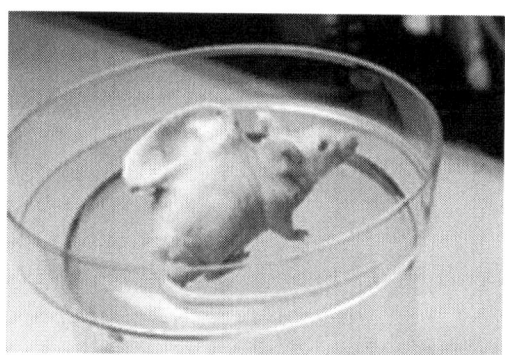

Image 24.1 The Vacanti mouse.

Genetic engineers are creating bizarre hybrid life forms, such as the spider-goat (a web-spinning goat that produces silk from its udders), glow-in-the-dark cats, enviropigs ("environmentally friendly" pigs), fast-growing salmon and mice which are partially human. This act of playing God is by no means an entirely modern fascination.

> "What has been done will be done again; there is nothing new under the sun." (Ecclesiastes 1:9).

Transgenics: The Post-Human Era

Transhumanism is the modern international movement which aims to utilise and streamline the evolutionary process with the use of technology. The ambition is to redesign humans and enhance intellectual, physical and psychological capacities in order to assist the transition to becoming a superhuman (and eventually reach immortality). Juan Enriquez, chairman and CEO of Biotechonomy, claims that we are: "... on the verge of becoming a new unique species, Homo Evolutis... there are opportunities to go beyond basic fixes and perform more elaborate enhancements." Essentially, from the evolutionary perspective, the next phase in development is to redesign the biological operating system (thus the freemasonic ambition of "rebuilding the temple" and the Kabbalist's quest for immortality is coming to fruition).

Elongated Skulls: Deliberate Cranial Deformation

Before stepping further into the realm of the bizarre, some common misconceptions that surround this subject must be confronted. From the days of antiquity, traditions such as head boarding were employed by ancient cultures to cause a deliberate cranial elongation. Fastened by cloth or rope, infants would have wooden sticks or boards strapped to their heads. As the child aged, their skull would grow in an elongated or flattened form. The device would be removed after several months (or years) and the skull would continue to grow in an elongated shape until the child reached adulthood. It has not been ascertained as to why various tribes and civilisations practised such techniques, but one could assume it was an elitist practice (to separate from the lower classes) or an attempt to increase intellect and psychic ability. Whilst these skulls are rarely displayed in museums and exhibits, the practice of deliberate cranial deformation has been present throughout the globe (even on remote islands), but it is unclear as to why this practice is so widespread. Upon first glimpse, somebody who was unfamiliar with the mysterious elongated skulls might be both fascinated and shocked by their appearance (before learning of the conventional techniques used to cause the elongation).

However, as David Childress and Brien Foerster demonstrate in their book, *The Enigma of Cranial Deformation*, some great mysteries do surround *some* of the elongated skulls. A clear distinction can be made between (at least) two types of elongated skull. As mentioned, the first type of skull is a homosapien (human) skull which has been exposed to a deliberate cranial shaping. The second type of elongated skull *appears* to be of a natural formation, which indicates that the shape is a genetic feature. As we shall see, these naturally elongated skulls show various physiological differences to that of an average human, indicating that they are a sub-species of homosapien or a different species entirely (foetuses and infant coneheads have also been discovered, which further indicate that the feature was hereditary). The DNA of these anomalous skulls needs to be analysed in order to determine if they are human. Carbon-14 dating and DNA testing is expensive and complex for these types of projects, but thanks to some independent researchers, at the time of writing this testing is underway and some of the results have just been announced.

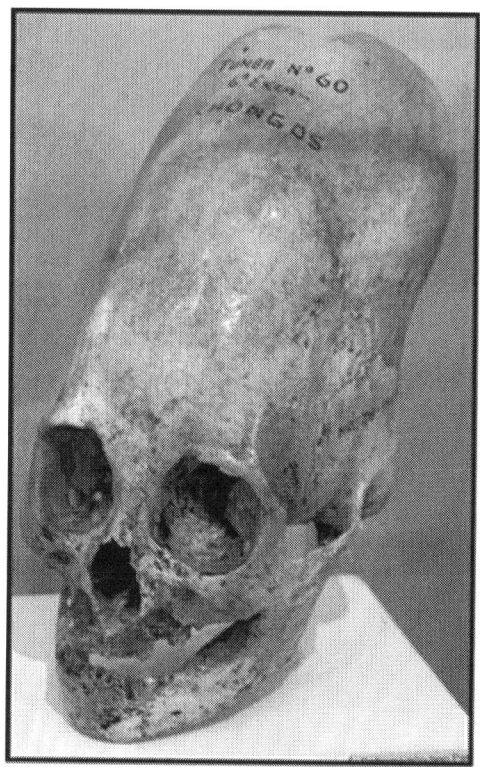

Image 24.2 An elongated skull
(courtesy of Hidden Inca Tours).

From America, Africa, Europe, Asia and Australia, various anomalous human remains have been uncovered all over the world, which include elongated skulls and giant human skeletons. The largest collection of the elongated skulls is on display at the Paracas History Museum in Peru. Brien Foerster is assistant director at the museum and his research reveals that some of these skulls have a cranial volume of 2.5 times the size of the average human. Foerster's field investigations demonstrate that they are commonly found in close proximity to ancient megalithic structures. Based on the analysis of both Childress and Foerster, "true" coneheads have the following features which set them apart from human skulls:

- The average human has a cranial capacity (volume inside the skull) of 1,400 cubic centimetres. Some of the conehead skulls have a cranial capacity of 2,800+ cubic centimetres – twice the size of a conventional human skull. Deliberate cranial shaping changes the shape of the skull and does not increase the volume.
- The "true" coneheads have two small holes in the back of the skull (holes that are not present on normal human skulls), which indicates that blood vessels were present, circulating blood to that area of the brain (in the same way, a human jaw has two small holes on either side for nerves and blood vessels to feed the tissue).
- A human skull is composed of three cranial plates; the frontal plate ends at the upper part of the forehead; the two parietal plates lie behind this and intersect the frontal plate, making a "T" shape.[cxcvi] The coneheads have only two plates with larger eye sockets and fewer teeth than an average human.
- They always maintain their natural convolutions, which indicate that no deliberate shaping techniques were used.

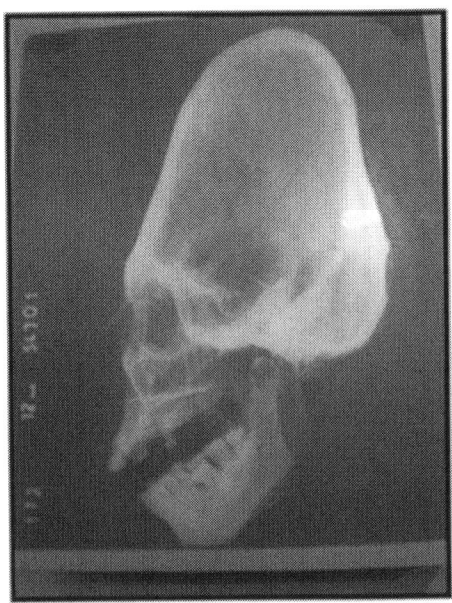

Image 24.3 An X-ray of an elongated skull (courtesy of Hidden Inca Tours).

These "star-gods" lived in tribes together, but who (or what) are they? It sounds like the concoction of a science-fiction writer, but based on the aforementioned physiological differences, these skulls *appear* to belong to a sub-species of human – the humanoid coneheads look like the outcome of genetic modification or the offspring of humans reproducing with non-human entities.

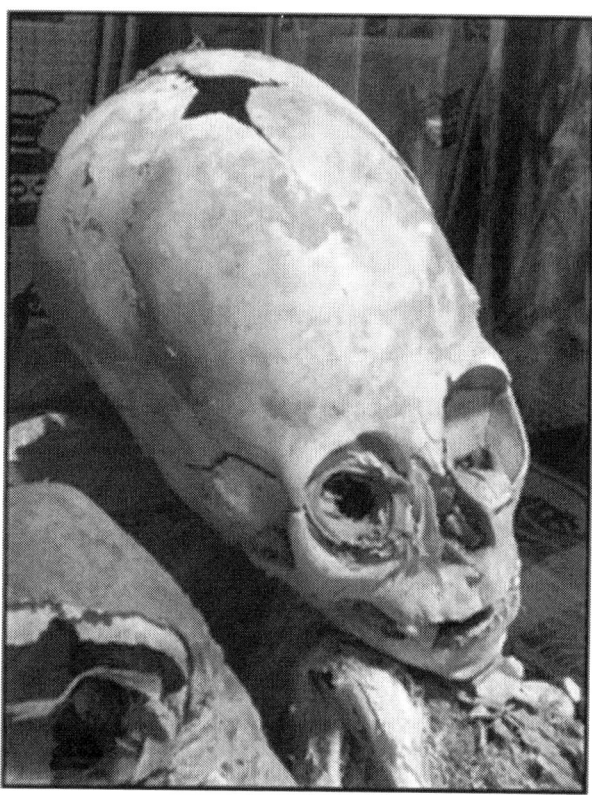

Image 24.4 An infant conehead
(courtesy of Hidden Inca Tours).

Elongated Skull Summary

The genetic trait of the elongated cranium *seems* to have become extinct. The practice of human head binding (which is clearly an attempt to imitate these true "coneheads") has gradually died out. As stated earlier in this work, many isolated tribes and civilisations all over the globe have common characteristics:

- Ancient mythology:
    - Stories of "divine beings" descending from the skies to teach man.
    - Stories of giants, para-humans and animal and human-hybrids.
    - Stories of mass floods that almost wiped out mankind.

- Extremely complex architecture and monuments (which demonstrate the use of ancient high technology).

- Similar practices (such as head-binding, mummification of dead bodies, rituals and human and animal sacrifices).

- The divine right of kings.

Image 24.5 A comparison of an elongated skull from South America (from the Pre-Inca or Incan period) to that of Egypt in Africa.

In the previous chapter it was concluded that although UFOs do manifest to a degree of physicality, they are non-physical in nature. After extensive research for this project, I do not believe that there is advanced life on other planets. However, "alien" life has evidently walked the Earth and intermingled with the human race. So what are these entities, if not visitors from other planets?

The Origins of "As Above, so Below"

Whilst a certain type of divine messenger, known as the "b'nai ha elohim" (or the divine sons of God) in the Bible are considered to be spiritual beings, they can engage in physical activity such as eating and wrestling. Whilst the spiritual realm itself is intangible, it can manifest to a degree of physicality – just as UFOs do. The most profound account of the "As above, so below" concept is recorded in the Bible, in Genesis 6 – this is where the concept originates. It states that the sons of God joined with the "daughters of men" to produce an offspring (the genetic information of humans and that of the divine sons of God were merged to produce a race of human-hybrids).

"When human beings began to increase in number on the earth and daughters were born to them, the sons of God [b'nai ha elohim] saw that the daughters of men were beautiful, and they married any of them they chose." (Genesis 6:1-2).

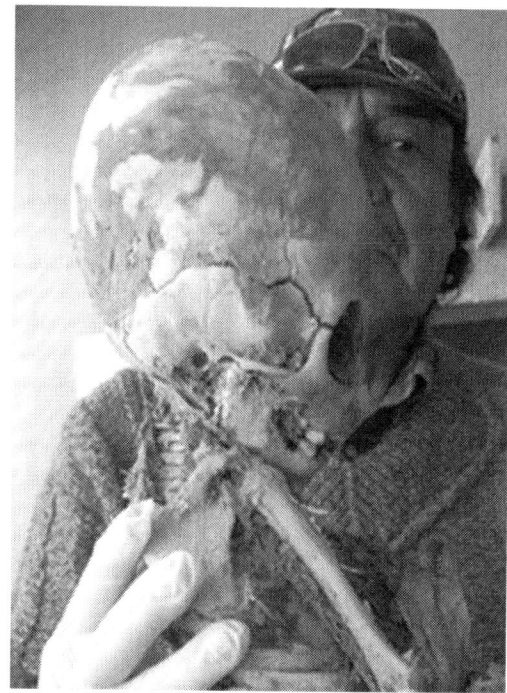

Image 24.6 Infant conehead.

Chuck Missler states: "These bizarre events are also echoed in the legends and myths of every ancient culture upon the Earth."cxcvii The horrific fusion of the heavenly realm with the earthly realm was a corruption of the image of God and led to a judgment like no other. These early days of depravity, wickedness and peril suffered the ultimate judgment and the reason for the worldwide flood is now clear – it was due to the widespread corruption of human and animal flesh.

God allowed for Noah and his family to survive in a boat before sending a flood to wipe out the hybrids. When the waters receded, Noah and his family emerged from the earthly cleansing, ready to repopulate and rebuild civilisation in the Middle East.

There were giants in the Earth in those days; and also after that, when the sons of God came in unto the daughters of men, and they bare children to them, the same became mighty men which were of old, men of renown. (Genesis 6:4).

And God saw that the wickedness of man was great in the Earth. And it grieved him at his heart (Genesis 6:5).

As recorded in Genesis 3:15, after Satan led Adam and Eve's descent into sin, God responded: "I will put enmity between you [Satan] and the woman, and between your seed [genetic information] and her seed; He shall bruise you on the head, and you shall bruise him on the heel." The first ever prophecy given by God was His plan for the redemption of mankind – it was the promise of a Messiah who would be born of a virgin. Men are always regarded as having the "seed" (sperm) and thus, by talking of the woman's "seed", God implied that the Messiah would be born of a virgin and "born of the spirit". This promise from God marked the beginning of a battle waged by Satan and the demonic realm to destroy the "seed", to corrupt the image of God and prevent the arrival of mankind's saviour. The supernatural birth of a coming Messiah was common knowledge in pre-diluvian culture and a clear indication of why "mother and child" cults were widespread in antiquity. In an attempt to prevent the birth of our Messiah, Satan and his "fallen ones" assisted in the corruption of human genetics in order to defile the image of God. Originally, as an angel of God, Satan had a divinely appointed position within the heavenly realm – he was one of the most highly exalted beings. Upon his rebellion, he deceived a vast number of angels into descending with him – perhaps he promised them that they would be worshipped as gods. Upon Adam and Eve rejecting God's authority in the Garden of Eden, Satan became the god of this world. Satan's kingdom is a complex hierarchy of demons and fallen angels which has been in close connection with many cultures all over the world.

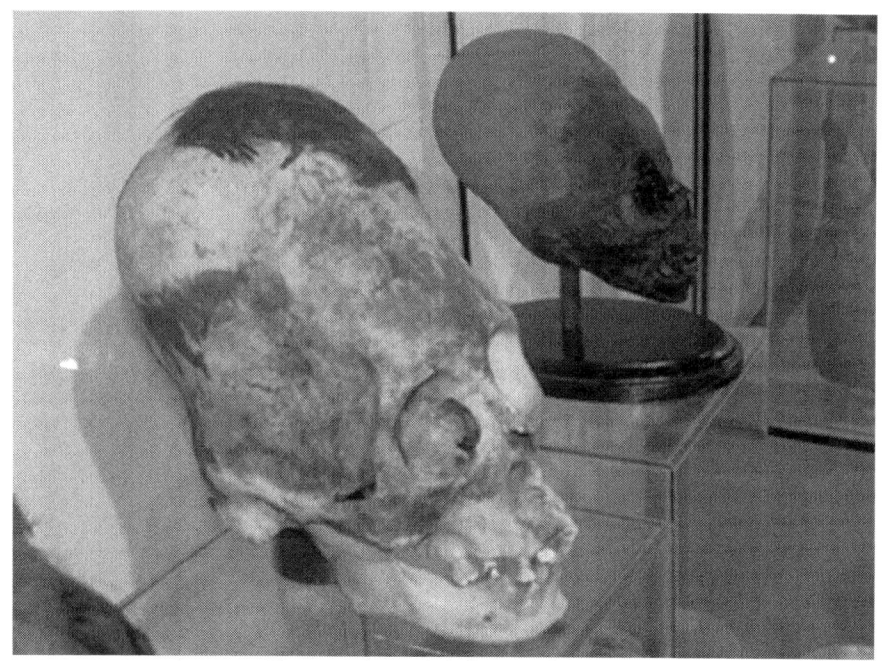
Image 24.7 Adult conehead.

25. Closing Statements

The ancient philosophy "As above, so below" is profound to say the least. The merging of heaven and Earth is the ultimate connection for which man has strived to accomplish since the rebirth of civilisation. A vast quantity of ancient mythology from all over the world is a retelling and distortion of the events recorded in Genesis. As a demonstration of how the spiritual realm can be manifested to a degree of physicality, the elongated skulls reveal how close the link between man and "god" became: "As above, so below". This is an indication as to why the pharaohs, kings and emperors on many continents, in many eras, have claimed themselves to be divine or the "son of god". "As above, so below" is a concept that has been represented in esoteric art, architecture and symbology throughout countless generations. The Bible tells us that it was not intended for man to live in a linear reality restrained by time. Eternal life is granted through Jesus alone, yet regardless of this, man is attempting to supplant God, reach salvation and become a god himself. Potentially, we are approaching the "post-human" era – the transhumanists have foolishly begun to toy with the source code for life (DNA). However, the problem is that the Master Programmer (God) has exclusive rights over all of creation. As the only true Son of God, in Matthew 24:37, Jesus warns that the events which occurred before the floods would reoccur just before He returns: "As it was in the days of Noah, so it will be at the coming of the Son of Man." As we witness a blurring of the distinction between man, animal and machine we are, once again, entering into the "days of Noah". As foretold by Paul in Thessalonians, a final tyrannical leader will deceive many into worshipping him:

> "Let no man deceive you by any means. That man of sin be
> revealed, the son of perdition who opposes and exalts himself
> above all that is called God, or that is worshipped; so that he as
> God sits in the Temple of God, shewing himself that he is God."

Is Paul's reference to the temple of God literal, referring to the Third Temple which will be built in Jerusalem, or is it symbolic of man's body? Either way, don't be deceived into accepting Babylon's mark of the beast.

> "And no one could buy or sell anything without that mark,
> which was either the name of the beast or the number
> representing his name." (Revelation 13:17).

The ultimate victory is fast approaching and the kingdom of the Messiah is soon to come. As mankind was forewarned many centuries ago by the prophets of Israel, a giant phoenix has swept down upon humanity and is carrying us back to Babylon. After briefly reviewing scientific evidence, various historical events, geopolitics, ancient civilisations, secret societies and the supernatural, we have aligned ourselves with the Bible to gain an understanding of life's origins, meaning, morality and destiny. It's time to realise your eternal destiny. According to the word of God, this purpose-built, physical environment was an expression of His glory, the opportunity to create children and to establish a relationship with us.[cxcviii] As the apex of creation, mankind is in rebellion against the Creator, but we have the chance to mature and overcome evil before we are delivered from this physical realm. There is a new, eternal creation, governed by alternative laws of nature, outside this space-time where there is no possibility for the existence of evil, death and decay. The Bible is a record of God's attempt to bring mankind back into fellowship with Him – and for this, He made the ultimate sacrifice. We are not worthy of admission to the kingdom because we abide by a self-determined standard of morality. The Bible reveals Yehushua (Jesus) as the one and true Messiah – the Author of Life not only lived here on Earth and walked amongst us, He served us and then died at the hands of His enemies, so that we may receive His gift of eternal life. No religion demonstrates this level of intimacy, love, or sacrifice. Jesus aligns with moral perfection and this qualifies Him to atone for the sins of mankind. At the cost of His conviction, through His crucifixion, the problem of sin has been dealt with – this is the redemption for mankind.

"Babylon the great is fallen, is fallen...
Come out of her my people." (Revelation 18).

BABYLON
RESURRECTED

[i] Louise Anthony, quoted in *Moral Argument* by William Lane Craig. Article available at: http://www.reasonablefaith.org/moral-argument (accessed June 23, 2013).

[ii] Professor Antony Flew, *Theology and Falsification* (1950).

[iii] David Flynn, *Temple at the Centre of Time* (Anomalos Publishing, 2008), p. 10.

[iv] Chuck Missler, *The Myths of Science* (Koinonia House, recorded lecture).

[v] Stephen Hawking, *A Brief History of Time: From the Big Bang to Black Holes* (New York: Bantam, 1988), p. 127.

[vi] Dr. Ravi Zacharias, *Apologetics* (RZIM, recorded lecture).

[vii] Daniel Beresniak, *Symbols of Masonry* (Assouline Publishing, 2000).

[viii] Chris Everard, *The Illuminati*, motion picture documentary (Enigma Productions).

[ix] *The Revelation of the Pyramid*, motion picture documentary (Optimum Home Entertainment, 2010).

[x] David Flynn, *Temple at the Centre of Time* (Anomalos Publishing, 2008), p. 1.

[xi] Richard Cassaro, *Suppressed By Scholars*. Available at: http://www.richardcassaro.com/suppressed-by-scholars-twin-ancient-cultures-on-opposite-sides-of-the-pacific (accessed October 10, 2014).

[xii] Christopher Dunn, *The Giza Power Plant* (Bear & Company, 1998), p. 59.

[xiii] Ibid, p. 51.

[xiv] Ibid, p. 56.

[xv] *The Revelation of the Pyramid*, motion picture documentary (Optimum Home Entertainment, 2010).

[xvi] Estimate provided by Merle Booker, director of the Indiana Limestone Institute of America, to Richard Noone, author of *5/5/2000 Ice: The Ultimate Disaster*.

[xvii] Andrew Collins, Baalbek - Lebanon's Sacred Fortress. Available at: http://www.andrewcollins.com/page/articles/baalbek.htm (accessed June 12, 2013).

[xviii] Michel Alouf, *History of Baalbek* (Book Tree, 1999).

[xix] Astronomy, The Sun. Available at: http://www.astronomy.com/en/News-Observing/Astronomy%20Kids/2008/03/The%20Sun.aspx (accessed June 23, 2013).

xx Answers in Genesis, Is the Sun Shrinking? Available at: http://www.answersingenesis.org/articles/cm/v11/n2/sun (accessed June 23, 2013).

xxi Astronomy, The Sun. Available at: http://www.astronomy.com/en/News-Observing/Astronomy%20Kids/2008/03/The%20Sun.aspx (accessed June 23, 2013).

xxii Wikipedia, Ice Age. Available at: http://en.wikipedia.org/wiki/Ice_age#Major_ice_ages (accessed June 26, 2012).

xxiii Wikipedia, Last Glacial Period. Available at: http://en.wikipedia.org/wiki/Last_glacial_period (accessed June 26, 2012).

xxiv Wikipedia, Last Glacial Maximum. Available at: http://en.wikipedia.org/wiki/Last_Glacial_Maximum (accessed June 26, 2012).

xxv S.A. Austin et al., *Catastrophic Plate Tectonics: a Global Flood Model of Earth History* (Proceedings of the Third International Conference on Creationism, 1994), p. 609–621.

xxvi Graham Hancock Library, The Study of Submerged Structures off Yonaguni Island of Japan: The Preliminary Results from Recent Expedition. Available at: http://www.grahamhancock.com/library/uw/c27.php?p=3 (accessed June 26, 2012).

xxvii Joshua Mark, Sumer. Available at: http://www.ancient.eu/sumer/ (accessed October 10, 2014).

xxviii Origin, meaning, morality and destiny: four questions Dr. Ravi Zacharias has discussed throughout his career as a Christian philosopher.

xxix Embassy of the United States in Baghdad, Iraq Cultural Heritage Project. Available at: http://iraq.usembassy.gov/projects.html (accessed July 1, 2012).

xxx John Hooper, Pope Calls for a New World Order (The Guardian, 2004). Available at: http://www.guardian.co.uk/world/2004/jan/02/catholicism.religion (accessed August 12, 2012).

xxxi George W. Blount, Peace Through World Government (Moore Publishing Company, 1974).

xxxii Jeffrey Winters, *Oligarchy* (Cambridge University Press, 2011).

xxxiii Webster G. Tarpley, How the Venetian System Was Transplanted Into England (New Federalist, 1996). Available at: http://tarpley.net/online-books/against-oligarchy/how-the-venetian-system-was-transplanted-into-england/

xxxiv Benjamin Disraeli, *Coningsby* (1844).

xxxv Wikipedia, Most royal candidate theory. Available at: http://en.wikipedia.org/wiki/Most_royal_candidate_theory (accessed August 1, 2013).

xxxvi Huberman and Sweezy, Introduction to Socialism (Monthly Review Press). Quote available at Marx Mail: http://www.marxmail.org/faq/socialism_and_communism.htm (accessed February 20, 2013).

xxxvii Dwight L. Kinman, *The World's Last Dictator* (Whitaker House, 1996), p. 29.

xxxviii Wikipedia, Manhattan Project. Available at: http://en.wikipedia.org/wiki/Manhattan_Project (accessed August 12, 2012). This estimation was taken from the Federal Reserve Bank of Minneapolis, Consumer Price Index (Estimate) 1800–2012.

xxxix Wikipedia, Manhattan Project. Available at: http://en.wikipedia.org/wiki/Manhattan_Project (accessed December 1, 2012). This estimation was taken from a 1945 Life magazine article.

xl William Blum, United States bombings of other countries. Available at: http://williamblum.org/chapters/rogue-state/united-states-bombings-of-other-countries (accessed May, 2013).

xli The Guardian, How Bush's grandfather helped Hitler's rise to power. Available at: http://www.guardian.co.uk/world/2004/sep/25/usa.secondworldwar (accessed September 22, 2012).

xlii Wikipedia, Business Plot. Available at: http://en.wikipedia.org/wiki/Business_Plot (accessed September 22, 2012).

xliii Antony C. Sutton, *America's Secret Establishment* (Liberty House, 1986).

xliv George H. Bush, *Address Before a Joint Session of the Congress on the State of the Union*, January 29, 1991. Transcript available at: http://bushlibrary.tamu.edu/research/public_papers.php?id=2656&year=1991&month=01 J (accessed December 9, 2012).

xlv Tom Horn, *Apollyon Rising 2012* (Defender, 2009), p. 3.

xlvi Bill Hughes, The Secret Terrorists (Truth Triumphant Ministries, 2002).

xlvii The Rules. Available at: http://www.therules.org/en (accessed July 10, 2013).

xlviii David Wood, Iraq reconstruction cost U.S. $60 billion (Huffington Post, 2013). Available at: http://www.huffingtonpost.com/2013/03/06/iraq-reconstruction_n_2819899.html (accessed June 23, 2013).

xlix Charles Forrester, BAE Systems announces preliminary 2012 financial results amid sequestration uncertainty (IHS Jane's 360, 2013). Available at: http://www.janes.com/article/10967/bae-systems-announces-preliminary-2012-financial-results-amid-sequestration-uncertainty (accessed June 23, 2013).

[l] Seth Doane, Battling obesity in America (CBS News, 2010). Available at: http://www.cbsnews.com/2100-18563_162-6069163.html (accessed April 6, 2012).

[li] Indian Food Industry. Available at: http://www.indianfoodindustry.net/ (accessed April 6, 2012).

[lii] US National Debt Clock: http://www.usdebtclock.org/ (accessed December 4, 2012).

[liii] Positive Money, How Banks Create Money. Available at: http://www.positivemoney.org/how-money-works/how-banks-create-money/ (accessed October 10, 2014).

[liv] Ibid.

[lv] Seumas Milne, *Private banks have failed – we need a public solution* (The Guardian, 2012). Available at: http://www.theguardian.com/commentisfree/2012/jul/03/private-banks-failed-barclays-scandal

[lvi] Henry Makow, *Illuminati: The Cult that Hijacked the World* (BookSurge Publishing, 2008), p. 26.

[lvii] Richard C. Cook, US housing market boom and crash engineered by the Government (Market Oracle, 2008). Available at: http://www.marketoracle.co.uk/Article6936.html (May 10, 2013).

[lviii] *China* leaves behind the US as world's leading trade partner (Russia Today, 2012). Available at: http://rt.com/usa/news/china-us-trade-partner-169/ (article accessed December 5, 2012).

[lix] Charlie Cooper, *Five ways the state could discourage people on benefits from having large numbers* of children (The Independent, 2013). Available at: http://www.independent.co.uk/news/uk/politics/five-ways-the-state-could-discourage-people-on-benefits-from-having-large-numbers-of-children-8562625.html (accessed June 23, 2013).

[lx] Bureau of Labour Statistics, Employment Situation Summary (2013). Available at: http://www.bls.gov/news.release/empsit.nr0.htm (accessed June 23, 2013).

[lxi] Dark Government, Afghanistan producing more heroin than ever. Available at: http://www.darkgovernment.com/news/afghanistan-producing-more-heroin-than-ever/ (accessed June 26, 2012).

[lxii] Larouche Pac, *Afghan 2013 poppy production headed for record; opium boom poses new threat* to the region (2013). Available at: http://larouchepac.com/node/26250 (accessed June 23, 2013).

[lxiii] *Afghan opium* fuels global chaos (BBC News, 2009). Available at: http://news.bbc.co.uk/1/hi/8319249.stm (accessed August 24, 2012).

lxiv David Flynn, *Temple at the Center of Time* (Anomalos Publishing, 2008), p. 65.

lxv Dr. John Coleman, *The Committee of 300* (Global Insights, 2000).

lxvi Carl A Trocki, *Opium, Empire and the Global Economy* (Routledge, 1999).

lxvii Romesh Dutt, *The Economic History of India under early British Rule* (originally printed in 1906, republished by Ulan Press, 2012).

lxviii Editors of the Executive Intelligence Review, *Dope Inc: Britain's Opium War Against the World* (Progressive Press; Fourth Edition, 2010), p. 67.

lxix William P. Litynski, *An Illustrated History of the China Trade & the Opium Wars.* Available at: http://www.scribd.com/doc/31032550/The-China-Trade-and-The-Opium-Wars (accessed June 26, 2013).

lxx Kathy Marks, *City law firms investigated over drug cartel money laundering* (The Independent, 1998): http://www.independent.co.uk/news/city-law-firms-investigated-over-drug-cartel-money-laundering-1186746.html (accessed June 23, 2013).

lxxi Rob Davies, *HSBC Let Drug Gangs Launder Millions* (Daily Mail, 2012): http://www.dailymail.co.uk/news/article-2174785/HSBC-scandal-Britains-biggest-bank-let-drug-gangs-launder-millions--faces-640million-fine.html (accessed June 23, 2013).

lxxii Heather Stewart, *£13tn hoard hidden from taxman by global elite* (The Guardian, 2012). Available at: http://www.guardian.co.uk/business/2012/jul/21/global-elite-tax-offshore-economy (accessed June 23, 2013).

lxxiii Editors of the Executive Intelligence Review, *The Coming Fall of the House of Windsor* (The New Federalist newspaper, 1994).

lxxiv Roger Cohen, *Who Really Brought Down Milosevic?* (The New York Times, 2000). Available at: http://www.nytimes.com/library/magazine/home/20001126mag-serbia.html (accessed March 20, 2013).

lxxv *The Revolution Business*, motion picture documentary (Journey Man Pictures, 2011).

lxxvi *America's Syrian friends and Afghan foes are same people* (Russia Today, 2012). Available at: http://www.rt.com/news/america-friends-enemies-islamists-812/ (accessed July 11, 2012).

lxxvii General Wesley Clark, *Winning Modern Wars* (page 130) quoted on Global Research, *Secret 2001 Pentagon Plan to Attack Lebanon.* Available at: http://www.globalresearch.ca/secret-2001-pentagon-plan-to-attack-lebanon/2797 (accessed April 8, 2013).

lxxviii *Saving the world economy from Gaddafi* (Russia Today, 2011). Available at: http://rt.com/news/economy-oil-gold-libya/ (accessed December 20, 2012).

lxxix NATO, *Statement by the NATO spokesperson on Human Rights Watch report* (2012). Available at: http://www.nato.int/cps/en/natolive/news_87171.htm (accessed January 5, 2013).

lxxx Ralph McGehee, *Deadly Deceits: My 25 Years in the CIA* (Ocean Press, 1983), p. 192.

lxxxi *Depleted uranium used by US forces blamed for birth defects and cancer in Iraq* (Russia Today, 2013). Available at: http://rt.com/news/iraq-depleted-uranium-health-394/ (accessed August 12, 2013).

lxxxii Bureau of Educational and Cultural Affairs, *Iraq Cultural Heritage Initiative.* Available at: http://eca.state.gov/cultural-heritage-center/iraq-cultural-heritage-initiative (accessed February 16, 2013).

lxxxiii Niels H. Harrit et al, *Active Thermitic Material Discovered in Dust from the 9/11 World Trade Center Catastrophe* (The Open Chemical Physics Journal, 2009).

lxxxiv JAN UTZON quoted in an interview for Architects and Engineers for 9/11 Truth, 2010. Available at: http://www.ae911truth.org/en/news-section/41-articles/108-jan-utzon-a-compassionate-architect-who-cares-about-the-truth.html (accessed May 17, 2013).

lxxxv Medical Professionals for 9/11 Truth Petition. Available at: http://mp911truth.org/ (accessed June 6, 2012).

lxxxvi C. Thurston, *Can Physics Rewrite History?* (2006). Available at: http://911research.wtc7.net/materials/contrib/911_physics_v12b_w_cov.pdf (Accessed November 25, 2012).

lxxxvii Dr.Lynn Margulis, *9/11: Explosive Evidence – Experts Speak Out for Architects and Engineers for 9/11 Truth*, motion picture documentary (2011). Quote available at: http://www.ae911truth.org/en/news-section/41-articles/590-dr-lynn-margulis-1938-2011-a-beacon-of-light-for-911-truth.html (accessed June 20, 2013).

lxxxviii Fire Fighters for 9/11 Truth (2008). Available at: http://firefightersfor911truth.org/ (accessed June 19, 2012).

lxxxix George H Bush, *Address Before a Joint Session of the Congress on the Persian Gulf Crisis and the Federal Budget Deficit,* September 11, 1990. View the transcript: http://bushlibrary.tamu.edu/research/public_papers.php?id=2217&year=1990&month=9 (accessed December 8, 2012).

xc Dr.John Coleman, *The Committee of 300* (Fourth edition, Global Insights, 2000).

xci *The First Global Revolution: A Report by the Council of the Club of Rome* (The Club of Rome, 1991).

xcii David Rohde, *Ted Turner plans a $1 billion gift for UN agencies* (NYTimes, 1997). Available at: http://www.nytimes.com/1997/09/19/world/ted-turner-plans-a-1-billion-gift-for-un-agencies.html (accessed November 4, 2012).

xciii *Turner's depopulation plan*, (Life Site News, 2008). Available at: http://www.lifesitenews.com/news/archive//ldn/2008/apr/08040306 (accessed May 26, 2013).

xciv *Gina Rinehart calls for sterilisation of the poor* (Before its News, 2013). Available at: http://beforeitsnews.com/ (accessed June 3, 2013).

xcv Dwight L Kinman, *The World's Last Dictator* (Solid Rock Books, 1995), p. 81.

xcvi *International Technical Guidance on Sexuality Education* (UNESCO, 2009). Available at: http://unesdoc.unesco.org/images/0018/001832/183281e.pdf (accessed June 12, 2013).

xcvii Melanie Hall, *Jimmy Savile satanic abuse claims as unlikely as 'alien abduction', says leading barrister* (The Telegraph, 2013). Available at: http://www.telegraph.co.uk/news/uknews/crime/jimmy-savile/10167684/Jimmy-Savile-satanic-abuse-claims-as-unlikely-as-alien-abduction-says-leading-barrister.html

xcviii *The UNESCO Courier* (UNESCO, 1991). Available at: http://unesdoc.unesco.org/images/0009/000902/090256eo.pdf (accessed 21st November, 2014).

xcix Bertrand Russell, *The Impact of Science on Society* (1953), p. 49-50.

c Paul Simon, *Agenda 21: The Earth Summit Strategy to Save Our Planet* (Earthpress, 1993).

ci *Recommendations from the Vancouver Plan of Action* (United Nations Conference on Human Settlements, 1976). Available at: http://www.un-documents.net/vp-d.htm (accessed May 17, 2013).

cii*Billionaire club in bid to curb overpopulation* (The Sunday Times, 2009). Available at: http://www.thesundaytimes.co.uk/sto/news/world_news/article169829.ece (accessed November 25, 2012).

ciii *Bill Gates on energy: Innovating to zero* (Ted, 2010). Available at: http://www.ted.com/talks/bill_gates.html (accessed May 24, 2013).

civ Vashisht N et al, *Polio programme: let us declare victory and move on* (Department of Paediatrics, St Stephen's Hospital, Delhi) (PubMed, 2012). Available at: http://www.ncbi.nlm.nih.gov/pubmed/22591873 (accessed May 12, 2013).

cv William Engdahl, *Bill Gates wants vaccines to reduce population* quoting from his book *Seeds of Destruction: The Hidden Agenda of Genetic Manipulation* (Global Research, 2007), 79-84. Available at: http://www.conspiracyplanet.com/channel.cfm?channelid=8&contentid=6746&page =2 (accessed March 17, 2013).

cvi Mike Adams, *Bill Gates says vaccines can help reduce world population* (Natural News, 2012). Available at: http://www.naturalnews.com/029911_vaccines_Bill_Gates.html (accessed December 8, 2012).

cvii Ibid

cviii Dr.Russell Blaylock stated this during a video interview titled: "Chemical dumbing down".

cix *Social & Economic Injustice* (World Centric, 2004). Available at: www.worldcentric.org/conscious-living/social-and-%20economic-injustice (accessed September 17, 2012).

cx *Population Facts* (NYC Department of City Planning). Available at: http://www.nyc.gov/html/dcp/html/census/pop_facts.shtml (accessed January 27, 2013).

cxi *Over population is a myth* (Research Population Institute). Available at: http://overpopulationisamyth.com (accessed November 27, 2013).

cxii Ibid

cxiii Sean Poulter, *Enough to make you shudder!* (Daily Mail, 2013). Available at: http://www.dailymail.co.uk/news/article-2260490/UK-temperatures-plunge-minus-10-average-heating-elderly-soars-1-350.html (accessed February 24, 2013).

cxiv Dion Dassanayake, *20,000 pensioners died from the cold last winter* (Express, 2012) Available at: http://www.express.co.uk/news/uk/361382/20-000-pensioners-died-from-the-cold-last-winter (accessed June 27, 2013).

cxv *The Coming Fall of the House of Windsor* (The New Federalist, 1994). Slide-show presentation available at: http://members.tripod.com/~american_almanac/fallhous.htm (accessed May 26, 2013).

cxvi *League of Cambrai* (Encyclopaedia Britannica, 2008). Available at: http://www.britannica.com/EBchecked/topic/90599/League-of-Cambrai (accessed May 2, 2013).

cxvii *Venice & the League of Cambrai* (Centre for the Study of the Renaissance, 2008). Available at: http://www2.warwick.ac.uk/fac/arts/ren/news_and_events/callsforpapers/venice_and_the_league_of_cambrai_call_for_papers.pdf (accessed May 25, 2013).

cxviii Webster Tarpley, *How the Dead Souls of Venice Corrupted* Science (1994, ICLC Conference). Available at: http://tarpley.net/online-books/against-oligarchy/how-the-dead-souls-of-venice-corrupted-science/ (accessed June 8, 2013).

cxix *Jesuit Order* (World Scope Encyclopedia, 1955) quoted on Amazing Discoveries. Available at: http://amazingdiscoveries.org/R-Jesuits_history_political_power_Pope (accessed June 14, 2013).

cxx *The New York Times*, July 14, 1880.

cxxi Leo H Lehmann, *Behind the Dictators* (Agora Publishing Co., 1942), p. 26.

cxxii Malachi Martin, *The Jesuits* (Simon & Schuster, 1988), p. 27.

cxxiii The Jesuit Provinces. Available at: http://www.jesuit.org/aboutus?PAGE=DTN-20130625090119&SUBPAGE=DTN-20130520123642 (accessed November 9, 2013).

cxxiv Ibid

cxxv Image https://commons.wikimedia.org/wiki/File:House_of_the_Temple.JPG#/media/File:House_of_the_Temple.JPG

cxxvi John Daniel, *The Grand Design Exposed* (CHJ Publishing, 1999), p. 302.

cxxvii Helena Blavatsky, *The Secret Doctrine, the Synthesis of Science, Religion and Philosophy*, Volume II (The Theosophical Publishing Company, 1888), p. 200.

cxxviii *Albert Pike and Three World Wars*. Available at: http://www.threeworldwars.com/albert-pike2.htm (accessed June 12, 2013).

cxxix *The Arab-Israeli War of 1948* (The Office of the Historian). Available at: http://history.state.gov/milestones/1945-1952/ArabIsraeliWar (accessed June 22, 2013).

cxxx *Secret Societies* (Amazing Discoveries, 2010). Available at: http://amazingdiscoveries.org/S-deception-secret-societies-Jesuit-knights (accessed June 14, 2013).

cxxxi*Agreement between the Swiss Federal Council and the Bank for International Settlements to determine the Bank's legal status in Switzerland* (Bank of International Settlements, 1987). Available at: http://www.bis.org/about/headquart-en.pdf (accessed March 18, 2013).

cxxxii Albert Pike, *Morals and Dogma* (p.870) quoted on Amazing Discoveries. Available at: http://pdf.amazingdiscoveries.org/Study_Guides/TO/212-Hidden_Agendas.pdf (accessed June 9, 2013).

cxxxiii Order of Malta, *Frequently Asked Questions*. Available at: http://www.orderofmalta.int/faq/26466/faq/?lang=en#4 (accessed June 17, 2013).

cxxxiv Martin A Lee, *Their Will Be Done* (Mother Jones archives, 1983). Available at: http://www.motherjones.com/politics/1983/07/their-will-be-done (accessed July 20, 2013)

cxxxv Ibid

cxxxvi Ibid

cxxxvii Paul Farhi, *Hersh rebuked on 'crusaders'* (Washington Post, 2011) http://www.washingtonpost.com/wp-dyn/content/article/2011/01/20/AR2011012005783.html (accessed July 6, 2013).

cxxxviii Kabbalah, *Kabbalah, Science, Islam & Armageddon with Billy Phillips*, video lecture, 2012. Available at: http://www.youtube.com/watch?v=5QPY1e0mb1E

cxxxix Chris Everard, *The Illuminati 2: The Anti-Christ Conspiracy*, motion picture documentary (Enigma Productions).

cxl Hugh Ross, *The Creator and the Cosmos* (NavPress, 1993), p. 43.

cxli Michael Heiser, *The Nachash and His Seed*. Available at: http://www.thedivinecouncil.com/nachashnotes.pdf (accessed March 9, 2013).

cxlii Jason Lisle, *The Ultimate Proof of Creation* (Master Books, 2009), p. 42.

cxliii Brian Cox and Jeff Forshaw, *The Quantum Universe: Everything That Can Happen Does Happen* (Allen Lane, 2011), p. 2.

cxliv Werner Gitt, *In the Beginning Was Information* (Master Books, 2006).

cxlv David Abel and Jack Trevors, *Three Subsets of Sequence Complexity and their Relevance to Biopolymeric Information* (National Center for Biotechnology Information, 2005). Available at: http://www.ncbi.nlm.nih.gov/pmc/articles/PMC1208958/#B47 (accessed October 15, 2014).

cxlvi Robert Wiener, *Control and Communication in Animal and Machine* (MIT Press, 1961).

cxlvii Robert Hotz, *Future of Data: Encoded in DNA* (Wall Street Journal, 2012). Available at: http://online.wsj.com/article/SB10000872396390444233104577593291643488120.html (accessed June 3, 2013).

cxlviii Hubert P Yockey (National Center for Biotechnology Information, 2000). Available at: http://www.ncbi.nlm.nih.gov/pubmed/10642883 (accessed October 15, 2014).

cxlix Dr.Don Johnson, *Programming of Life* (Big Mac Publishers, 2010), p. 48.

cl Dr.David Abel, *The 'Cybernetic Cut': Progressing from Description to Prescription in Systems Theory* (The Open Cybernetics & Systemics Journal) Available at: http://benthamopen.com/tocsj/openaccess2.htm (accessed October 10, 2014).

cli Werner Gitt, *In the Beginning Was Information* (Master Books, 2006), p. 52.

clii http://www.worldscientific.com/doi/pdf/10.1142/9789814508728_0017

cliii Lee Spetner, *Not by Chance, Shattering the Modern Theory of Evolution* (Judaica Press, 1996).

cliv Harun Yahya, *The Collapse Of The Theory Of Evolution In 20 Questions*. Available at: http://harunyahya.com/en/books/964/The_Collapse_Of_The_Theory_Of_Evolution_In _20_Questions/chapter/2206 (accessed October 17, 2012).

clv Michael Behe, *Darwin's Black Box: The Biochemical Challenge to Evolution* (Simon & Schuster Ltd, 2006).

clvi Dr.Don Johnson, B*iocybernetics*. Available at: http://www.worldscientific.com/doi/pdf/10.1142/9789814508728_0017 (accessed October 15, 2014).

clvii Dr.Don Johnson, *Programming of Life* (Big Mac Publishers, 2010), p. 84.

clviii Hugh Ross, *Anthropic Principle: A Precise Plan for Humanity* (Reasons to Believe, 2002). Available at: http://www.reasons.org/articles/anthropic-principle-a-precise-plan-for-humanity (accessed October 10, 2012).

clix Hugh Ross quoted on *The Residual UFO Hypothesis* (Reasons to Believe, recorded interview).

clx Grace Church Bellingham, *The Jewish Trinity: How the Old Testament Reveals the Christian Godhead*. Available at: http://gracebellingham.org/media/Jewish_Godhead_Wk1.pdf (accessed June 19, 2013).

clxi Dr. Michael Heiser, *The Concept of a Godhead in Israelite Religion*, 2008. Available at: http://www.michaelsheiser.com/TwoPowersInHeaven/ETS2008.pdf (accessed May 26, 2013).

clxii Michael Heiser's commentary on *Two Powers in Heaven*. Available at: http://www.twopowersinheaven.com/ (accessed June 23, 2013).

clxiii Chuck Missler, *UFOs and the Bible* (Koinonia House, recorded lecture).

clxiv Ibid.

clxv Samuel Sandmel, *Parallelomania* (Journal of Biblical Literature, 1962). Available at: http://www.biblicalstudies.org.uk/pdf/parallelomania_sandmel.pdf (accessed February 17, 2013).

clxvi Chuck Missler, *What is Prophecy?* Available at: http://www.khouse.org/articles/2006/664/print/ (accessed June 2, 2013).

clxvii Walter Vieth, *Truth Matters* (Amazing Discoveries, 1997), p. 47.

clxviii Simon Sebag Montefiore, *Jerusalem: The Biography* (Phoenix, 2012), p. 26.

clxix Gershon Salomon (The Temple Mount Faithful, 2011). Available at: http://www.templemountfaithful.org/Events/details-of-the-2011-chanukah-march-of-the-temple-mount-faithful.htm (accessed April 14, 2012).

clxx *Josephus: The Complete Works.* (Thomas Nelson, 1998).

clxxi Charles Dyer, *The Rise of Babylon: Sign of the End Times* (Moody Publisher, 2003), p. 162.

clxxii David J. Stewart, *Oprah Winfrey's Teachings EXPOSED!* Available at: http://www.jesus-is-savior.com/Wolves/oprah-exposed.htm (accessed January 25, 2013).

clxxiii Manly P. Hall, *The Secret Teachings of All Ages.*

clxxiv Manly P. Hall, *The Secret Teachings of All Ages*, p. 20.

clxxv Albert Pike, *Morals and Dogma of the Ancient and Accepted Scottish Rite of Freemasonry*, p. 15-16; 472.

clxxvi John Daniel, *Scarlet and the Beast: A History of the War Between English and French Freemasonry*, Vol. III, p. 6-7 (Source: Misc Study - The All-Seeing Eye)

clxxvii Iraq U.S. Embassy, *Iraq Cultural Heritage Project.* Available at: http://iraq.usembassy.gov/projects.html (accessed July 1, 2012).

clxxviii William Peterson, *Masonic Quiz Book: "Ask Me Another, Brother"* (Charles T. Powner, 1951).

clxxix Manly P Hall, *The Secret Teachings of All Ages* (Tarcher, 2004).

clxxx Wikipedia, *Triangulation.* Available at: www.en.wikipedia.org/wiki/Triangulation (accessed July 14, 2012).

clxxxi David Flynn, *Astronomical Procession*, recorded video lecture.

clxxxii London Town, *London Borough* http://www.londontown.com/LondonStreets/

clxxxiii Stanford News, *The Strange Case of Solar Flares.* Available at: http://news.stanford.edu/news/2010/august/sun-082310.html (accessed June 25, 2013).

clxxxiv Secrets in Plain Sight, *33.* Available at: http://www.secretsinplainsight.com/2011/07/04/nazis-nasa-freemasons-and-33/ (accessed May 14, 2013).

clxxxv Leonard Ulrich, *NWO: Secret Societies and Biblical Prophecies Vol. 1* (motion picture documentary).

clxxxvi Vatican Observatory, *History of the Vatican Observatory.* Available at: http://vaticanobservatory.org/VOF/index.php/about-us/history (accessed April 20,

2013).

clxxxvii USA Today, *A third of Earthlings believe in UFOs, would befriend aliens.* Available at: http://www.usatoday.com/news/nation/story/2012-06-26/ufo-survey/55843742/1 (accessed July 22, 2012).

clxxxviii Hugh Ross et al., *Lights in the Sky and Little Green Men* (NavPress, 2002), p. 37.

clxxxix Hugh Ross, *The Residual UFO Hypothesis,* recorded interview (A Reason to Believe production).

cxc Hugh Ross et al., *Lights in the Sky and Little Green Men* (NavPress, 2002), p. 31.

cxci Ibid.

cxcii BBC News, *Animal mutilations linked to UFOs says Walsall man.* Available at: http://news.bbc.co.uk/local/blackcountry/hi/tv_and_radio/newsid_8718000/87180 28.stm (Accessed April 11, 2012).

cxciii Animal Pathology Field Unit. Available at: http://apfu.org/ (April 30, 2012). This website is now unavailable.

cxciv Catholic News, *Vatican Astronomer says if Aliens Exist, they may not need Redemption.* Available at: http://www.catholicnews.com/data/stories/cns/0802629.htm (Accessed June 20, 2013).

cxcv Slate, *Manimal Rights.* Available at: www.slate.com/articles/health_and_science/superman/2013/05/human_animal_hyb rids_chimeras_with_mice_pigs_and_goats.html (accessed June 20, 2013).

cxcvi Graham Hancock Forum, *Elongated Skulls Of Paracas: A People And Their World* by Brien Foerster http://www.grahamhancock.com/forum/FoersterB6.php?p=4 (accessed August 2, 2012).

cxcvii Koinonia House, *Mischievous Angels or Sethites?* Available at: http://www.khouse.org/articles/1997/110/#articles (accessed May 12, 2013).

cxcviii Hugh Ross, *The Physics of Sin,* (Reasons to Believe, 2002). Available at: http://www.reasons.org/articles/the-physics-of-sin (accessed August 20, 2012).

Printed in Great Britain
by Amazon